MW00649242

Psychoanalytic Participation

RELATIONAL PERSPECTIVES BOOK SERIES

Volume 16

RELATIONAL PERSPECTIVES BOOK SERIES

STEPHEN A. MITCHELL AND LEWIS ARON
Series Editors

PSYCHOANALYTIC PARTICIPATION

Action, Interaction, and Integration

Kenneth A. Frank

THE ANALYTIC PRESS

1999   Hillsdale, NJ   London

© 1999 by The Analytic Press, Inc.
All rights reserved. No part of this book may be stored, transmitted, or reproduced in any form whatsoever without the prior written permission of the publisher.

Published by
The Analytic Press, Inc.
   Editorial Offices:
   101 West Street
   Hillsdale, New Jersey 07642
   www.analyticpress.com

   Some material in Chapter 10 appeared originally in the *International Review of Psycho-Analysis*, 19:57–79 (1992), © Institute of Psychoanalysis.
   Some material in Chapter 11 appeared originally in the author's chapter (pp. 79–104) in *The Impact of Managed Care on the Practice of Psychotherapy: Innovation, Implementation, and Controversy*, edited by R. M. Alperin and D. G. Phillips (New York: Brunner/Mazel, 1997).

   Designed and typeset by Compudesign, Charlottesville, VA.
   Index by Leonard S. Rosenbaum.

Library of Congress Cataloging-in-Publication Data

Frank, Kenneth A.
   Psychoanalytic participation : action, interaction, and
   integration / Kenneth A. Frank.
      p.   cm.
   Includes bibliographical references and index.
   ISBN 0-88163-273-2
   1. Psychotherapist and patient.   2. Psychoanalysis—
   Methodology.   I. Title.
   [DNLM: 1. Psychoanalytic Therapy—methods.
   2. Physician–Patient Relations.   WM 460.6 F828p 1999]
   RC480.8.F69 1999
   616.89'17—dc21
   DNLM/DLC
   for Library of Congress   99-24906
                                                                    CIP

Printed in the United States of America

10   9   8   7   6   5   4   3   2   1

To Linda, Sara, and Jonathan

CONTENTS

PREFACE

It is said that a long journey starts with a single step. The step that launched this book was taken in the fall of 1985. At that time, following formal training and many years of practice as a psychoanalyst, I decided to enter the certificate program at the Center for Cognitive Therapy in Philadelphia. I hasten to state that I did not take that step out of disillusionment with psychoanalysis. Rather, it was stimulated by very practical concerns, including the need for a treatment program for cardiac patients, a clinical group with whom I had worked for many years at the Columbia-Presbyterian Medical Center in New York City. Cardiac patients, like so many others with psychosomatic problems, often see themselves not as candidates for psychotherapy but as medical patients. They may wish to change certain risk-related behaviors, or to rapidly learn skills that help them manage their illnesses, but they are not always interested in undertaking a time-consuming process of self-exploration that may result in changes in their personalities. Consequently, I wanted to master some short-term techniques that might help this group of patients achieve specific behavioral changes.

The program in cognitive-behavior therapy itself was hardly inspirational to me, and by no means did I become a convert to this new way of approaching clinical problems. In fact, at times, perhaps to the detriment of my classmates, I had lively exchanges with my professor based on our very different approaches to clinical material. The course served its purpose, however, as a useful introduction, and the spectacular success I experienced with my first treatment case—in which I used cognitive-behavior therapy to treat a bridge phobia—

convinced me that it was a modality deserving of my serious consideration. Soon enough, I would encounter other clinical realities that revealed the limitations of this modality, which at that time seemed so impressive to me for work with symptoms. Thus, quite early in the process of learning cognitive-behavior therapy, my clinical experience suggested that the desirability of an integration with analytic processes could more effectively accomplish certain other objectives. The realization that transference reactions developed and could be analyzed with an analyst who was truly active, so obvious to me now and yet seeming so groundbreaking at the time, fueled my interest further.

Despite these stimulating beginnings, all this might never have amounted to very much were it not for other contemporaneous developments. Stephen Mitchell's (1988) book, *Relational Concepts in Psychoanalysis*, came to my attention as soon as it was published, and I read it with enthusiasm. I realized that Mitchell's relational synthesis, emphasizing both internalized relational patterns and external interactions, represented a psychoanalytic framework valuable for thinking about and actively implementing some of the practical advantages of the action-oriented modality I was studying. I (Frank, 1990) began publishing these ideas, first seeking to extend the "cyclical psychodynamic" view that Paul Wachtel had advocated and by grounding integration in relational theory instead. Other psychoanalytic conceptualizations were beginning to emerge, reshaping the ways analysts thought about action, reality, and the therapeutic process within a two-person model, which also supported my thoughts about integration. I also discovered personal meaning in the emerging issue of the analyst's contribution to the analytic process as an individual, an issue that had fascinated me from the earliest stages of my career and that I explored in an earlier book (Frank, 1977), an edited volume concerned with the "human dimension" in analysis. That earlier work has been refined and extended here.

In fact, this psychoanalytic direction allowed me to bring together several other important interests of mine. For one, so forceful had been the behavioral/learning theory emphasis of my undergraduate training in psychology that even then, before I had a right to claim a personal point of view, I felt myself closing off behaviorist ideas and championing the deeper, alternative hypotheses offered by the psychoanalytic position. As the years passed and my psychological and psychoanalytic studies deepened and expanded, my appreciation of the depth, richness, and comprehensiveness of the psychoanalytic approach grew. Yet, although I rejected many of their teachings, I always appreciated and retained the critical thinking and empirical grounding that my earliest mentors had encouraged. Empiricism, parsimony, validation, and operationism all remained important concepts in my clinical thinking, and were especially active ones in those significant parts of my career that were concerned with behavioral medicine and biomedical research. The pragmatism of cognitive-behavior therapy, its grounding in a hard-nosed empiricism and desire to achieve demonstrable results, appealed to those early foundations. But how would I reconcile the approach I was learning with my fundamentally analytic convictions?

As I look back, several other personal factors also helped to cultivate this project. I struck up a collegial relationship with Paul Wachtel, who later became my friend. He encouraged my efforts and became increasingly supportive as we both discovered that the way in which I was thinking about psychotherapy integration, compatible in many fundamental respects with his own, found a receptive audience in the psychoanalytic community. Fortunately, too, I was operating in two uniquely supportive professional settings. At the National Institute for the Psychotherapies (N.I.P.), many individuals expressed enthusiasm for these ideas. Had the analytic community I regarded as my home base been more closed minded and restrictive, as so many others were, I might have been discouraged from developing and expressing these ideas. It is a serious hindrance to progress in the field of psychotherapy that many practitioners experience a pressure that discourages them from exploring and expressing creative ideas that emerge from responsible clinical experimentation, but that deviate from the clinical mainstream.

Also, the Consultation-Liaison Psychiatry Service and Behavioral Medicine Program of the Department of Psychiatry at Columbia University College of Physicians and Surgeons, where I am a senior staff member, offered a supportive clinical setting for the further development of these ideas. Ethan Gorenstein, Kenneth Gorfinkel, Kenneth Greenspan, Donald Kornfeld, Daniel Seidman, Richard Sloan, and, later, Catherine Monk were among the principals in that program. In fact, Donald Kornfeld, heading up the Behavioral Medicine Program, and always my supporter, underwrote my initial studies at the Center for Cognitive Therapy. In addition to many of the ideas offered here, that support eventually led to the formulation and implementation of a psychological rehabilitation program for cardiac patients. Further, the clinical psychology interns at Columbia-Presbyterian Medical Center, like the psychoanalytic candidates at

N.I.P., also were extremely receptive to the ideas leading up to those presented in this book. Thus I realized that many of the younger professionals entering the field experienced a greater openness than many senior colleagues, who were committed to more traditional forms of clinical understanding and practice. In my view, the fields of psychoanalysis and psychotherapy are changing for the better, and these ideas come across as far less radical today than when I first engaged them over a decade ago.

When I first conceived the idea of writing this book, I saw my focus quite narrowly in terms of psychotherapy integration. I recognized a need to make analysts aware of the valuable resources available to them in cognitive-behavior therapy. Paul Wachtel (1977, 1987) had written in this area in a way that was very satisfying to me as an analyst, but his penchant was theory building; and, aside from Wachtel's work, there was very little in the literature that, from an analytic perspective, could guide practitioners with integrative technique. As time passed, my ideas about the book's focus broadened. I came to appreciate the many ways that analysts' and patients' actions played a role in the analytic change process. Action-oriented methods and concerns with coping in everyday reality, foci that are emphasized in cognitive-behavior therapy, had become blended with my analytic ways of working. I realized that it was possible while working analytically to use action-oriented interventions to help people take effective action, reduce symptoms, and concentrate on achieving life goals, among other applications. Meanwhile, psychoanalytic theorizing had shifted from the drive-structure model and Freudian metapsychology toward a model emphasizing the intrinsically social nature of the individual. Theorizing now placed interpersonal interaction, especially with the analyst, at the center of the therapeutic action, as reflected in the "two-person" treatment model. This development facilitated a more participatory way of working analytically.

I believe that progress in analytic technique has lagged behind that in theory and that the field, as a whole, needs to appreciate more fully the treatment implications of relational developments, and especially the two-person model. Thus, while retaining psychotherapy integration as a significant part of this book, I decided to extend the scope of this project, and stressing the broader topic of the psychoanalyst's participation, positioned psychotherapy integration within that broader context. Rather than write a book about psychotherapy integration alone, I felt there might be greater value, and certainly greater fidelity to my own way of working, in calling attention to the participatory nature of the emerging two-person model. Such a study includes the importance of the analyst as an active individual who can intervene in many ways, including through psychotherapy integration, to influence patients' real-life adaptations. It became my hope that such a book, while psychoanalytically sound, might also have value for the many practitioners who ground their work in cognitive and behavioral insights.

Many friends and colleagues have taken their valuable time to read and react to some part or parts of this book. Among them are David Altfeld, Karen Antoshkiw, Margaret Black, Pam Feldman, James Fosshage, Henry Grayson, Dorothy Griffiths, Emanual Kaftal, Judith Kaufman, Donald Kornfeld, Stephen Levitan, Clem Loew, Valarie Oltarsch, Kenneth Porter, Merrill Schneiderman, Dennis Schulman, Sandra Shapiro, and Neil Skolnick. I wish to thank Clem Loew for his support and for the jacket photograph. Special thanks, too, to my good friend Richard Rubens, who supported my efforts to write about these ideas by meticulously reading and criticizing drafts of my early articles. In a rewarding dialogue, we discovered our agreement on fundamental points, but it was our disagreement on others that helped me articulate and establish the limits of my own beliefs about a two-person model and its impact on traditional technique. Stephen Mitchell has been a masterful editor. After helping me with a task I found impossible—cutting hundreds of manuscript pages—he acted with a delicate hand in helping me fine tune the material that remained. A few subtle suggestions went a long way toward solving difficult problems. I thank him for encouraging this entire process. I am deeply grateful to those colleagues, students, supervisees, and especially patients who provided clinical material that is disguised within these pages. My patients have helped me to pose many of the questions and, more important, to find the solutions that are proposed here.

Finally, I wish to thank my wife, Linda Reckler Frank. For more than five years, both at home and at our Stockbridge retreat in the Berkshires, this book occupied a major portion of my "free" time. The manuscript became a traveling companion during trips to the West Coast, England, France, and Italy and, needless to say, asked a great deal of Linda. Her unselfish "coparticipation" in this project—her patience, steadfast support, and encouragement, as well as her discerning commentary and skillful editing—is further testimony to the advantages of a two-person model.

CHAPTER 1

INTRODUCTION AND OVERVIEW

*N*ot long ago, a book about the psychoanalyst's participation could not have been written. Rather than being seen as a valid psychoanalytic project, an exploration of this sort would have been viewed as a foolish concern with an oxymoron. For what was crucial about the psychoanalytic process in the past—indeed, what distinguished it from other psychotherapeutic modalities—was the analyst's striving to remain a *non*participant, an objective observer who was emotionally detached from the analysand's reactions. Today, a convergence of historical developments provides the analyst's participation with new meaning. Once seen as a kind of "noise" and an interference to be minimized and even eliminated during the conduct of analytic treatment, now the analyst's personal participation is recognized not only as inevitable but also as an important source of information about the patient and the interaction, and even as a powerful factor in the therapeutic action.

Forms of psychoanalytic participation thus are being redefined. The mutative or curative role of the treatment relationship itself and of the analyst's participation within it are receiving renewed attention. The once iron-clad rule of abstinence has been modified by the participatory idea. The special, inside track to reality that the detached analyst once claimed, on the basis of a positivist epistemology, has been superseded by a perspectival realism (Nagel, 1995) that emphasizes instead the differences that exist between the analyst's and the analysand's personal perspectives. For many analysts, Freud's (1912a) recommendation regarding "evenly-suspended attention" has given way to more active and directed ways of listening and relating to patients' material. Fundamental philosophical shifts have occurred, therefore, that involve analysts' ideas about their own participation, involvement, objectivity, activity, and even authority in the psychoanalytic situation.

The winds of change have brought ambiguity, uncertainty, and confusion, and many analysts are now attempting to redefine the most productive ways of bringing their participation to bear in the psychoanalytic situation. How can the analyst's individuality best be integrated into the treatment process so as to potentiate analytic work? When are activities like self-disclosure most constructive? At what point does the analyst's participation become intrusive and interfere with analytic growth? What is the relationship between the analyst's self-expressions and new relational experience? Can the analyst intervene to influence change directly, and yet remain analytic? How much is too much? And how much is too little?

This book seeks to clarify and extend aspects of the important participatory shift in psychoanalytic thinking and, especially, to offer technical insights that put the therapist's participation, which is in any event inevitable, more fully to therapeutic advantage. Ultimately, I wish to promote ways of expanding, while deepening, the therapist's participation, based on the newer "two-person" insights, in order to enhance the efficacy of analytic therapy. The view I outline is psychoanalytic, based on crucial psychoanalytic assumptions emphasizing the importance of profound sources of unconscious motivation, conflict, the individual's resistance to change, and, especially, the experience shared by the patient and the therapist (transference and countertransference) within the treatment relationship. But it may reflect a more thoroughgoing application of the insights of a two-person treatment model than is familiar to many readers. I attempt to elaborate forms of psychotherapeutic participation that take into account the interplay between conscious and unconscious levels of the treatment process, action and insight, intrapsychic and interpersonal factors, and transference-countertransference ramifications. I propose analytic ways of understanding and making use of an active, participatory dimension that may seem unfamiliar to many analytic therapists who are accustomed to working in more traditional ways. The role of enactments and adaptive action, external reality, new relational experience, and therapist self-disclosure, among other ideas, all are explored to highlight ways that analysts' active participation can most constructively be employed. I also wish to make readers aware of the limitations, contraindications, and even dangers of a more participatory approach. I hope, thereby, to develop a framework that places the therapist/reader in a better position to evaluate and choose whether, when, and how to participate more fully and to intervene more actively, when it seems that that approach might be most helpful.

Developments advancing analysts' participation have been inhibited in the past by the influence of the "basic model" or "standard" technique—the traditional model. The efficacy of the traditional (or one-person) analytic model, emphasizing the endogenous origins of patients' disturbances, depends on the central triumvirate of analysts' anonymity, abstinence, and neutrality, which sharply delimits the appropriate range of their participation. The view advanced here is that analysts' attempts to frustrate patients, to minimize their own participation and activity, and to obscure or avoid the role and impact of their personal participation and their uniqueness as separate persons are impediments to treatment. I seek to develop the opposing advantages—of the analyst's involvement, of intervening actively while remaining cognizant of and putting to constructive analytic use, the analyst's individual contribution.

The ambiguous "one-person" and "two-person" distinction that has recently received much attention from psychoanalysts (Greenberg and Mitchell, 1983; Modell, 1984; Mitchell, 1988; Ghent, 1989; Gill, 1994; Aron, 1996, for example) is clarified and employed throughout this book in order to guide the investigation. Applied to the psychoanalytic situation, it has a meaning more specific than the more general term relational and is defined here in a very particular way that highlights the differences between alternative treatment models. These two models involve assumptions with very different, often contrasting, treatment implications. Often we see analytic therapists compromising what I would call a true two-person model that fully develops the implications of the idea of psychoanalytic interaction; these analysts instead follow a hybrid model and a technique closer to the classical in that it is satisfied to deal with others at a level of internalization while avoiding the full impact of the analyst's presence and the patient's real, external interactions with others.

Thus personality functioning and psychotherapeutic change are not understood using the drive metaphor in the traditional psychoanalytic manner here, that is, by explaining psychological phenomena through concepts elaborating instinctual strivings, energy transformations, and their manifestations. Rather, recent relational developments (Greenberg and Mitchell, 1983; Mitchell, 1988) have influenced these ideas. Relational views emphasize as fundamental the ways in which the individual seeks attachment to others. They revise the earlier classical emphasis on the instinctual foundations of personality and instead propose that the individual psyche is best understood as an open system that is formed by and operates through transactions with others. Thus I emphasize the ongoing transactions between internalized relational representations, or object relationships, and actual interpersonal interactions. To a more limited degree, insights stressing the development and cohesiveness of the self and related adaptive processes also have influenced these ideas. One's unique perspective on the outer world and how one maintains it are regarded as integral.

With fundamental psychological motivations seen as "object-seeking," patient's relationships—with the psychotherapist as well as with others—are seen as the primary field both for the expression of the patient's difficulties and for personality change. Personality organization and disturbance are understood as processes through which early interpersonal experiences were internally symbolized, organized, and thereby "structured" into rigidly enduring action patterns that shape maladaptive aspects of a person's contemporary functioning. Consideration is given here to the complex ways in which people change, and how an approach that actively addresses both internalized and external relationships, by combining both insight-oriented and "action-oriented" techniques, can facilitate and potentiate profound and lasting personality change. In this respect, the role of new relational experience in the therapeutic action will be probed carefully, both as it pertains directly to the interaction between therapist and patient and to everyday interactions that occur outside of therapy.

With a full awareness of the complexity of the therapeutic action, to which the current multiplicity of psychoanalytic and therapeutic perspectives provides ample testimony, I advance the position that the analytic therapist must be recognized unequivocally as a participant in the treatment, involved uniquely as another person, and not just as a technician, or a vague or ambiguous figure through which the patient's inner world is expressed and grasped. He or she must be willing to be authentically known, to engage, to be active, to initiate, and to examine collaboratively—at times in an open and direct manner—the fullness of the possibilities that develop within and between the participants in the unique analytic matrix formed by their presences. Thus the dynamics of treatment are articulated here with a recognition of therapists as persons in their own right, who have unique impact through their individual personalities and actions. The treatment relationship itself is seen as a "real" one that is continuous with the patient's (and therapist's) relationships in ordinary life. With the therapist seen as a real, involved person, his or her uniqueness, affectivity, and directness cannot be minimized but come to play a crucial role in the therapeutic action.

Among psychoanalytic approaches, the one offered here may strike the reader as particularly pragmatically oriented. While structural change is seen as the overriding goal of analytic therapy, it is balanced with a concern for the quality of a person's life adaptations and level of personal distress. The acquisition of self-knowledge, insight, and intrapsychic change is most meaningful when it is integrated with, and consolidated in and through, a person's everyday problem solving, coping, and functioning. This view is compatible with more intensive forms of therapeutic participation than are customary, and therapists are encouraged to become involved, at times in active ways, that are dealt with analytically. Too often analysis becomes an intellectual exercise, an exploration of a segregated psychoanalytic reality that offers a patient too little traction for dealing with his or her life outside and that may even neglect the very problems that have brought the patient to treatment (Renik, 1998).

The idea of the psychoanalytic situation's providing a sanctuary from real-life stresses and strains, and from the intrusions of others, including the analyst, while advantageous in certain respects, is problematic in others (Renik, 1996). For instance, while creating a space in which open-ended self-exploration can be intensively conducted, such an approach also deprives the patient of the opportunity to experience new forms of relatedness with the therapist that can play an important role in the change process. Through transforming pre-structured interactions with the analyst, the patient must learn about himself or herself in ways related to extrasession living. New relational experience thus becomes more than mere analytic neutrality, but new and reparative ways of analysts' relating that foster constructive interactions that patients can internalize. Moreover, when psychotherapists face the reality that analysis happens in "real time," they recognize that the practitioner who waits and does not take action may actually be squandering an opportunity that the patient will never experience again (Hoffman, 1996). That is one of the reasons the approach I describe is capable of becoming action oriented and that one of the chapters of this book (chapter 11) concentrates on analysis as a short-term modality.

Many psychoanalysts have tended to see the realities of the patient's life outside the analyst's office as having limited importance, and only then as a surface that may make the full scope of the patient's inner world accessible to interpretive influence. This orientation is understandable in the light of traditional psychoanalytic emphases that have encouraged exploration of the patient's intrapsychic world and discouraged interest in an external reality. There is no doubt that when a patient's difficulties come alive in the therapeutic relationship the subsequent therapeutic work can acquire a sense of immediacy and emotional conviction that is difficult to replicate through work with the patient's other relationships. Yet there is also reason to appreciate the mutative role of other forms of lived experience and to value an integration of "life" goals with "treatment" goals (Ticho, 1972). Thus the therapist thoughtfully balances intraanalytic exploration with a concern with the patient's outside progress, process elements with real-life problem solving, and resistance analysis with an appreciation of the patient's real-life yearnings and joins transference exploration with that of outside relationships. Throughout this book, I emphasize a quality of *realism*, including that of the analyst as a person and of the authentic aspects of the analytic relationship, which may be unfamiliar to certain practitioners (Bader, 1995; Renik, 1998).

While therapists who operate from nonanalytic orientations may find such assertions unremarkable, those who are psychoanalytically oriented will recognize the complex and even radical ramifications of this position. For, traditionally, it has been reasoned that the patient's transference to the analyst—that is, the fantastic, or distorted, aspects of the patient–therapist relationship—holds the key to change in psychoanalytic therapy. The importance of the "real" or "total" relationship existing between patient and therapist was minimized in the past. Seen mainly as an alliance to foster insight in earlier views, the analytic relationship, and the analyst's responses within it, had to be stereotypically limited, with the analyst acting as a "blank screen" or "reflecting mirror." Even classical critics of the earlier blank screen idea, such as Greenson (1971), who emphasized the importance of the patient's ability to accurately perceive the analyst's benign aspects and his or her countertransference expressions, did not alter in the slightest the standard understanding of transference as distortion and the dichotomy of transference as opposed to the undistorted perception of the analyst (Hoffman, 1983). If the analyst's personal presence or influence were to become strong, therapeutic efficacy would be compromised and analysis of the endogenous origins of the patient's distortions would become impossible. Today we realize that if psychoanalysis is nothing else it is an interpersonal-influence process. I believe analysts do well to acknowledge their influence, while moderating it, sometimes by bringing it openly into their work.

As psychoanalytic understanding moves progressively into a relational realm, many of the traditional distinctions between psychoanalysis and psychotherapy are breaking down (Wallerstein, 1986; Renik, 1993b). Relational, experiential, and participatory factors are now seen by most psychoanalysts as critical. It is recognized that therapists' involvement, actions, and joint enactments, the avoidance of which once represented the very criteria of psychoanalysis, are integral and even play a crucial role in the therapeutic action. Psychoanalysts, who in the past have striven mightily to set analysis apart from other therapeutic modalities, now are beginning to acknowledge elements that analysis has in common with other psychotherapeutic modalities. That strategy will go far to reverse directions followed in the past that threaten the very viability of psychoanalysis as a modality in the current social and economic environment.

Beyond interactions with the therapist, another important arena for change that is stressed here is the patient's "real-life" or "extrasession" interactions with others, especially the new relational experiences that can occur within those interactions. This approach encourages therapists to be concerned not only with the "psychoanalytic reality" and with the patient's "psychic reality," but also with the patient's "everyday reality." Here is another departure from traditional psychoanalytic views and a point where realism enters into analytic therapy. There is an important role for extrasession changes at the level of adaptive action in the process of structural change and thus for interventions that may facilitate them. In introducing some relevant technical resources from cognitive-behavior therapy, I appraise the idea of analytic activity within a historical framework, and I consider both the theoretical commitments and, importantly, the politics that have impeded the assimilation of action-oriented ideas into psychoanalysis. In fact, I show that such methods can be employed in analytic ways that enhance and expand the analytic relationship and its mutative potency. Thus, I encourage analysts to enter territory formerly forbidden to them—to allow themselves to become reflectively involved with patients and to attempt, deliberately, to shape their patients' actions, while always acting analytically.

In addition to transference analysis, I acknowledge the value of a body of specialized procedures/methods, for teaching patients to calm themselves, for example, or to become more assertive, and describe how some of these methods can be used analytically. Yet it is certainly not the application of techniques alone that makes treatment effective. Ambitious research projects sponsored by NIMH (Elkin et al., 1996) and by the Menninger Foundation (Wallerstein, 1986) have suggested what analysts long have known: that the therapy relationship itself, and not particular techniques, is primarily therapeutic. Therapists' personal impact extends far beyond any specific techniques that they may selectively apply, the formal manner in which they may apply them, or how they may explain or even think about these interventions. All interventions encompass unconscious elements of both therapist and patient that the other, consciously or unconsciously, may perceive. The therapist communicates on many levels—actions, forms of speech, feelings, metamessages, who he or she actually *is* with and toward each patient. Nonverbal and affective responses may communicate far more powerfully than intended verbal meanings, with every analytic intervention itself forming an interpersonal interaction that can be internalized. Here we explore some ways analysts might work with inadvertent forms of their self-expression, since, ultimately, it is the way all of this comes together and is processed by the patient that determines efficacy.

Many authors from a variety of schools have realized that analytic therapists can be highly effective, and treatment extremely powerful, when therapist and patient become deeply involved with one another (e.g., Little, 1951, 1957; Tower, 1956; Wolstein, 1959; Bird, 1972; Levenson, 1972, 1983; Singer, 1977; Searles, 1979, 1986; McLaughlin, 1981; Ehrenberg, 1982; Mitchell, 1988). What ultimately is profoundly mutative, then, is the application of techniques within a highly significant and meaningful human encounter that is made possible through the negotiation and reworking of that relationship. Throughout this book I emphasize this very important concept. Here is where the therapist's personal involvement and authenticity become so important.

That is not to say that a therapist's participation should not be guided by carefully considered therapeutic goals and professional boundaries; indeed reflection and discipline are key, and I fear that many young professionals who have witnessed only the deconstruction of classical psychoanalysis have not been adequately helped to appreciate the very real need for analytic discipline. But, from the two-person perspective I am advancing, the ideal clearly is not to operate in a manner that is detached or suppressed—"anonymous," as many analysts have characterized their roles in the past—but to participate more openly and directly, while balancing that involvement within a framework that acknowledges the importance of maintaining specific forms of "asymmetry" in the therapist's and the patient's roles (Aron, 1996). In chapter 8 I offer a model for self-revelation, balancing these considerations.

Although they may seem quite diverse, the chapters of this book all are linked by their exploration of different aspects of the analytic therapist's participation—its conceptual framework, sources, applications, advantages, and problems. I build my case from the ground up, as it were, in order to make it as accessible as possible to analysts at different levels of theoretical appreciation, and also to those less familiar with analysis, especially cognitive-behavior therapists who may find these ideas helpful. Some of the ideas that are set forth undoubtedly will seem familiar to analytic readers; timely themes, such as the therapist's self-disclosure, have recently received considerable attention from psychoanalysts. Here this topic is discussed in a way that extends the implications of the two-person model by encouraging the analyst's authenticity and willingness to be known. The approach that is described, rather than systematically obscuring the analyst as a separate person, introduces the possibility of bringing the analyst's participation and related interpersonal elements openly into the therapeutic exchange. This approach considers how enactments, new relational experiences, and the analyst's authenticity, for example, ultimately become integrated into the patient's transformation. Other ideas, such as deepening and extending the structural change process by analytically employing action-oriented techniques, may seem extreme.

Expanding analysts' participation, encouraging them to become more involved, active, and willing to be known by their patients causes a dilemma for those practitioners who believe they must maintain a low profile in order to foster the emergence of the patient's psychodynamics in ways that can be modified. Throughout this book, I address these and other concerns, many of which are derived from the one-person model and, I believe, applied inappropriately in the light of the thoroughgoing articulation of a two-person model of the psychoanalytic situation I advocate. How can a psychoanalysis that for nearly a century has urged analysts to limit their participation and to actively minimize their significance as real persons now be reconciled with a methodology emphasizing the centrality of action, and the analyst's personal participation and influence in the process? That is one of the crucial questions with which this book grapples.

CHAPTER 2

THE MEANING OF A TWO-PERSON
TREATMENT MODEL

*F*reud's original ideas about the psychoanalytic situation—the use of the couch, free association, and dream analysis—and his formulations about mental structure, personality functioning, pathogenesis, and change, all were of a piece. Predisposed by the positivistic scientific spirit of his time, and, more specifically, by his medical background and training in neurology, he viewed people as separate, self-enclosed systems. Many analysts have continued to understand the interpersonal processes occurring between the patient and analyst in terms of the individual psychology of the patient; an event occurring between the two is examined as an event represented within the patient's mind. The analyst remains, traditionally, a "reflecting mirror"—removed, uninvolved, and objective. Minimizing the effects of actual interactions, classical analysts trace interpersonal phenomena back to, and understand them in terms of, the patient's endogenously arising drives and related defense mechanisms. As Rycroft (1968) defined the Freudian approach, "psychoanalysis is a psychology of the individual and therefore discusses objects and relationships only from the point of view of a single subject (p. 101).

Although classical psychoanalysis has expanded its interest in interpersonal phenomena, its major thrust still reflects the proposition that the individual's mental functioning is isolated from the direct influence of the external world. Moore and Fine (1990), in a glossary that carries the imprimatur of the American Psychoanalytic Association, offered analysts a prescription for anonymity, a "state of being unknown," as crucial for the smooth functioning of the therapeutic action. These authors, eschewing analysts' self-defining interventions, assert that "self-revelation (the opposite of anonymity) may occasionally be unavoidable with severely pathological patients, but it usually impedes psychoanalytic progress by limiting the breadth of transference projections and their availability for interpretation" (p. 23). According to this view, when the analyst acts in self-defining ways, the study and modification of the analysand's personal psychology becomes compromised.

The Emergence of the "Two-Person" View

Following a one-person model, Freud (1912a) discussed the need for the surgeon's attitude and advised analysts to remain "opaque" to their patients. Yet, contrary to the spirit of most of his scientific writings, some of what Freud expressed, and especially his reported clinical work with patients, revealed an appreciation of relational factors—that the analyst's personality and the patient–therapist relationship have an impact on the patient and the process. Freud (1913) realized the need for the analyst's responsiveness in appreciating the role of the analyst's "sympathetic understanding" and suggesting that "serious interest" must be made available to the patient in a manner similar to "people by whom he was accustomed to be treated with affection" (pp. 139–140). Freud (1912a) also identified the "unobjectionable positive transference" and described the patient's positive attachment to the analyst as "the vehicle of success in psychoanalysis" (p. 105). Freud also seemed, unofficially at least, to acknowledge the role of the interaction. For instance, discussing a young analyst's faulty technique in a letter to Pfister, he noted that the analyst "spoils the effect of analysis by a certain listless indifference, and then neglects to lay bare the resistance *which he thereby awakens* in his patients" (quoted in Gill, 1983, p. 207, italics added). Overwhelmingly, however, until recently, American orthodox analysts selectively advanced the one-person elements of Freud's model and ignored the relational seeds that existed in his ideas. Thus, as Gill (1994) pointed out, transference for a very long time was based on a one-person view and was not understood in terms of a *relationship* between analyst and analysand but as a distortion by the analysand of the *situation* between analysand and the analyst.

Balint (1950) was among the first to call attention to the inadequacy of traditional formulations to articulate important treatment processes related to the role of interaction. He called for a "two-person psychology" to complement the existing "one-person" method of conceptualizing clinical technique.[1] Observing that the concepts of psychoanalysis were up to that point based on and limited by a one-person psychology, Balint reasoned, "That is why they can give only a clumsy, approximate description of what happens in the psychoanalytical situation which is essentially a Two-Body Situation" (p. 124). Recognizing that clinical events that were described only from the point of view of the individual were incomplete, Balint urged analysts to develop an independent object relations theory that would be comparable to the prevailing "biologizing" theory of the development of instincts.

Balint (1950) referred to the unpublished work of Rickman (1951) who described a one-person psychology as concerned with "what goes on inside one person taken in isolation" (p. 218). Defining the one-person view as the realm of *individual* mental functioning, Rickman concentrated his definition on what he regarded as neurological functions—sensation, reaction time, learning and forgetting, memory, imagery, hallucinations, introspection. Rickman explained that a two-person psychology is concerned with "reciprocal relationships . . . It studies the relation existing when two persons are in a more or less closed region and are tied to one another by simultaneously acting aims, tasks or needs" (p. 219). He reasoned that the psychoanalytic situation was simultaneously a one-person and a two-person situation: transference and countertransference, seen as one-person phenomena, were thought to originate in the past and to become accessible through memory traces; but the here-and-now experience of the analytic pair was thought to be largely a two-person matter.

The Impact of the Relational Paradigm Shift

Rather than seeing people as separate, self-enclosed systems reacting to instinctual strivings, relational conceptualizations of personality organization and functioning emphasize the importance of a person's interactions within a relational field—what Balint and Rickman had in mind by a two-person psychology. In the relational paradigm, personality structure is understood as aspects of early relationships that have become internally represented. These relational configurations form

---

1. Although Balint (1950) and Rickman (1951) originally introduced it, Langs (1981) and Modell (1984) can be credited with the more recent attention to this distinction.

the building blocks of psychic structure and regulate the person's internal functioning, including affects, and also the expression of fundamental needs for attachment. Relationships thus replace the drives, with personality seen not as fundamentally isolated, as in the traditional view, but as social and interactive. What motivates the person endogenously is not drives, not blind instinct pushing the person to seek the satisfaction of specific needs that involve others—be they sexual, aggressive, pleasure-seeking or even object-seeking—but relatedness as an expression of our essentially social nature. As Mitchell (1998) stated when discussing Fairbairn, "Object-seeking is not the vehicle for the satisfaction of a specific need, but the expression of our very nature, the form through which we become specifically *human* beings (p. 117).

Important early relationships shape what follows; they are expressed through real actions in the outer world, including those involved in ongoing relations with others that reciprocally affect internal relational patterns. Even psychological structures that may appear to have become sealed off, or dissociated, remain intrinsically transactional. Throughout life, one's perceptions, experience, and actions result both from present actualities and from transactions involving past relational experience. Where personality disturbance results, it is caused by a person's developmental efforts to adapt to the idiosyncrasies of past caretakers; these adaptations, which have "structured in" rigid relational patterns, are resistant to external reality and to change. Acting as closed systems, these ways of relating, based on preset structures, shape personality inflexibly and limit one's ways of reacting.

Thus, with the relational paradigm shift, the very subject matter of psychoanalysis, the mind, became reframed. Formerly defined as a self-contained entity, one to be modified appropriately within the one-person model of the psychoanalytic setting, the mind has become understood in terms of transactions between internalized relational patterns and actual interpersonal interactions. With the conceptualization of mental functioning as encompassing a person's actions within a relational field, the one-person model is inadequate. Now two-person articulations of the psychoanalytic setting are required. The paradigm shift transformed the psychoanalytic *situation* into a *relationship*.

Eliminating Ambiguity from the One-Person and Two-Person Distinction

The one-person–two-person distinction has been used in a number of very different ways. It has been employed as an analogue for "intrapsychic" and "interpersonal," "individual" and "social," "alone" and "together" processes, self-regulation and mutual regulation (Aron, 1996), and even synonymously with classical and relational theories. Sometimes the distinction refers to different places—like private thoughts versus public transactions; at other times, to different types of experiences—like dreams versus conversations; it has been used to distinguish past influence from present, and even as a shorthand for higher level theoretical metaphors. So disparate have its applications been that this distinction, so valuable historically, now has limited utility.

Further ambiguity results from theoreticians' using the distinction to denote different conceptualizations of the psychoanalytic situation and process, or "models," as well as different "psychologies" to describe the mental functioning of people. With the prevalent tendency of some analysts to equate intrapsychic with one-person and interpersonal with two-person realms of overall psychological functioning and to treat the two dichotomously, it is understandable that others have made concerted efforts to combine the two domains. They have asserted that one-person and two-person "psychologies" for understanding a person's overall functioning are overlapping and complementary, rather than incompatible or opposing (see Modell, 1984; Ghent, 1989; Aron, 1990, 1996, for example). A dialectical formulation of a person's psychological functioning as alone and yet together with others captures a vital duality of human existence and holds compelling psychoanalytic appeal (Modell, 1984). Discussed in these ways, compatibility is not only possible but necessary for presenting a complete picture of the overall psychological functioning of an individual.

Intrapsychic and interpersonal phenomena, one-person and two-person psychologies—but not one-person and two-person models of the psychoanalytic situation—are complementary. As integrated parts of a unified whole, intrapsychic and interpersonal functioning can usefully be understood as dialectical, interpenetrating, and interactive aspects of a person's psychological functioning. But combining psychologies is not the same as combining alternative constructs for understanding the therapeutic action of the psychoanalytic situation. Thus I propose the advantages of restricting the use of the one-person and two-person distinction to *alternative models of the psychoanalytic situation.*

Distinguishing One-Person and Two-Person Treatment Models and the Analyst's Participation

Although the psychoanalytic literature reveals considerable progress on the part of analysts, including contemporary classical practitioners, toward integrating relational ideas—which represents an enormous gain for psychoanalysis—nevertheless, there is evidence of the continuing and often inappropriate influence of the monadic model in the clinical functioning of relational analysts. One-person and two-person models are considered in this book as alternative treatment models. Based on very different ways of understanding personality development, organization, functioning, treatment, and change, they are seen as fundamentally incompatible. That point cannot be emphasized enough and has far greater therapeutic significance and applicability than often is appreciated.

Accordingly, in describing a two-person model of the treatment situation, I am not referring simply to a different psychology—to different aspects of the psychological activity of the patient within the psychoanalytic situation. In that view, intrapsychic activity, such as transference fantasies or dreams, might be seen as one-person psychological processes; and interpersonal phenomena, such as analytic enactments, as two-person. Rather, I refer specifically to the way analysts define the structure of the psychoanalytic situation, based on their views of personality organization and change, and the particular psychoanalytic functions that follow from that structure.

The one-person and two-person conceptualizations, or models, of the psychoanalytic situation and process are not to be confused with a one-person and two-person psychology, which are systems for understanding the mental functioning of the patient. In the one-person model of the psychoanalytic situation, the analyst ordinarily understands the patient's mental functioning on the basis of a one-person psychology; that is, psychological developments within the patient, which are the focus of study, are seen as arising endogenously and are largely independent of the characteristics of the individual analyst. Although the two paradigms are seen here as alternative ways of articulating the psychoanalytic situation, some practitioners attempt to combine the two models, endorsing two-person psychological concepts such as internalized object-relations, role-responsiveness, and even enactments, while still maintaining a strong commitment to ways of working that have been traditionally associated with the one-person model. Here it is assumed that the contribution of the analyst's actual presence, while a consideration, does not alter the character of the analytic work fundamentally. Theorists such as Boesky (1990) take this position. He makes a sharp distinction between attempts to refine an understanding of the interaction between two persons and the idea of shifting from the intrapsychic to the interpersonal domain of discourse and theory. As Boesky sees it, a concentration on the patient's intrapsychic, but not interpersonal, processes can adequately account for the important dyadic aspects of the interaction between analyst and patient.

The two-person model for understanding the psychoanalytic situation and process (as distinct from a two-person psychology of the patient) conceptualizes the analyst's presence as an actual, external person and his or her individual impact on the patient through transference-countertransference interactions. That assumption, so very different from the fundamental assumption of the one-person psychoanalytic paradigm (and its one-person psychology of the patient) leads the analyst to deal differently with what goes on within each of the partners, and also to focus on what goes on between them interpersonally. Within the two-person model, but not the one-person, new relational experience, one form of interaction, may assume a position of prominence equivalent to that of insight in the therapeutic action. In contrast with Boesky's orientation, Ehrenberg's (1992) participatory analytic approach exemplifies a thoroughgoing application of the insights from the two-person psychoanalytic model.

By its nature, a relational understanding of personality introduces a two-person model of the treatment situation. In a two-person model, the personal involvement and contribution of the analyst, rather than being eliminated, become crucial. Now, instead of striving to keep their personal contribution to a minimum as in one-person models, analysts are challenged to develop ways of making their analytic participation, which is seen as inevitable, most therapeutically beneficial. Relational views highlight the contribution of the analyst as a person and emphasize the new and constructive ways in which the patient and therapist may interact in order to transform pathogenic forms of relationship and thus, psychological structure. Although practitioners are offered a great deal of individual latitude in applying relational treatment approaches, the two-person model tips the technical balance toward involvement rather than detachment, participation rather than observation.

I employ the one-person and two-person models throughout this book to clarify and apply new developments supporting an active, participatory psychoanalytic approach. A major point is that a thoroughgoing elaboration of the two-person model creates a theoretical framework permitting—even encouraging—that analytic therapists draw more actively, expressively, and expansively from a much wider range of intervention possibilities, at times including methods that may shape patients' new behaviors, compared with the monadic model. Among the unique corollaries of the two-person model I include the centrality of action, interaction, mutuality, intersubjectivity, and perspectivism—all related to a psychoanalytic role for external reality that is very different from that in the one-person model.[2]

As I employ it, the two-person model for understanding the psychoanalytic situation is related to Hoffman's (1983) designation of "asocial" and "social" forms of analytic participation and his (1991, 1992b) broader social-constructivist framework. In the one-person (Hoffman's asocial) paradigm it is assumed that the patient's experience occurs in a way that is largely divorced from the immediate impact of the therapist's presence. Hoffman has called attention to the "naive patient fallacy," the idea being that the analysand cannot plausibly perceive the analyst—his or her attributes, actions, and experience, including reactions to the patient—as a real person. That concept is similar to the way Greenberg and Mitchell (1983) have described the drive-structure model: "The analyst's position vis-à-vis the patient is similar to the position, within the drive model, of an individual's objects. As the object is external to drive-derived aims, so the analyst is external to the neurotic process" (p. 388).

The success of applications of a one-person model depends on the extent to which the analyst can minimize his or her personal impact on the patient. The analyst seeks to achieve personality modification not through interactions, but almost despite them—by turning the patient's mind in upon itself, as it were, so as to examine and explicate the patient's transference neurosis, which is ultimately infantile in form, structure, and content. In this view, the analyst must therefore behave in a very circumscribed manner in order to create conditions conducive to gaining access to the patient's encapsulated internal world through a regressive unfolding. Thus, the traditional analyst enters the therapeutic equation in a limited role—not so

---

2. In discussing the one-person model, I refer primarily to the drive-conflict model that has dominated American psychoanalysis. However, the Kleinian view also is based on a one-person model, differently conceptualized, and I discuss it later in connection with object relations theory.

much as another person but as a purveyor of insight. Analysts' actions other than interpretations are thought to bring the analyst intrusively into the transference-analytic field. Modifications of technique recognizing the role of the actual person of the analyst and integrating the interactive idea are not achieved easily within one-person views.

Hoffman (1983) has pointed out that the social view—what I am calling the two-person model—cuts across theoretical allegiances and elaborates the role of interaction in the psychoanalytic relationship. Among the precursors of this view, he has identified Gill (1982a,b, 1983), Levenson (1981, 1983), Racker (1968), Sandler (1976a, 1981), Searles (1979), and Wachtel (1981). The two-person model provides the foundation for many of the ideas presented in this book. Hoffman (1991) has written that the terms social and participant define a set of conditions designating the analyst's involvement *and* that he or she and the patient both shape the participation of the other. The term constructivist, which is integral here as in Hoffman's view, indicates that each participant understands the other from his or her own *perspective.* Distinct from the one-person model, the two-person recognizes the significance of the analyst as a separate person. The model's underlying assumptions assert that the analyst's functioning, like the patient's, cannot be understood as removed, as in the one-person model. Rather, the analyst's contribution, like the patient's, is communicated in ways that are both conscious and unconscious. Therefore, whatever happens must be understood in ways that take account of both parties' unwitting as well as deliberate influence.

A two-person model defines the psychoanalytic situation in a way that involves interactions with the analyst as a person. The individual analyst becomes drawn into roles that are congruent with the patient's internal mental structures, understood in terms of relational patterns. The analyst may sometimes become influenced by the patient's old objects and sometimes by consciously experienced, as well as disavowed, aspects of the self of the patient. As a participant-observer, the analyst is thus affected by, yet in part creates, what he or she observes. Rather than being preset and unfolding, as in the one-person conception, analytic events are seen as cocreated through the interactions involving two persons' individual psychodynamics and actions.

There can be no standardized set of conditions, no ability to view the analysand more or less "in vitro," as in the monadic conception. It is recognized instead that *any* way in which the psychoanalytic situation and the stance of the analyst is structured—neutrality, anonymity and abstinence included—will figure into the patient's (and analyst's) transference. In fact, these stances have been seen as very powerful stimuli (Lipton, 1977, 1983). Further, unlike the "naive patient fallacy" inherent in the monadic view, the patient in the two-person view is seen as fundamentally reality oriented, directed toward actual people in the interpersonal world, and thus quite capable of realistically perceiving the analyst and his or her reactions.

The triumvirate of abstinence, anonymity, and neutrality, which organizes the analyst's attitude and smooth functioning in the one-person model, has no place in the two-person model, at least as these defining concepts have been understood traditionally. That is not to say that the participation of the analyst and the analysand in the two-person psychoanalytic situation is fully symmetrical; the analyst's and the analysand's orientations and tasks are structured differently on the basis of the primary concern with how *the patient's* patterns are replicated and can best be favorably modified. Considerations such as the analyst's participation (versus abstinence) and individuality (versus anonymity) must be taken into account and dealt with in the two-person model, and neutrality must be redefined in ways that accommodate an awareness of the role of the analyst's involvement and ongoing processes of interaction and enactment.

I do not mean to imply that, dichotomously, one model is fully participatory and the other is not at all. As Gill (1983) pointed out, there is a certain "inevitability of significant involvement" (p. 214), and the degree to which an analyst participates varies widely, regardless of orientation. Gill found it useful to distinguish "major" from "minor" forms of participation: Wolstein (1981) is seen as a major participant (see chapter 5); Tarachow (1963), an example of the latter, reasoned that therapy is psychoanalytic (rather than therapeutic) to the extent that the analyst succeeds in resisting engaging in the interaction. Nevertheless, the two models endorse basically different analytic stances. The one-person model analyst, aided by Anna Freud's (1936) recommendations regarding "equidistance" from the patient's material, pursues an anonymous, neutral and abstinent ideal, striving to remain removed form the patient's influence. In the two-person model, the analyst is seen as being inevitably involved in a mutual influence system with the patient and works with its data to be effective within that system, which the one-person model analyst attempts to remain outside of. Because the historical predominance of the earlier, one-person model has inhibited the full emergence of a thoroughgoing two-person treatment model, there are dangers in understating the very real differences between the two.

The underlying assumptions of the one-person and two-person models prescribe treatments that often are in conflict with one another, and analysts run into serious problems when they try to combine these alternative conceptualizations in the psychoanalytic situation. In combining these alternative understandings, each loses its interpretive power. Thus, operating within the one-person conceptual system, the participatory, self-revealing analyst spoils the possibility of unfolding endogenous transferential phenomena that are, within that system, critical for a successful analysis. Reciprocally, the removed analyst weakens the potency of the two-person model approach; by operating at a remove, the analyst is unable to put to therapeutic advantage crucially mutative interaction processes.

The two-person model sometimes is seen as more superficial, external, or ancillary as compared to the one-person articulation of the psychoanalytic setting, which is regarded as dealing with the individual's psychic reality on more profound levels. It is important to clarify that the two-person model does not exclude the unconscious and dynamic features that one-person theorists emphasize; by incorporating them into a more comprehensive conceptual structure, it deals with those parts of the psychoanalytic situation that were previously explained less adequately by one-person concepts. The one-person model cannot adequately account for what goes on between the two participants in actuality, but the two-person model can account for what goes on within the individuals. Two-person models permit a continuing focus on the psychic reality or subjectivity of each member of the analytic pair—understanding what each participant brings to the interaction from his or her prior experiences, fantasies, wishes, and motives, and how each one organizes, experiences, and influences the events of an analysis. But these processes are understood and elaborated within the context of ongoing interactions between the members of the pair.

Internal Objects and Real Objects

A pronounced difference between one-person and two-person treatment models, which clarifies a major source of difficulty in attempting to combine the two, relates to the very different ways "objects" are treated within these different theoretical understandings of the psychoanalytic situation. Real people are their own centers of initiative and agency. In addition to acting, they evaluate and respond to others' actions toward them, including others' feelings about them, as they are revealed in others' actions and nonverbal behavior. Internal objects, in contrast, are not autonomous persons but fantasies that are constructed by others and that are manipulated by them. Not all relational formulations acknowledge the importance of real persons; instead they deal only with the mental representations of individuals. A two-person model takes account of the person's real interactions with others, including the analyst, as well as internalized representations.

A very different approach to technique results when one concentrates on the role of *internal* object relations alone in psychodynamic psychology, as compared with emphasizing the mutative role of interactions with *real* people. While some theorists (Hoffman, Mitchell, and Wachtel, for example) express a balanced concern with structural and actual relationships, many theorists (Kernberg, 1976; Klein, 1946; and Sandler, for example) emphasize internalized object relations but not real interactions in the therapeutic action. In emphasizing internalized relationships alone, a shift in the analyst's ways of conceptualizing based on these ostensibly two-person or interpersonal insights is not necessarily followed by an appropriate modification of technique. Rather, a one-person emphasis on understanding the relationship only from the point of view of the single subject, the patient, still applies.

A two-person articulation of the psychoanalytic situation addresses the analyst not just in terms of the analysand's fantasy or internal representation of the analyst or just as the object of the patient's actions. Analysis is not only about what the analysand has in mind, as it were, but also what the analyst has in mind, and what goes on between the partners. In a two-person model, the very real, individual initiatives, actions, and overall participation of the analyst as a subject, conveyed through verbal and nonverbal expressions, are recognized as continually shaping the phenomena the analyst seeks to understand and change, and are actively integrated into technique.

Models of analysis that deal with internalized object relations but fail to deal with the analyst as a real person, with his or her unique contribution, or with the analytic relationship as a real (or total) relationship, do not meet the criteria of a two-person model. Interpretations of the interaction between patient and therapist—but at an intrapsychic level, as Rycroft (1968) described—may represent an attempt to balance these considerations. But working in that way is shadow boxing and does not go far enough toward relating the expressions of the patient's internal world to the interpersonal reality with the analyst. It is only by doing so that the fullest development of new relational experience is made possible, that the potentials of active methods can be fully tapped, and that the patient is able to gain insight into the workings of his or her psychology in relation to others, and thus in ways applicable to the individual's interpersonal world, where they matter most. If the two-person idea is to be realized fully, then the analyst must be systematically integrated into the treatment as an actual person. The implications of this conclusion have far-reaching and even radical implications for the conduct of psychoanalysis.

CHAPTER 3

THE PSYCHOANALYST'S PARTICIPATION AND THE NEW ROLE FOR ACTION AND EXTERNAL REALITY

*T*o help us arrive at a working definition of participation, consider an example of the internal process of the analyst at work:

The analyst listened silently as her patient sensitively described reading a bedtime story to her three-year-old daughter. The tenderness with which the patient spoke and the poignancy of her description moved the therapist. As the session progressed, the therapist, also a mother, became aware of an array of feelings toward the younger patient—some positive, such as admiring her caring for her daughter, but also envy and competition. The therapist was even aware of experiencing jealousy toward the child as the recipient of her mother's adoration. For a few moments, the therapist's attention turned to loving recollections of similar moments with her own daughter, now grown. She felt a fleeting awareness of regret of opportunities missed with her own child, with whom she had recently experienced conflict. As her thoughts drifted toward her relationship with her own daughter, she became aware of feeling distracted and wondered whether she had become more concerned with issues of her own, rather than her patient's. She considered briefly whether and how these reactions might relate to her patient's, and then, feeling uncertain and perhaps partly, too, to avoid the distress of the personal topic, the therapist refocused her attention on what the patient was saying.

As the patient continued to speak, the therapist became aware of her patient's posture—soft and open, and her melodic tone. Attending both to her patient's and to her own feelings, the therapist became particularly aware again of her own admiring feelings, mixed with envy related to her patient's nurturing qualities, which at this moment, she was aware, felt superior to her own. Momentarily, she entertained the thought, reassuring to her, that her patient's personal growth in treatment had been substantial. Then, reflecting again on her own experience, she began to wonder why it was that as the patient continued to speak about her experience lovingly, tenderly, her own associative drift took a somewhat negative, competitive, and even self-recriminatory direction, and why she was having so much difficulty remaining empathically attuned to her patient. She wondered, had her patient acted to stimulate this, was it a reflection of her patient's psychodynamics, or was this an idiosyncratic response of her own? Made uncomfortable by what she was feeling, she began to attend more closely to the meaning of her own experience in the light of the patient's. She wondered about the possibilities of guilt, rivalry, and an avoidance of them, and what these reactions might have to do with her patient, herself, with elements of the patient's formative relationships, and with the interaction. As she listened, a dream the patient had had about the two of them came to mind. . .

Although the therapist in this example was not technically active, at least overtly, and did not speak a word, she was profoundly personally involved internally—some might even say overinvolved with her patient. Yet an observer might plausibly construe the analyst's silence as noninvolvement or nonparticipation. What exactly do we mean when we speak of psychoanalytic participation?

Definitions: Action, Participation, Involvement, and Activity

Following Schafer (1976), I define *action*, generally, as purposeful or goal-directed behavior. Thinking, wishing, and fantasizing are forms of action. Defenses also may be understood as unconsciously performed actions to prevent other actions. The analyst, like the patient, when deliberately silent, acts not to speak and continues acting in internal, nonpublic, or private ways—in thinking and fantasizing, for example. I distinguish action from *activity*, which is restricted to the therapist, as relatively intensive or extensive action. Sharing openly and introducing extensive interventions that are intended to promote behavioral changes are examples of a therapist's *active* technique.

Participation and involvement refer to interdependent actions, and each implies the other. Webster (1988) defines the active verb to participate as "to take part," "to have a part or share in something." "To involve" is "to engage as a participant . . . to occupy (as oneself) absorbingly; esp: to commit (as oneself) emotionally." Internally, the analyst in the example, having become emotionally absorbed, was *involved* with her patient. As pertains to the analyst, private listening or any of these nonpublic actions may be associated with a greater degree of involvement than is a therapist's more open participation. An analyst's deep, personal involvement, even if only felt and not deliberately expressed, often may have a powerful impact on treatment. But what is critical from the viewpoint advanced here is that action and activity not be viewed as opposing insight; like involvement, the analyst's activity and overall participation, including overt behavior, are implemented analytically.

In summary, *action* is purposeful, continuous behavior, including both overt and private forms. *Involvement* refers to the active, emotional engagement of the analyst with the patient and his or her material. Therapist *activity* designates intensive or extensive therapist's action. I employ the term *participation* inclusively with regard to all of these. Throughout this book, I show how action, once construed as opposing the role of reflection and thus as antithetical to the analytic change process, actually plays a crucial role in the complex, multifaceted process of structural personality change. I show how both the analyst and the patient are able to potentiate the action dimension in change.

Action, One-Person and Two-Person Models

Analysts who use active forms of psychoanalytic participation run a risk—according to followers of the one-person model—of surrendering neutrality, of becoming overinvolved, perhaps personally influential, or of shifting attention from the analysand's inner life, where it belongs, to external reality. From this point of view, therapists' and patients' actions and the processes involved in achieving insight are antithetical to one another. That is, of course, precisely the opposite of what we might assert within a two-person model—that the analyst is inevitably involved, cannot but influence the patient with his or her every act, and can be *analytically* active. Using active techniques analytically not only involves higher levels of therapist activity and initiative than is traditional but may also incorporate the radical objective of directly affecting the patient's actions in external reality. As we will see later, active techniques that are designed to promote patients' adaptive actions can be linked with the analytic process. The one-person model analyst, following traditional methodologies, frowns on these methods.

Prior to the last decade, one-person-model analysts regarded action primarily as opposing the psychoanalytic process. Freud (1914) was, of course, the first to take note of patients' needs to repeat certain neurotic conflicts during an analysis rather than recall their traumatic origins. He treated transference itself as a form of acting out and responded by establishing the requirement that the analyst not join with the patient's action because that would prevent recollection and thus insight. Freud (1915) wrote, "The patient's need and longing should be allowed to persist in her, in order that they may serve as forces impelling her to do the work and to make changes" (p. 165). He (1920) came to see the "compulsion to repeat" as a manifestation of the death instinct and explained it in terms of the conservative nature of the instincts and the patient's need to bind tension and eliminate excitation. Concentrating on instinctual vicissitudes, Freud viewed the analysand's repetitive actions as transferential "new editions" of painful childhood memories that were grounded in biological inheritance. That conceptualization has been criticized by a number of classical analysts (Kubie, 1939; Schur, 1966), and most recently by Interbitzin and Levy (1998). Critics often observe that it is impossible to distinguish clinically between the specific repetitiveness of a repetition compulsion and the repetitions common to all neurotic phenomena.

Following Freud's lead, classical analysts came to emphasize that, through their countertransferential actions—that is, by reciprocally "acting in" with their patients—they might block patients' verbalizations and recollections and therefore the achievement of insight. Rather than dealing with the analyst's actions as a source of information about the patient and the analytic interaction, which later became crucial, early analysts regarded their own potential for action, like patients', as a problem. Given the narrow (pathologic) view of countertransference, analysts' actions were seen primarily in relation to the possibility of counterresistive collusion with their patients' resistance and psychopathology. Apart from interpreting, analysts were encouraged to curtail their actions overall.

With the two thought to be incompatible, action and insight thus became polarized by classical psychoanalysts, and the negative attitude toward acting out was extended, in less direct and more subtle ways, to all forms of action—patients' and analysts' alike—as being opposed to the progression of the analytic process (Bernstein, cited in Atkins, 1970). The prevailing tendency was to equate all action with acting out (and acting in, that is, acting out within the psychoanalytic situation), associating it thereby with aspects of resistance and defense that were activated by the analytic process. Action thus acquired the pejorative connotation of "bad behavior," and it became associated with acting out, denial, and other defenses opposing introspection, memory, verbalization, and insight, all prized in the psychoanalytic endeavor (Laplanche and Pontalis, 1973; Boesky, 1982; Moore and Fine, 1990). This association finds linguistic support in Webster (1988), where the term active is "characterized by action *rather than* by contemplation or speculation" (italics added).

Seeking to replace Freudian metapsychology with an "action language," Schafer (1976, 1983) was among the first to reformulate the role of action in psychoanalytic theorizing. This trend toward conceptualizing psychoanalysis in terms of action reflects a growing emphasis on personal agency—a recognition of the individual as a choosing, meaning-creating, active agent in the process of change. Many analysts have begun to recognize and describe the indispensable role of action in the psychoanalytic process, and the patient's actions, both with the analyst and even in external reality, gradually became an integral element in the analytic endeavor for many analysts. It has been acknowledged that experience is encoded in *praxis*, the semiotic of practice, with meanings that are represented and communicated not only through words but through actions as well (Fourcher, 1992; Stern, 1997). As Stern explains, "To the extent that we are unaware of what we are doing, or cannot 'find the words to say it,' our relatedness is encoded in the mode of action" (p. 19). With an emphasis on process rather than content, nonverbal and affective interactions have come to represent an extremely important semiotic medium and form of analytic data (Levenson, 1983; Ehrenberg, 1992).

Some authors, stressing the inevitability of enactments within the psychoanalytic situation (Sandler, 1976a; Gill, 1982a; Jacobs, 1986; Poland, 1986; Smith, 1990; Renik, 1993b), have suggested that understanding of the transference *follows* the analyst's responses to them. Mutual actions, or enactments, move interpersonal developments toward actualization and thus analyses of patients' internal worlds (Sandler, 1976a). Renik (1993b) asserts that, rather than the analyst's fantasies being the major source of countertransference awareness, it is common for analysts to become aware of their countertransference as a result of acting toward their analysands in some way. In this view, analysts' attentions to prescriptives about what they *ought* to be doing can dull their awareness of what they actually have been doing. With these developments, analysands' and analysts' nonverbal actions, both deliberate and inadvertent, have come to play an integral role in the analytic process.

When we stress the role of adaptive action in psychoanalysis, especially outside the psychoanalytic situation, we are challenging the traditional, one-person model emphasis on action as antianalytic. Yet we are simply attending to what always has been there—in Freud's repetition compulsion and Strachey's (1934) early discussion of vicious circles: an awareness of the role of the analysand's need to recreate neurotic patterns through action and the analyst's attempts to thwart these counterproductive developments. Distinguishing adaptive forms of action from acting out, other analysts thus gave attention to patients' extrasession actions. Wachtel (1977, 1987, 1997), concentrating on this aspect of the patient's capacity for action, has postulated that the relations among the person's manifest behavior, the situations it leads to, the desires that are aroused, and the fantasies that guide and interpret experience all are interlocking, with no aspect any more basic or causal than any other. Rangell (1981a, 1990) notes that analysis moves "to a point in treatment where positive actions become desirable if not necessary both in the analysis and in life" (p. 130). Gedo (1988a,b) has described "apraxias," or skills deficiencies, as a factor in psychopathology. Mitchell (1988) has elaborated how a person's actions proceed in cyclical patterns from internalized structures that are expressed through enactments and result in the reinternalization and consolidation of the original, internalized structures.

Action and interaction have taken center stage in the two-person psychoanalytic model. Thinking of personality organization as enduring relational patterns enables analysts to conceptualize their efforts in terms both of internal relational patterns and of external object relationships, as well as the transactions between them. As Wachtel (1997) wrote, "The putatively intrapsychic and interpersonal are seen together as part of a mutually interpenetrating and mutually shaping and sustaining relationship between fantasies, fears, and desires on the one hand and the actions and experiences of living and interacting with people on the other" (p. 347).

Interaction, Mutuality, and Intersubjectivity

Three important corollaries of the two-person model of psychoanalysis are interaction, mutuality, and intersubjectivity. Each of these three interrelated concepts assimilates the consequences of recognizing the presence of the individual analyst and his or her actions and impact within the psychoanalytic situation. Let us consider them in turn. Webster defines interaction as "mutual or reciprocal action or influence"; interacting, as "to act upon one another." The participants' actions and the interaction between them, like the analyst's presence and impact, are, and of course always have been, inherent in the practice of psychoanalysis. Yet for many years it was thought that interaction belonged within the province of psychoanalytic psychotherapy versus analysis (Oremland, 1991). "True" psychoanalysis, which regarded the actions of patient and therapist as inimical to insight, remained equated with observation, *non*interaction, and *non*participation. Thus it is not surprising that the term *interaction* cannot be found in Moore and Fine's (1990) standard glossary. The "pure gold of analysis," as Freud (1919) put it, was not to be alloyed with the copper of suggestion, which, associated with interaction, was seen as a lesser form of psychotherapy.

Instead of the implications of patient–therapist interactions in treatment being explored—and we definitely have seen the seeds of it contained in Freud's work—its role and effects deliberately were downplayed in the one-person schema. That methodology formed the foundation for the basic model, or standard psychoanalytic technique, which limited the role of external reality and the attention paid to interpersonal meanings and explorations. The term interaction obviously is a two-person concept that refers to the mutual influence operating between the patient and the therapist.

Interaction and mutuality imply that the expressions of each person influences the other in ongoing and reverberating ways. We find the term mutual defined as "having the same relationship each to the other." Aron (1996), dealing with the topic of mutuality comprehensively, has described three forms: mutuality of *regulation*—the two analytic participants create a unique, bidirectional system that regulates the affects, subjectivity, and behavior of one another; mutual *recognition*—both analyst and analysand see one another as separate people, each with his or her own separate subjectivity (which I later emphasize as a treatment *goal*); and mutual *data generation*—the participants share and coparticipate in generating and interpreting data together, as compared with the more asymmetrical one-person model, in which the analyst elicits data from the patient that the analyst may interpret. Aron reasons that virtually all analytic processes are affected by mutuality—empathy, interpretation, even regression (Aron and Bushra, 1998). Although the relationship is mutual in psychoanalysis, individual roles are different, a characteristic discussed later in terms of the asymmetry of the analytic relationship.

In addition to interaction and mutuality, every analytic moment can be understood as an expression of intersubjectivity. Thus, the unconscious and conscious mental states or actual experience of each participant is in part a response to the influence of the other. Benjamin's (1990) definition of intersubjectivity is compatible with the way I am defining a two-person model. Accordingly, it aims to change psychoanalytic theory and practice so that "where objects were, subjects must be" (p. 34). Benjamin sees intersubjectivity as referring to that zone of experience or theory in which the analyst or analysand is not merely the object of the other's need, drive, cognition, or perception, but has a separate and equivalent center of self.

Diverse Views of Psychoanalytic Interaction

During the past two decades an interactional point of view has progressively become implicit in the work of many practitioners from virtually all schools. On the whole, the controversy over whether or not analysis is interactional is subsiding. Interaction, however, is a concept that can be interpreted and applied in a variety of ways. Because there is no single formula for integrating two-person or interactional ideas with traditional psychoanalytic methods, it is hardly a straightforward matter to integrate two-person insights such as interaction with the basic one-person schema that traditional psychoanalysis has been based on; and observers have taken a variety of positions with respect to the theoretical and technical significance of these ideas. The debate among those advocating different interpretations is highly significant because an analyst's understanding of the role of interaction is embedded in his or her fundamental theoretical commitments; how he or she relates to the one-person or two-person question plays an integral role in determining the forms the analyst's participation will take. Let us consider how several theoreticians have integrated the interactional idea.

If the analyst's functioning is guided by a strict interpretation of the rule of abstinence, analytic anonymity, and neutrality, then recognition of the impact of the analyst's own personal psychology, activity, and thus interaction is, of course, inimical. The formulations of Arlow and Brenner (1990) provide an example of that extreme. Rather than seeing psychoanalytic interaction as a process occurring between two *persons*, they characterize it very narrowly in terms of the interactions between "the patient's conflicts and the analyst's technical interventions" (p. 686). Although Arlow and Brenner (1988) recognize the role of the analyst's theory in shaping analytic events, beyond that they do not acknowledge the impact of the analyst's personal psychology. Thus, although these authors concede that the analytic process is interactive in this limited sense, they downplay the role of bidirectional influence processes.

Boesky (1990) is among a number of commentators who have attempted to reconcile classical psychoanalytic views with the idea of interaction. He sees resistance and its successful negotiation by the analyst, most often through interpretation, as the basic psychoanalytic unit. Resistance develops uniquely in every situation, even being unconsciously negotiated by the patient and the analyst—a sort of "benign iatrogenic resistance" (p. 572). While granting that the psychoanalytic process is interactive, he shifted attention to the controversy centering instead on whether change more significantly involves intrapsychic or interpersonal processes. Boesky cautions analysts to distinguish between attempts to refine an understanding of the interaction between two persons and the idea of shifting from the intrapsychic to the interpersonal domain of discourse and theory. He reasons that there is "abundant room" within the boundaries of a one-person psychology to account for the important "dyadic" aspects of the interaction between analyst and patient. Holding the line with regard to the primacy of intrapsychic exploration, he takes the position that the domain of psychoanalysis should be restricted to the intrapsychic sphere to explain all observations.

Addressing the question of interaction, Dewald (1990) has described the dialectical ways in which intrapsychic and interpersonal

experiences operate within the psychoanalytic situation. He con-
cludes that new interpersonal experience plays a significant psychotherapeutic role, but one that is ancillary to the more profound
aspects of structural change. The role of the interaction is seen as
"facilitative," or preparatory, versus "definitive." Facilitative changes
are thought to precede the analysand's exposure of intrapsychic "core
structures" through a transference neurosis and the definitive
changes that result from the interpretation of them.

Acknowledging the role of interpersonal interaction opens the
door to that of new relational experience, and many analysts thus are
reluctant to do so since that emphasis would threaten the very foundations of the monadic emphasis on the mutative role of insight. The
strategy of arguing for the predominant mutative importance of interpretation rather than relational factors, or of emphasizing only those
relational factors (neutrality, anonymity, and abstinence) that are
inherent in the psychoanalytic situation as it is defined within a one-
person model, is fairly typical of classical analysts who have addressed
the role of interaction (Pine, 1993, for example). Some, such as
Boesky (1990), have reasoned that the major benefit of an appreciation of interactional factors is that it modifies the view of the analyst
as impermeable and encourages the analyst to reflect on his or her
subjectivity in order to understand the antecedents of inadvertent
countertransference intrusions, interpretation, and, especially, counterresistances. Thus, intrapsychic investigation can be productively
applied to the experience of the analyst as well as that of the patient.
Boesky explicitly stated his opposition to attempts to emphasize interpersonal therapeutic processes such as the corrective emotional experience and techniques such as countertransference disclosure. Such
approaches are emphasized as part of the participatory approach
advanced in this book.

With views similar to that which I am recommending, some
authors (Levenson, 1972, 1983; Ehrenberg, 1982, 1984, 1992;
Wachtel, 1983; Stern, 1989; Renik, 1993a, 1995) take the importance
of interaction to the next level, integrating it more actively with
understandings of the analyst's participation and the therapeutic
action. Rather than seeing the patient's personality as isolated, and
intrapsychic insight as key, these practitioners see work with the relationship that is coconstructed by the two participants, rather than by
the patient, as the basic psychoanalytic unit. They also emphasize the
mutative or healing aspects of the interaction. From the point of view
of these theoreticians, therapeutic benefits derive not from trying to

overcome or to minimize the influence of interaction but from collaboratively articulating the ways in which the members of the analytic pair actually engage and act to influence one another. As Wachtel (1983) put it, the patient's difficulties require "accomplices" to maintain them. Thus, in describing the psychoanalytic situation, he wrote:

> It is in the very act of participating that the analyst learns what is most important to know about the patient. And it is in coming to see their joint participation in what is for him a familiar pattern—but a joint participation, with the crucial difference of reflectiveness—that the patient too learns what he must in order to begin the process of change [1983, p. 179].

In Levenson's (1983) words, "What the patient and the therapist talk about will simultaneously be shown or played out between them. . . . The power of psychoanalysis may well depend on what is said about what is done" (p. 88). Verbalization and behavior are seen as transforms of one another, and interactions—what happens between the analytic participants, are as important as what is said. What is "done" that is of interest is done not only by the patient but by the participant-analyst as well, and there is value in clarifying the correspondence between verbal and action levels of communication. The view that interaction is inevitable and therapeutically integral results in the collaborative attempt to understand mutual impact as the analytic medium.

Ehrenberg (1982, 1984, 1992) also has described the patient and the therapist as continually influencing and being influenced by each other in a dialectical way, often without awareness. Ehrenberg (1992) wrote:

> Focusing on the interface of the analyst-patient interaction is not the same as focusing on the patient or the analyst. Rather, it is the nature of the integration, the quality of contact, what goes on between, including what is enacted and what is communicated affectively and/or unconsciously, that is addressed [p. 33].

Stern (1989) described the necessity of analyzing the analytic interaction, that is, articulating and clarifying it. He wrote:

> As long as patient and analyst are reacting to one another without questioning what they are doing, they are caught in the grip of the field. . . . But of course the grip is only useful because

sometimes it is broken. This happens only when patient or analyst becomes able to observe the interaction and question it, i.e., formulate it [p. 21].

In summary, the one-person psychoanalytic situation, structured to minimize interaction, has been transformed by those theorists who make therapeutically central that which formerly was avoided—the transference-countertransference interaction. Every moment of an analysis, every single development is to be understood in terms of the converging influence of the two individuals and the ways that the two participants cocreate them. For this group of two-person-model analysts, elucidating these interactions constitutes the core of the psychoanalytic work.

The Need for Psychoanalytic Realism

A one-person model regards external reality, the analyst included, as little more than an external screen onto which the patient projects meaning reflecting his or her inner world. The individual's inner world and its imprint on external reality are held in the foreground by analysts following this model; the actual external reality, including the patient's interactions within it, and the analyst's personal contribution to those interactions, are of secondary importance. Externals must be eliminated or carefully controlled. Thereby, a special sort of analytic reality is established, a reality regarded as separate from the patient's (and analyst's) ordinary life, that must be carefully maintained.

Many analysts, among them those influenced by relational ideas, continue to see the psychoanalytic situation as a unique domain (Renik, 1998). Accordingly, it has been described as a "different level of reality," an "'unreal' context," or "unlike anything else in ordinary life" (Modell, 1991). It is seen as occurring in "potential space," within "the realm of illusion" (Winnicott, 1951), or as creating a unique "analytic third" subjectivity (Ogden, 1994). The psychoanalytic relationship has been conceptualized as "an analytic space, a sort of vacuum which the patient can fill [with] his own internal theater" (Sandler and Sandler, 1993). In other words, a special analytic environment is defined that is distinguished qualitatively from ordinary relationships and does not conform to the same conceptual framework used in describing other relationships, such as temporal reality (Green, 1975; Viderman, 1979). Davies (1998), in reinforcing safe boundaries for a patient who was beginning to experience emerging, erotic transference feelings, defined the analytic relationship as "a place of thought, not action; a place that could never exist in real time and space; an imaginary place unbridgeable with the real world" (p. 764). But when analysts emphasize the psychoanalytic relationship as a special reality in these ways, a great deal may be lost. I think we do so as a carryover from a one-person model.

I do not wish to minimize the importance of that which is unique in the analytic relationship. Each analysis is a singular relationship, uniquely cocreated by two individuals and elaborated within a uniquely psychoanalytic, asymmetrical structure. But that is not the special sense many of these theorists intend when they characterize the analytic medium as a very different realm and reality (or unreality). Implicitly, many of these theorists de-emphasize the ways in which the psychoanalytic relationship is like others occurring in ordinary, everyday life. I believe there is value in seeing the analytic relationship as governed by the same principles as any other relationship, but expressed through and elaborated within a very particular asymmetrical structure. Conceptualizing the psychoanalytic relationship as a unique domain supports analysts' performing certain of their essential functions. Specifically, metaphorical conceptualizations that privilege the role of fantasy in the analytic relationship help analysts avoid imposing themselves on patients, enabling patients, in turn, to give the fullest expression to their innermost worlds—their deepest feelings, fears, expectations, and other potentially unrealistic experiences, in an atmosphere of safety. These conceptualizations support the asymmetry that permits patients' structures to emerge, recognizably, into the work, while honoring the delicate balance between the analyst's influence and the patient's autonomy (Mitchell, 1998). It should be noted, however, that these ways of understanding psychoanalytic participation and personality change do not depend on metaphorical conceptualizations defining a unique sort of psychoanalytic reality or space; indeed, they are understood quite practically.

In emphasizing that the psychoanalytic relationship is uniquely paradoxical or dialectical, an extraordinary space, analysts must not overlook or minimize the ways in which other social relationships also can be understood in terms of paradox and dialectics. For instance, all relationships, even our most intimate ones, and not just the analytic relationship, impose certain limits on the closeness that is possible and require us to find ways of making accommodations to them. Likewise, while we certainly do not collect a fee for listening to or advising a friend who may need a sympathetic ear, there are nevertheless other expressions of the quid pro quo that comes into play in everyday relationships. Further, we are normally, and not just in analytic roles, required to find a balance between expressions of self-interest and the perceived interests of others, and thus to maintain a sensitivity to others while trying to accomplish personal or professional goals. These and the many other self-contradictory elements that operate within the psychoanalytic relationship are not unique to it, but are defined and elaborated in very specific ways, receiving closer and more explicit attention within the asymmetrical structure, than in outside relationships.

Renik (1998) has criticized ideas of a dialectical or paradoxical psychoanalytic reality that imply an equilibrium, a static condition lacking progression. Certainly Modell's (1991) formulations can be understood in that way; he stresses the value of an acceptance of contradictory phenomena without a striving for synthesis. Even Pizer (1998), who develops his ideas about negotiation within the psychoanalytic dyad so usefully, asserts the need for the analyst's "preservation" of paradox. As an alternative to these views, Renik emphasizes the Hegalian idea of a progressive dialectical process in which contradictory propositions contend with one another until one prevails or until they reach a new integration—the familiar thesis, antithesis, and synthesis, analogous to conflict resolution. This progressive way of thinking about the psychoanalytic relationship, related to a process I call righting the relationship (chapter 5), can be extremely useful. Accordingly, rather than emphasize the need to preserve paradox and unreality, the analyst engages the patient in a dialectical sort of reality testing in analysis, that is, articulating and clarifying the sources of the patient's views of reality through a comparison with those of the analyst. Through such negotiations, both partners are enabled to adjust subjective realities and, especially in the patient's case, to discover new and more adaptive ways of viewing and experiencing life in general.

When, at the expense of acknowledging continuities with ordinary reality, we focus on and maintain paradoxical elements as unique in the analytic relationship, we run the risk of reinforcing schizoid elements in the analyst's stance. Thus I emphasize a different sort of paradox—that the psychoanalytic relationship is different from all other relationships and yet the same, unreal in that its asymmetrical structure gives play to powerful residues of the past, but also real in that, as in other relationships, the actions of both participants also are shaped by reality-oriented processes and adaptations. Differences between the analytic and other relationships are, in such a view, a matter of degree and thus wrongly characterized as an imaginary place unbridgeable with the real world. Rather, I find advantages in regarding patients' experiences with their analysts—how they make sense of, adapt to, and work with their individual analysts' personalities and the paradoxes that are built into the analytic relationship—in terms of their similarities to the efforts patients make with other persons in ordinary reality, and how they learn new and more adaptive ways of relating. What is significant from this point of view is not that the paradoxes of analytic reality are unique or distinct; indeed, contradictory aspects are common, if manifested differently, in all our intense relationships. In addition to playing a major role in patients' and analysts' reworking their personal relationship together, paradoxical and dialectical aspects of the analytic relationship become significant as they reveal how individuals function with others—specifically, how they go about negotiating with others many of the very same contradictory and conflictual elements that are expressed in ways different from, yet in ways similar to, their relationships with their analysts.

Advantages exist in attending to what the psychoanalytic relationship has in common with other, ordinary relationships, and with day-to-day, or extraanalytic reality, as well as appreciating what defines it as singular. Approaching the psychoanalytic relationship in a pragmatic spirit of realism encourages a concern with how the patient actually copes with life's challenges and lives daily life in extraanalytic reality. This orientation to the patient becomes of the utmost significance in chapters 9 and 10 when our interest in action and change is extended to the analyst's attempts to influence patients' maladaptive behavior patterns.

Perspectival Realism

The detached monadic analyst's functioning is based on a simple positivist assumption drawn from the natural science tradition. In that view, it is assumed that there is a single knowable reality and distortions of it, and that the psychoanalyst can be the arbiter of the two. Analysts following the one-person model either argue against the analyst's attention to external reality and reality testing (Stein, 1966), suggesting that it forecloses exploring a patient's fantasies (Abend, 1982); or, from a positivist perspective, discuss reality and reality testing in a way that assumes the existence of a single, determinable reality (Interbitzin and Levy, 1994, for example). These one-person-model analysts believe, further, that focusing on the real, or external, aspects of a patient's life—the reality of the analyst, the patient's extrasession life or behavior—interferes with the patient's observation of his or her own mental processes (Laplanche and Pontalis, 1973; Boesky, 1982; Gray, 1994). They reason that such an orientation directs attention outward to the perceptual world rather than inward toward one's own mental processes, where, in one-person models, it belongs. Stein (1966), for example, explains that analysts should not introduce their own judgments about patients' assessments of reality but instead, by analyzing, reduce patients' distortions of reality. Stein writes, "By attaining a clearer vision of his own mental processes, by unsparing honesty with himself, we hope that our patient's distortions of perceptions of the outer world will be reduced to a minimum" (p. 276). The logic here is consistent with the one-person idea of individuals as separate, self-enclosed systems and with the anonymous analyst's investment in maintaining a pure analytic field for the emergence of the patient's transferences and their interpretation.

That reasoning opposes the intrinsically transactional way of understanding mental functioning that prevails in relational views. A two-person model accommodates the importance of the real characteristics of the analyst and of the features of the psychoanalytic situation. There has developed a perspectivist view of realism (Nagel, 1995), combining that which may exist independently in reality and how it is individually grasped or understood. This model for understanding the analysand's experience is radically different from one-person model psychoanalytic conceptualizations that isolate intrapsychic functioning. Thus analysts have turned their attention to mental processes and the ways that people *construct* their reality. Constructivism, social constructivism, narrative theory, the Piagetian paradigm, and postmodernism all reflect different attempts of this sort (Stern, 1997). Let us consider the perspectivist idea further.

Winnicott (1971), writing of the given and the made, noted that they constitute a paradox. As Stern (1997) described, "We take given experience and make it into something that is our own; but it is just as true that we make or construct experience only by avoiding violations of the givens that define what the experience can be" (p. 3). Constructivist and hermeneutic accounts (see Stern) have had a profound influence on two-person-model psychoanalysts. These accounts of the patient's experience assume that there exists no natural or intrinsic organization—that it is "fundamentally ambiguous" (Mitchell, 1993, p. 57)—until it is engaged and organized through interpretation, which is accomplished once the patient takes a perspective on it. Accordingly, inner and outer are understood as a dialectic in continuous flux, with experience seen as the joint creation of interacting influences from within and without—from social life as well as the enduring structures of one's inner world. All experience, even the most ordinary and familiar, is interpretive or perspectivistic activity. We organize whatever is given in the present emotionally and cognitively from past relational experience.

Drawing from her academic background in philosophy, Orange (1995) explains that all experience is both given and made—not just conceived in either way, like the particles and waves of quantum physics or the ducks and rabbits of Gestalt theory. The given, the brute, or that which is at least partly unprocessed is undeniable events or occurrences. The given, she points out, is a necessary epistemological, logical, and psychological condition for the possibility of experiencing, that is, for creating the made. The act of making relates to subjective and relational organizing activity. To experience is to organize the given. No longer does the resolution of maladaptive transference elements depend on the patient's recognizing his or her own contribution in pure culture, as with a blank screen, or an anonymous analyst, for example; rather, transference becomes clarified through refining the patient's recognition and understanding of his or her participation in relation to that of the analyst and what each makes of the given.

What the patient understands about the analyst, as well as what the analyst understands about the patient, is subject to individual organizing activity and thus is a matter of perspective. That involves the analyst's psychodynamics, like the patient's, played out within the context of mutuality in the intersubjective psychoanalytic situation. Countertransference can be the patient's, as the analyst's. Subjectivity and perspectivism reign in the two-person view, tending to equalize the participants' claims to truth. The analyst's knowledge, like the patient's, is perspectival; it cannot transcend their respective psychodynamics, the reverberating effects of interpersonal interactions, or the analyst's theoretical commitments.

There are many forms of constructivism. "Radical constructivism," which connotes a virtually solipsistic relativism, can be distinguished from "critical constructivism," connoting an interaction between a partially independent reality and the activity of human subjects

(Mahoney, 1991). The latter view corresponds to the perspectivist position taken here. Analysts following radical forms of perspectivism interpret as constructions *whatever* the patient makes of the analyst. Taking perspectivism to an extreme, these analysts run the risk of returning to the notion of the analyst as a reflecting mirror since that approach deals with the patient's mental processes alone and overlooks the real characteristics and actions of the analyst that the patient is adapting to. This point is key in understanding the two-person perspective I am advancing; ideas failing to acknowledge the importance of the given do not allow analysts to thoroughly cultivate the two-person implications of the analyst's participation and to grapple with the dynamic meanings given by the patient to the contribution of the analyst.

The Analyst as a Real Person

Historically, the fantastic, or transference, aspect of the therapy relationship and its analysis were thought to carry the therapeutic action. In that view, the nontransference relationship with the analyst was minimized, being appreciated mainly as an alliance that had the primary function of fostering insight into the patient's distortions. But once it is understood that internal structures both shape and are shaped by the patient's external world, and the patient's actions within it, there can be no avoiding the reality of the analyst and the role of the total relationship that exists between the analytic pair. This expression of realism has far-reaching and compelling ramifications for our understanding of psychoanalytic technique and the therapeutic action. What, specifically, each analyst may choose to do, technically, with that awareness, is an individual matter; but, although the analyst's individual contribution may be incorporated in a variety of alternative ways, somehow it must be dealt with.

Therapeutic objectives are not realized by avoiding the reality of the analyst, but rather by incorporating the analyst's personhood into the treatment. Interactions with the analyst now have significance not only at the level of the patient's fantasy but also in terms of the patient's perspective on the real contribution of the analyst and the very real and potentially healing interaction between the two persons. Conceptualizing in terms of perspectival realism accommodates a recognition of both aspects of the analytic relationship—that which is real as well as that which is constructed. Some analysts are, in reality, depressed, serious, cautious, or anxious in ways as noticeable as an analyst's consistent lateness, for example. The reality of these analysts' characteristics and the actions related to them, while certainly less readily objectifiable than punctuality, must somehow be dealt with technically. To treat patients' perceptions of these analyst characteristics as if they were entirely the patients' creations clearly is not, in the two-person model, a valid way to conduct transference analysis.

The perspectivist, or constructivist, mode of understanding the participants' experience meets the requirements of a two-person psychoanalytic model. Interventions now become based on the assumption that the patient may always be responding to something real about the analyst, but doing so in his or her own way. Analysis is thus conducted on a perspectivist foundation—that is, not on the assumption that the patient's (or analyst's) perception is either constructed or actual, but that it is both and as such is only one of many possible perspectives on what has happened and one of many ways that what has occurred might be perceived or experienced. The individuality of the analyst, expressed in his or her real contribution, is not excluded but now can become incorporated into transference analysis.

The patient and the therapist bring the same propensities to treatment that they bring to all their other relationships. For the patient, of course, this assumption provides the very basis of the analyst's ability to make any therapeutic claims. That is not to say that the therapy relationship does not have some unique characteristics, among them its asymmetrical structure and primary interest in advancing the emotional growth of the patient; in this respect it resembles a parent –child relationship. Other relationships also have many of the same attributes that we are inclined to assign only to the analytic relationship—limits that must be negotiated, a quid pro quo, selecting what to disclose and what not to, accommodating to another individual's communicative characteristics, and tact, to name a few. Likewise, other relationships, not just the analytic one, involve paradoxes—intimacy within limits, for example. In other words, the treatment relationship is real, like any other; it varies along the same parameters as ordinary relationships, with differences being those of degree.

Many analysts have tended recently to emphasize the role of negotiation in the analytic relationship. As Pizer (1998) put it:

> We shape, and, in turn, are shaped by our partners. . . . Collusive
> relationships are forged around the negotiation of mutually
> invested defenses and repetitions, and therapeutic or mutually

enhancing relationships are created and evolved through an ongoing negotiation that allows for self-expression, spontaneity, and self-revelation in a context of safety, respect, and reciprocity [p. 3].

Yet it is erroneous to suggest that these processes of negotiation are qualitatively distinct from those that occur in ordinary relationships.

The analytic relationship, when understood on the basis of a two-person model, has unique attributes that foster authentic contact and an unusual sort of intimacy; but they exist within ordinary or everyday reality. As Renik (1996) has pointed out, if the goal of treatment is to enable the patient to explore within the analytic relationship how he or she operates in the world, with an eye toward making constructive changes, then the patient is best served when both analyst and patient think of their relationship as "ordinarily real." The patient and the therapist progressively make contact as real people—what Fairbairn (1958) described so many years ago as "behavior [or relationship] in an open system in which inner and outer reality are brought into relation" (p. 381). Fairbairn's idea of bringing inner and outer reality into relation corresponds to the perspectival idea and to the more familiar and very useful terminology of Piagetian cognitive psychology—in particular, to the simultaneous operation of the processes of assimilation and accommodation, the one assimilating new experience into old structures, and the other promoting adaptations to the new and the real. Now transference analysis is concerned with the analyst as a real person, and the ongoing resolution of transference proceeds concurrently with the development of mutual recognition and intimacy as goals of an analysis.

CHAPTER 4

THE ANALYST AND THE ROLE
OF ENACTMENTS

*A*ction language, paradoxically, is our original "mother tongue" (Schafer, 1976). Mothers typically respond to their babies' messages long before their children can reach them through words. Babies, too, are able to read and respond to nonverbal communications. Even before spoken language is learned, one's facial expressions, posture, gestures, rhythm, and vocalistics become capable of requesting, giving, withholding, expressing contentment—in other words, capable of *influencing* others. These nonverbal skills, the very first form of communication, are practiced and mastered long before words, as each mother-infant pair works out its own subtly choreographed, unique interaction system, attuning to one another's affective states (Stern, 1985; Beebe and Lachmann, 1992). That first vocabulary, consisting of a language of action, is an effective one that never is relinquished. Instead, although it becomes integrated with a vocabulary of words that eventually seems to predominate, the continuing language of action shapes and, in turn, is shaped by each participation in the process of intersubjective exchange.

Interest in enactments reflects the ongoing shift within psychoanalysis toward a system acknowledging the inherent role of action. The concept of enactment has been understood in a variety of useful ways—on the basis of role-responsiveness, projective identification, and other mutual, regulatory processes that structure the psychoanalytic, like other relationships. Here I define enactments as automatic, preconscious interaction patterns involving both participants' unique, interlocking, personal psychodynamic systems. Enactments have real and symbolic meanings, and, depending on their nature and fate, they may be either adaptive or maladaptive within the framework of the psychoanalytic relationship. An awareness of the importance of enactments shifts the analyst's attention from verbal content alone to preconscious communication processes conveyed both verbally and nonverbally. Patients' and therapists' actions are thus seen as expressions containing important unconscious information about both participants and the interactions occurring between them. Although clinical decisions never can be prescribed, they are developed against a highly complex background involving a variety of theoretical and clinical variables; significant among them is the role of enactments.

While virtually all psychoanalysts agree that enactments play some role in the psychoanalytic process, the ways in which they are understood and the role they play remain ambiguous, with significant differences, especially, between understandings based on one-person and two-person treatment models.

Historical Background and Definition

The specific term enactment is of fairly recent origin. Although it is not even defined in Moore and Fine's (1990) standard psychoanalytic glossary, a panel (1992) of the American Psychoanalytic Association saw this concept as a needed and useful one for denoting resistive interactions that nevertheless offer a royal road to unconscious meanings that exist in both the analyst and the patient. Enactments were viewed by the panel mainly as a reflection of the patient's unconscious efforts to persuade or to force the analyst into a reciprocal action. It is in that sense regarded as a two-sided playing out of the patient's fundamental internalized configurations.

Hirsch (1998), exploring similarities, reasons that theorists of both classical and interpersonal psychoanalytic approaches have come to recognize the potentially positive role of action and enactments within an interactional psychoanalytic context. Still, there are some very real differences in the ways these two groups understand and apply the concept.

"Countertransference" Enactments

We have seen (chapter 3) that one-person-model analysts for many years understood the role of action, interaction, and thus enactments

as detrimental to the psychoanalytic process. These theorists emphasized how the actions of both the analyst and the analysand defensively substituted for words in a treatment modality depending
primarily on verbalization. Renik (1993b) has summarized the con-
sensual view among classical analysts as follows: "An analyst's *awareness* of his countertransference is an asset that contributes to analytic
work, while expression of his countertransference *in action* is a liabil-
ity that limits analytic work" (p. 136).

Enactments were first seen as "acting in," identified as resistive
forms of acting out that occurred within the analytic setting. The current understanding of enactments in classical circles can be traced to
the writings of Tower (1956), Bird (1972), and Sandler (1976a, 1981).
They approached an understanding of the concept as they acknowledged the importance of unconscious factors in the analyst's involvement, action, and the role of analytic interaction. These early papers
did not stimulate serious interest among those writing in the classical
tradition, however, until Jacobs's (1986) paper called attention to the
concept.[1]

Ahead of her time, Tower (1956) emphasized the importance of
the analyst's countertransference feelings, even calling attention to
the analyst's *transference* and to the analyst's expressions through
unwitting action, specifically, through interactions with patients' transferences. Noting the importance of the analyst's involvement, she
stressed the positive potential of an "emotional upheaval" in the relationship and the working-through of a mutual transference-countertransference neurosis that developed, with a resulting "new
orientation" on the part of *both* persons to one another. Tower also
recognized that such developments often could be recognized only
retrospectively. In a similar vein, Bird (1972) noted that analysts regularly became involved in their patients' transference neuroses and
developed "reciprocal transference reactions." Radically, he emphasized that analysts' becoming immersed in this way resulted in the
most profound forms of change. He explained that this development
was a way that the patient extended his or her intrapsychic conflict to
include the analyst, whereupon the analyst became the protagonist
and the patient the antagonist, or vice versa, in a very real conflict
within the analysis. According to Bird, the analyst's own transference
involvement was a necessary part of the therapeutic action.

---

1. Actually, Hoffman (1983) had described "enactments" in his classic paper.

Sandler (1976a, 1981), advancing his work within an object-relations framework, provided a very useful way of understanding enactments (although not using that term) that bridged intrapsychic and interpersonal processes. In the need for *actualization*, a person was thought to manipulate or provoke specific actions from others and to interact with them in ways that fulfilled wishful fantasies associated with early object relationships and with a feeling of safety. Sandler (1976a) observed, "The commonest way of making something 'real' or 'actual' is to act on the real world in such a way that our perception comes to correspond to the wished-for reality" (p. 39). He clarified that the analyst's participation in the analysand's old patterns through "role-responsiveness" was inevitable and that the analyst's responses always were, in fact, a compromise formation between the analyst's own propensities and a reflexive acceptance of the roles the patient forced on him or her. Significantly, Sandler noted that the analyst would "tend to comply with the role demanded of him [but] may only become aware of it through observing his own behavior, responses, and attitudes *after these have been carried over into action*" (p. 47).

Subsequently, other analysts began to appreciate the role of action and the analyst's involvement. McLaughlin (1981) saw the analyst as an involved participant-observer, fully capable of transferential (as distinguished from countertransferential) responses. In McLaughlin's view, the analyst's own perceptions were best understood in relativistic rather than positivistic terms; instead of setting off the analyst in a protected position that presumed to privilege his or her view of reality, McLaughlin emphasized the ambiguity of the analyst's perceptions and the ubiquitous role of the analyst's more or less evolved transferences. Later McLaughlin (1991) distinguished two forms of enactment. Accordingly, in the broadest sense, enactments are *all* the behaviors of both parties, including verbalizations, in consequence of the intensification of the action intent of our words created by the constraints and regressive push induced by the psychoanalytic situation. The analyst and the patient *both* are thought to act under pressure to create experiences that are consistent with their expectancies of self and other, thereby shaping a happening—an enactment. But McLaughlin further defined a second, more specific class of enactments—regressive (defensive) interactions occurring in the analytic dyad that are experienced by each person as a consequence of the behavior of the other. These involve the analyst's blind spots, representing regressions to "less evolved perceptiveness" that, according to McLaughlin, are caused by partially mastered conflicts that have been stirred up by the particular patient's dynamics and transference concerns. McLaughlin noted the ways these developments might be used to advance the analyst's understanding.

Boesky (1990) also has recognized the positive potential of the analyst's personal involvement. He writes, "If the analyst does not get emotionally involved sooner or later in a manner that he did not intend, the analysis will not proceed to a successful conclusion" (p. 573). Boesky appears to be describing enactments when he refers to the reciprocal action of adaptive or benign iatrogenic forms of resistance. He explains, "*The manifest form of a resistance is even sometimes unconsciously negotiated by both patient and analyst*" (p. 572). This concept refers to resistance as a "joint creation" to which the analyst inadvertently contributes as an unavoidable expression of his or her emotional involvement. Actualizing resistances, a central element of the psychoanalytic process, relates to the analyst's unwitting playing out of the patient's key internalizations; as such, enactments are crucial for analytic effectiveness.

Chused (1991) has defined enactments as "nonverbal communication (often cloaked in words) so subtly presented and so attuned to the receiver that it leads to his responding inadvertently in a manner that is experienced by the patient as an actualization of a transference perception, a realization of his fantasies" (p. 638). Chused does not take a fully bidirectional view in her account of enactments; instead she emphasizes the action of the patient on the analyst. Like McLaughlin, Chused stresses the advantages of an abstinent ideal. While she recognizes that it is rarely attainable, she takes a hard line:

> Sympathetic with a patient's pitiful state, he [the analyst] does not nurture; temporarily aroused by a patient's seductive attacks, he does not counterattack. . . . To want anything from patients, to want a cure, to help, even to be listened to or understood accurately, is to be vulnerable to the experience of one's own transference and thus be susceptible to an enactment [pp. 616–618].

Enactments and the Two-Person Model

Rejecting the narrow view of countertransference and more fully acknowledging their own ongoing participant roles in a two-person field, two-person model analysts are more inclined than the former group to accept and to find advantages rather than hindrances in enactments. In fact, many two-person-model theorists believe it is the dialectical relationship of enactments with new relational experience (see chapter 5), dealt with through negotiation, that drives important elements of the therapeutic action. Enactments thus are thought to be common in the psychoanalytic process. Rather than episodic lapses that occur under conditions of impasse, stress, or therapist regression, they are seen as forming an important semiotic dimension, with the relationship between patient and therapist continuously playing out in a patterned discourse of action (Levenson, 1983). Every dimension of the therapy—history, dreams, memories, acting out, transference and countertransference, the discourse of action—all are seen as interrelated parts of a whole. Thus, as Levenson put it, "The therapist's ability to range across these transformational variations of the patient's themes is . . . the therapist's true métier" (p. 83).

One narrative is spoken, and another may be communicated through action. According to Bromberg (1994), dissociated experience that has a weak or nonexistent linkage to the "me" as a communicable entity is normal, rather than psychopathological. Before these "not-me" states of mind can become objects of analytic self-reflection, however, they must first become "thinkable" and linguistically communicable through their enactment in the analytic relationship. Bromberg believes that the most powerful way dissociated elements become integrated is through the authentic analyst's ability to acknowledge the divergent realities held by discontinuous self-states and to create links to them through the immediacy of the analytic relationship. Distinguishing knowing one's patient profoundly and holistically through "direct relatedness," rather than mere understanding, he follows Ferenczi in advising, "Don't just listen to the words; try to see the dissociated speaker who is relating to you at that moment, the part of the self that 'lives on, hidden, ceaselessly endeavoring to make itself *felt*' (Ferenczi, 1930b, p. 122)" (p. 543, italics added).

So pervasive are enactments in the view of many interpersonal analysts that, no matter how the analyst conceptualizes what is occurring, there always is another prism of meaning through which it can be viewed, always another level of abstraction. Thus it is crucial that analysts become sensitive to what is being enacted while remaining aware that any effort to address it may itself constitute yet another level of potential enactment, one as complex as the interaction it seeks to illuminate (Ehrenberg, 1992).

We see that mutual enactments, a language of action, once held to be undesirable and avoidable, have come to be seen as pervasive, inevitable, and, potentially, a major factor in change. As Hoffman (1983) has described, the ubiquitous nature of enactments exists as "a certain thread of countertransference enactment throughout the analysis which stands in a kind of dialectic relationship with the process by which this enactment, as experienced by the patient, is analyzed" (p. 417). Renik (1993a,b, 1995, 1996) further emphasizes the role of the analyst's actions, especially unintended ones, in the therapeutic action. Like Bird (1972), he describes how the analysand's conflicts reach out to include the analyst; through enactments the transference-countertransference dialogue develops into a real relationship. Here a level of enactment is seen as ubiquitous, and awareness of it is *always* retrospective. Renik urges analysts to abandon their attempts to avoid enactments and to recognize that they are not only inevitable but *necessary* for the therapeutic action. In such a view, efforts to suppress countertransferential urges may be as detrimental to treatment as acting on those urges. Rather, analysts do well to wonder, on an ongoing basis, what am I caught up in right now, and why? And what does my experience have to do with the patient and his or her internal world?

A Clinical Example

Imagine eavesdropping on an ongoing therapy, simplified here for purposes of illustration. The analyst believes the work is proceeding smoothly as the pair successfully clarifies the patient's key psychodynamic issues, especially those related to the patient's extremely submissive orientation to others. The active agenda, to explore the patient's excessive passivity, understanding it mainly through his interaction with his pampering, slavishly overprotective mother, feels fitting and important to both participants. In addition to advancing insight, the process of inquiry seems to be encouraging the patient toward fuller self-assertiveness in his extraanalytic life, a therapeutic objective that is agreeable to both participants and that seems to confirm the value of the work. In general, the therapist has adopted a benevolent, encouraging stance with the patient, and the patient finds value in the analyst's overall posture and questioning, which the analyst (and perhaps the patient) would describe as appropriately "neutral."

However, this seemingly constructive interaction involves an enactment—an unconscious, collusive structuring of the relationship around some intersecting defenses and problematic dynamics of both participants. The therapist, an older sibling, is, among other transferences, indulging the constructive way he came to deal with his envy toward a younger brother, the obviously more cherished by a beloved parent. The patient, reciprocally, is expressing a compliant pattern that for him acted in the past as a shield from intensely competitive and rageful feelings toward his domineering father. Each participant thus inadvertently colludes to provide reinforcement for the self-protective behavior of the other. The result is an interaction that feels "therapeutic" enough to both of them and that facilitates the patient's growth by enabling him to see how he avoids being more self-assertive—at least with individuals other than the analyst. But, significantly, the enacted transference-countertransference configuration also provides both with safety from another, potentially threatening aspect of their relationship, as well as a very important, but unacceptable, side of their individual personalities. Neither participant is aware of his own participation on this protective level of exchange, or enactment, its impact, or its origins in past history. The therapist, although psychoanalytically sophisticated, is blinded and feels positive about the treatment, which seems to be going smoothly. However, clarity about what might hold the most power analytically and what does not is blurred for him.

As far as it goes, this way of interacting is "psychotherapeutic"; it affirms and liberates the inhibited patient's conflicted assertiveness in the external world and provides an adaptive role model for internalization, while offering the patient an apt narrative that supports a way of moving toward a more constructively assertive life adaptation. However, the approach is limited psychoanalytically; for while facilitating the patient's growth in certain respects, the therapeutic interaction also shields the patient (and analyst) from getting in touch with other important self and other configurations, the integration of which might be more empowering. This is the counterproductive sense in which we usually understand enactments—as a collusion around defensive ways of relating, or a discourse of joined action that inhibits verbalization and insight and fails to expand, optimally, the patient's capacity for relatedness.

So long as the analyst plays benevolent big brother, encouraging, indirectly, the patient's internalized sycophantic son's growth through greater assertiveness, the analyst will feel professionally worthwhile, safe from his own desires to outdo or even to taunt the patient (who represents his envied brother), and thus safe from stimulating similar, base inclinations in his patient. Of course the analyst is, in a strict sense, abusing the patient as the patient's father did, in the analyst's somewhat condescending analytic demeanor. The patient, correspondingly, is gaining from the therapist's seemingly benevolent attentiveness, safe thus far from having to grapple with his own competitive desires to outdo and even harm the analyst. So long as he is the "good" patient within this stifling framework, playing the "good son" to the analyst's "good" big brother, the patient (and analyst) can feel safe. But the price is great; aspects of his personality experienced as forbidden and potentially dangerous, and that inhibit self-realization, remain closed off, unintegrated.

Through this interaction, we see how the enactment both obscures, and yet holds the key to identifying and modifying, the patient's disturbance, and contains the potential for a new relational experience. That favorable outcome will become possible in the most meaningful sense only if the participants are able to become aware of, and to move out of the enactment. It seems reasonable to assume that these ways of relating probably are characteristic of both participants, to a degree, in their lives outside. If the two were to continue the analytic work in a thoroughgoing way, examining what the patient seems to want and need from the analyst and what he does not want, and how the analyst, in turn, for reasons of his own that might come to light, cooperates with those needs, then the two might grow to understand their relationship more and more intensively, revealing how and why they mutually avoid more aggressive forms of interaction.

Thus the enactment, including its origins in the pasts of both participants, eventually might come to light and be transformed. Negotiating both defenses and self-realizing voices, the pair can modify and extend their ways of relating; the patient might learn that he can feel safe with the analyst, even in aggressive states, integrating that sort of transference-countertransference configuration. What is enacted thus becomes a meaningful source of insightful structural change. In the view that is presented here, the ideal therapeutic result, at least for many patients, is one that is psycho*analytic*, involving more than practical changes alone but also an enhancing integration of avoided relational configurations and disavowed parts of the self.

Different Ways of Dealing With Enactments

Following the one-person model, it might be argued that the analyst in the example became "overinvolved," having suffered a lapse in analytic neutrality. In theory, at least, rather than being influenced by the patient's excessively friendly behavior, he should have been able to recognize and interpret the resistance involved in it. Reflecting the growing appreciation of the implications of the two-person model, many analysts who stress the advantages of intrapsychic psychoanalytic investigation (Boesky, 1990; Chused and Raphling, 1992, for example) reason that since enactments are inevitable it makes little sense to emphasize them as "lapses" in the analyst. Instead we should try to understand why they occur when they do, and we should increase understanding of the unconscious fantasies and conflicts in both participants which have prompted action. This development is an attempt to temper the prevailing view that enactments are extraordinary, episodic, regressive lapses in the analyst's ideal posture that reflect stressful phases in an analysis when the analyst's own unresolved conflicts are stirred up by the patient's psychodynamics. Yet, although the possibility of turning therapist action to therapeutic advantage is acknowledged, there remains the stronger implication that, ideally, it is to be avoided.

Analysts who emphasize the necessity of what has come to be called "optimal" abstinence strive to maintain a neutral position outside of the interaction and therefore beyond the reach of enactments. Sandler (1976a) pointed out, as Chused (1991) later implied, that "normally" the analyst is expected to "catch" this countertransference, especially if it seems inappropriate, and to regain an optimally abstinent stance. Thus enactments come to analysts' attention when they realize that they have done something "wrong." When enactments are identified—and they are thought in this model to occur relatively infrequently, perhaps because analysts are attending to what they should be doing, rather than what they actually are doing—they are to be traced back, privately, to the vulnerable analyst's own intrapsychic difficulties. As they are understood, especially in relation to the patient's psychodynamics, the analyst is enabled to restore a more evolved stance of neutrality and abstinence and then possibly interpret the enactment. The interpretive focus of the one-person-model analyst is to approach enactments through the internal experience of the patient, interpreting, for example, why the patient might wish to evoke a particular countertransference that the analyst has become aware of.

In a thoroughgoing two-person model, enactments can be understood more symmetrically and bidirectionally. They are understood intersubjectively as being shaped by ongoing interactions between the analyst's and patient's personal psychologies and the reverberating actions and influence processes occurring between them. For the two-person-model analyst, enactments and the negotiations that may follow from them operate at the very center of the therapeutic action, not just as the analyst struggles alone to avoid them but as the pair might struggle together to transcend their grip. The smooth-functioning one-person-model analyst, it is thought, can avoid action. In the two-person model, the inevitable role of the analyst's actual participation, and not abstinence, however, is stressed; involvement is the analyst's baseline stance. In this model, the unconscious, expressive languages of action and enactment, with their hold on the analyst manifested in degrees, are ubiquitous and must always be taken into account in working within the analytic process. There is no equivocation in this regard—enactments are continuous, not episodic; they are normal and potentially advantageous interpersonal occurrences, rather than expressions of pathological failures on the analyst's part. The two-person-model analyst, accepting that he or she may have unwittingly been pulled into an enactment, needs to be concerned with deleterious effects but also greets enactments as an opportunity to work toward new relational experiences in an emotionally immediate way. The analyst may choose to examine the analytic reality with the patient and, in order to explore it, sometimes might openly acknowledge that an enactment, in which the analyst played an active role, has occurred.

Fundamentally, enactments are a corollary of the two-person model of the psychoanalytic situation. They require a two-person model for their full understanding, and following the tenets of the one-person model limits the analyst's interpretive power in relation to them. The very term countertransference enactments, which classical (but not interpersonal) analysts have employed, emphasizes them as expressions of narrow, or regressive, countertransference and thus as therapist failures, rather than as normal interactive processes. Defining enactments within the markedly asymmetrical monadic structure that stresses the analyst's optimal abstinence results in a one-sided, intrapsychic formulation; specifically, instead of enactments being seen as actual interactions, they are understood in relation to the patient's experience and unconscious efforts to persuade or to force the analyst into undesirable, reciprocal action. This way of articulating the psychoanalytic situation does not integrate the idea of interaction in a thoroughgoing manner. And certainly the one-person-model approach discourages interest in understanding and exploring, together with the patient, the actual, unique role of the analyst's own participation, both deliberate and unwitting, in probing analytic developments. In the two-person model, it is not just the two separate one-person psychologies that matter—that is, using the data of enactments to clarify what is going on within each of the separate individuals, openly in the instance of the patient and privately for the analyst—but also the "space between us," as Mitchell (1988) put it—the interactive matrix comprising the complex interface of transference and countertransference.

Enactments and the Limitations of the One-Person Model

While finding a congenial framework in a fully developed two-person model, interactional conceptualizations like enactment are stretched to a conceptual breaking point when they are mixed with the treatment implications of the one-person model. To illustrate this point, let us consider Langs's (1982) theorizing about "rectification," a forerunner to later ideas about negotiation. With this idea, Langs attempted to advance a systematic way of understanding and working with enactments, a worthwhile project, but its application was stifled by the limiting influence of the monadic model. Langs's process of rectification is similar to my emphasizing monitoring the patient's reactions to the analyst's interventions as commentary on the contribution of the analyst (see chapter 5), but it is quite different in terms of the analytic actions involved in connection with such monitoring.

Rectification is a process introduced for managing countertransference. Countertransference is defined narrowly by Langs, compatibly with a one-person model; yet its manifestations are assumed to be inevitable, continuous, and even essential parts of the communicative interaction between therapist and patient. Every intervention, attitude, or response of the analyst, therefore, involves some degree of countertransference "disturbance." Recognizing the role of interaction, Langs believes that a therapist's countertransference is consistently under the influence of the patient's communications and always is but one element of the conscious and especially unconscious interaction between patient and therapist. He defines the process of rectification in terms of the need—before the therapist addresses "distorted," transference-based reactions to analysts' therapeutic interventions—first to review and monitor each of the patient's responses to interventions as potentially valid unconscious perceptions and responses to therapists' countertransference-based communications.

Langs points out that, paradoxically, countertransference, while detrimental, is nonetheless essential to the mutative process; once expressed inadvertently, it can be significantly modified and can ultimately contribute to a positive and insightful therapeutic resolution of the patient's neurosis. Langs sees the disturbed reactions of the analyst as having positive effects through their consistent recognition and rectification, and through the analysis of the patient's direct and derivative reactions to them. He even acknowledges that the patient might make strong therapeutic efforts on the analyst's behalf, with something inherently therapeutic in the patient's appreciation of the therapist's difficulties and the mobilization of the patient's therapeutic resources. Thus Langs sees countertransference and its positive potential as a dimension of every cure.

Langs's essential point was that, by carefully monitoring the patient's material for reparative efforts, the therapist could rectify countertransference influences while simultaneously analyzing the patient's responsive material. Through the process of rectification, including self-analysis, the analyst was to become aware of the underlying, unconscious fantasy that distorted his or her therapeutic functioning and overcome it. Langs states, "The therapist must implicitly reveal his or her ongoing struggle against countertransference expressions in order to provide the patient with a critical positive introject; the absence of signs of such a struggle is highly destructive to the therapeutic interaction" (p. 135). The process of rectification, while recognized by the analyst, was to be kept from the patient; the analyst acting alone would determine what "really" was countertransference and what, in fact, the patient could recognize of it. Calling direct attention to the interactions involved in rectification, or making them in any way manifest, was taboo. Aside from the indirect communication involved in the analyst's signs of "struggle" to conceal reactions, Langs prohibited any direct sharing of countertransference at all. That prohibition encompassed the subtle, potentially valuable communication processes involved in rectification, rich in both here-and-now as well as past determinants. A counterproductive level of mutual participation, although recognized and even mutually rectified, was to remain tacit. The royal road to the unconscious lives of both patient and analyst, as manifested through the subtleties of what was enacted between them, thus was not to be traversed. Instead, the analyst must strive for an unachievable analytic ideal, a preferable "countertransference-free" position from which the analyst could operate without undue subjective involvement. In this sense, the analyst was encouraged to concentrate attention on what *ought* to be happening, and to act accordingly, rather than analyzing what *actually* was happening in "the space between us."

Different from Langs's hybrid approach, which mixes one-person and two-person paradigms, the fully developed two-person model creates a more satisfactory framework for clarifying patients' psychodynamics as they are manifested in interactions with others (the analyst). Rather than striving to conceal the analyst's (and patient's) actions, the model provides the possibility of unraveling, directly and openly, the complex interactions between the participants' transferences, their sources in each person's psychodynamics, and shared attempts to rectify them. The "genuine, extensive, persistently constructive therapeutic efforts in the face of threat and danger" that Langs saw in the analyst's efforts to *withhold* countertransference and to work it through internally are nowhere more compelling, on the basis of the two-person model, than in the *joint* struggle of a patient and therapist to recognize and emerge from troubled transference-countertransference enactments and act collaboratively to right the relationship. (This idea, "righting" the relationship, is further developed in chapter 5.)

A thoroughgoing interpretation of the two-person model provides a more adequate way of thinking about enactments. It takes a view that is continuous with, and offers insight that can be grasped within the framework of, the patient's relationships with others as well as the analyst, and also internalized relationships. Here analytic exploration is not necessarily confined to the patient's internal experience, but also may include interpersonal interactions. In this view, it is a mistake to emphasize that enactments alone provide the analytic relationship with its immediacy and reality. The total relationship contributes to that reality, including the discovery, reworking, and transformation of enactments—that is, the transition to new relational experience, which enhances the emotional and personal significance of the experience for the patient.

Once the therapeutic importance of new relational experience is acknowledged as a significant element in the therapeutic action, it follows that the role of enactments, or "old relational experience," as it were, becomes defined in a different way. The residual influence of the one-person model, stressing interpretation and insight, causes a reluctance to grant importance to the role of new relational experience, and thus to integrate as pervasive the significance of enactments. Although enactments are seen as providing an important avenue to insight, they are thought to operate differently, and in a more limited way, as a factor in the therapeutic action.

Interactional conceptualizations such as those of Langs, stretched to a conceptual breaking point under the influence of the one-person model, find a congenial framework in the two-person model. With an action orientation emphasizing process, experience, and interaction, the two-person-model analyst need not defend against his or her subjectivity or necessarily avoid its expression. Instead, monitored subjectivity, sometimes shared and openly explored, becomes a powerful source of analytic data in unfolding a shared exploration of authentically lived experience that can lead to places neither participant might have anticipated.

In summary, differences are diminishing as analysts committed to both forms of theory (one-person and two-person) have come to recognize that enactments play an integral role in analytic communication (Hirsch, 1998). Merely recognizing that enactments play an analytic role, however, does not mean that they are understood in the same way, have the same significance, or that they are addressed therapeutically in the same manner. In fact, on each of these levels, there are significant differences among practitioners, based on how they draw from one-person and two-person models.

The Two-Person Model, "Unanalyzed" and "Therapeutic" Enactments

Extending the traditional opposition between action and insight, enactments are seen in the one-person model primarily as resistive phenomena. In the two-person model, enactments are not necessarily seen as resistive; they also can represent positive, growth-enhancing interactions. Many relational analysts have emphasized that the patient's interpersonal orientation to others (including, of course, the analyst) involves a desire for a constructive, reparative relationship that coexists with the fear associated with experiencing ironic success in re-creating the pathogenic past. Thus, through enactments the patient not only may act defensively but also may express strivings for a potentially more constructive, or reparative, attachment to the analyst. The selfobject transferences of psychoanalytic self psychology signify this sort of relating. Thus the pair may collude around mutual defenses and avoidances, but also may integrate mutually enhancing transference-countertransference configurations that involve spontaneous self-expression, self-realization, and reciprocity. Accordingly, my finding spontaneous humor in what a patient dreads, or aligning myself in a spontaneously affirming way with an emerging and previously unacceptable aspect of the patient's personality, may contribute to a patient's growth. From this vantage point, the one-person-model analyst's avoidance of involvement and participation can be seen as thwarting the patient's need for the constructive relatedness associated with self-reparative efforts and psychological growth.

As the role of action becomes increasingly recognized as inherent in psychoanalysis, there is value in distinguishing between patient-therapist enactments that represent a counterproductive collusion around defensive repetitions and the avoidance of potentially threatening interactions—what have been called "countertransference enactments," and therapeutic forms of enactment. The latter may or may not be conscious or deliberate on the part of the analyst. Enactments are counterproductive when the participants have been blinded to the realization that transference-countertransference configurations are constricted, that analytic developments have become rigidified, and that therapeutic growth processes have become stalemated. But they also can be therapeutic when, even without insight, the two individuals are able to achieve an authentically new, mutually-enhancing experience together.

The idea of deliberately interacting in ways that may to the analyst seem beneficial, and not necessarily analyzing these interactions, is, according to some relational analysts, compatible with the shift to a view of psychic structure based on relational patterns. Psychic structure can be favorably modified by new sorts of interactions because structure itself consists of internalized interactions represented in a particular way (Greenberg, 1992). As Gill (1994) pointed out, ideas such as Greenberg's about neutrality, involving the analyst's making himself or herself "available" in particular ways, "may imply witting maneuvers that are not analyzed" (p. 51). Indeed, attempts to analyze everything, even all the aspects of possible enactments, drains the important "real life" quality of the experience. The need to do that, itself, ought to be analyzed (Hoffman, 1996). Desirable or not, the analyst's unwitting participation in enactments occurs on an ongoing basis. Therapists actually have little choice in the matter, and, in any event, if enactments are not themselves forms of positive new relational experience, they may be forerunners to it. Additionally, the pair's becoming caught up in a stifling enactment and working their way out of it may constitute a very important aspect of the therapeutic action in the two-person model.

While it is often preferable for the patient to gain explicit insight, there is no doubt that certain *uninterpreted* enactments can, within limits, provide a form of new experience that has substantial psychotherapeutic impact. Transference-countertransference negotiations, including many that remain tacit and are never even identified, undoubtedly play a highly significant role in the reworking of the relationship. Analysts, of course, are always partially unaware of their actions and the sources of them, and thus of their participation in enactments. On the basis of considerations of intrinsic "fit" between patients' and therapists' personalities, therapists may quite spontaneously act in ways that allow patients to overcome salient maladaptive expectancies and to participate in and develop new and salutary relational patterns that become internalized. Every experienced analyst has had the experience of patients they find relatively easy to work with; without a great deal of deliberation or effort, therapists' instincts guide them to a stance that proves to be quite naturally therapeutic. At times, analysts may become as mystified as patients sometimes do as to how dramatically positive results were so readily achieved. Yet we know, too, that such developments also may be a cause for the analyst's suspicions.

The Limits of the Usefulness of the Concept of Enactments

In stressing the dangers of countertransference enactments, analysts run the risk of operating at a remove that closes off constructive participation and even limits access to their own experience. But too broad a concept of enactments, or one emphasizing their therapeutic value, threatens to leave the concept so broad as to be meaningless. Since the analyst's reactions to the patient, like those of the patient to the analyst, inevitably involve responses to the other's influence on all levels, all patient–therapist interactions must be considered as possible enactments. We might ask, are there any moments when the pair is not enacting something? It can be argued, plausibly, that every single interaction, including the pair's efforts at clarification, might involve levels of enactment encompassing each's attempts to influence the other, consciously and preconsciously, so as to maintain a safe attachment.

How can we understand enactments in a way that captures their broad meaning but preserves their analytic utility? Although the working analyst's self states are constantly shifting, one may find oneself moved in a direction that may feel extreme in relation to his or her more usual modes of analytic relating. For example, a depressed patient whom I saw for a short time seemed to me to be doing splendidly, taking to the analytic task like a duck to water. I saw him productively achieving insight, including work in the transference, and I felt excited about the work; my excitement was confirmed by his reports of improvement in his mood. It was only after months of our working "so well" together that I began to develop suspicions about our invigorating analytic partnership. My suspicions were stirred as I noticed how extreme was my enjoyment of the work with this patient, and how eagerly I anticipated sessions. My suspicions were furthered by a growing awareness that, rather than expanding, his insights remained at superficial levels as the work proceeded. I lost the sense of movement one develops when things seem to be going well. One day he speculated that I was depressed. I was not aware of feeling so. When we questioned and more closely examined what was going on between us, we gradually began to realize that some part of what was happening could be understood in relation to enacting a childhood role of his cheering up his depressive mother. The mother, locked into a dreary marriage and a life of thwarted personal achievement, had counted on my patient to be her "sunshine." Thus my patient and I enacted a behavior pattern that, appearing at first quite acceptable by psychoanalytic standards, proved to be motivated by a profound desire to cheer me up. My role was, of course, unclear to me. But I was not aware of feeling depressed, and that, plus the extraordinary enthusiasm I experienced about the treatment, was the discrepancy that led to an awareness of the enactment. I believe that any therapist would have been pleased with this patient's apparent gains, but he and I shared a common issue from childhood that might have predisposed me to "fall into" this pattern—a similar role with a depressive parent. It is a disturbing realization that prolonged, counterproductive enactments can go along disguised—that is, experienced by both participants—as "good therapy" while actually stifling more meaningful forms of analytic growth.

Consider another example, this time emphasizing how the mutual negotiation of an enactment resulted in a favorable analytic development. An analyst, intimidated by a long-term patient who raged, accused her of exploitation and greed, and threatened to leave whenever the idea of a fee increase was introduced, has worked for a ridiculously low fee for many years. The arrangement grew to feel intolerably demeaning and, finally, the analyst was prepared to take a stand. Placing the fee issue in a therapeutic perspective, the analyst announces that the patient must pay a more appropriate fee or she will consider ending the treatment. Following a brief struggle, the patient agrees to the increase, and the result turns out to be extremely favorable for their work. It removes a block that has inhibited areas of the work, and now for the first time, retrospectively, the two are able to talk about the many meanings the fee has had for the patient, including envy. The pair comes to realize that the analyst's "unilateral" decision was hardly that; without conceptualizing it, she had sensed that the patient was now able to tolerate the increase and handle such a confrontation, which in the past would have been narcissistically devastating and threatening to the viability of the relationship. The patient had somehow signaled that readiness. Undoubtedly, this promising development resulted from a *mutual* evolution, a negotiation that incorporated the regulation and recognition of each by the other, in terms of the pair's readiness to address their enactment around the fee.

The analytic "contract" varies from pair to pair. "Breaches" alert the participants to discordant patterns. The formal analytic contract, asymmetrically structured, involves the patient's goals of spontaneity, openness, awareness, insight, and ultimately change. It provides guidelines enabling the analyst to recognize gross resistances in the patient in the form of noncompliance, as when a patient makes small talk rather than getting down to analytic business, as it were. Yet in the foregoing examples we saw that other, "tacit" agreements also can develop within the relationship in the forms of happenings, enactments. The partners, collusively structuring a cheerful relationship, seemed to be following the formal contract while actually avoiding more serious, and especially potentially disheartening, concerns. A "special" fee is set. Moving toward familiar forms of attachment, each participant conforms to, and is, at some level, gratified by the subliminal beckoning involved in the other's actions, while inadvertently providing the other with a reciprocal, subliminal hook that prompts the other's corresponding unreflective participation. As long as the analyst and the patient are swept along in the enactment, finding mutual "gratification" and seeming to be in harmony, with each playing his or her part, it is virtually impossible for the interaction that is preconsciously enacted by the two to be identified and analyzed. Here I have in mind not constructive or therapeutic enactments, but counterproductive ones that typically have characterized the individual's dealings with others in outside relationships—and which led up to the patient's coming for treatment.

How are enactments revealed so as to become analyzed? When either the analyst or the patient comes to see the shared basis for the relationship and its smooth functioning differently from the other and experiences a need for something different (the therapist's need is more likely, but not always, to be grounded in and defined by the formal analytic contract), then there develops a discordant sense of the relationship with conflict developing between the two (Greenberg, 1995a). ("No. I really don't feel depressed. Why does that matter now? And why so much?"—leading to a discussion of his need to brighten my day.) An astute colleague, removed from the patient–analyst interactive field, might be able to help the analyst recognize enactments. Consultation can be enormously helpful in this regard. More commonly, something strikes the analyst as "off," especially if he or she is listening for that part of the patient that is endeavoring to make itself *felt* or is wondering about the sense in which the patient is "making use" of him or her. The analyst may shift from feeling pleased to noticing that the patient needs too much to be pleasing; the patient reports only successes, for example, apologizes for applying the analyst's wisdom clumsily, is too concerned with the analyst's good mood, tries too hard to be the "good" patient, or is too forgiving when the analyst is terribly late in starting sessions. The analyst feels bullied or, overcoming a nagging inhibition, takes a stand. Or the patient questions the way the analyst is working, enabling the analyst to discover unrecognized aspects of his or her own participation. Now the treatment has become skewed; the pair is no longer working in a way that suits both. With such a breach in the shared analytic contract the pair can begin to penetrate and formulate their enacted relatedness, develop new ways of interacting, and progress toward a growing intimacy in which their authentic voices can be increasingly expressed and heard by one another. The enactment can be recognized only retrospectively, and only then by the conscientious analyst who is vigilant about them.

In addition to breaches that may be noted, the examples show other features that might cue the analyst that a clinically meaningful enactment is occurring. The affective tone of the relationship had become inappropriate, exhilarating and yet constricted, or perhaps extreme, with sessions somehow routine and superficial. The interaction pattern resembles other, problematic relationships of the patient, present and past. Other indications include the analyst's inexplicable experience of affective intensity, pressure, distress, or a sense of the uncanny. The analyst may wonder, for example, why did I say or do that?

Enactments and Collaborative Technique

It was once believed that the less participatory the analyst was, the more limited was the potential for enactments. Now the validity of that observation, as well as the therapeutic price of the analyst's detached posture, is being questioned. The detached analyst avoids constructive forms of active participation without assurances of avoiding counterproductive enactments. In fact, it may be precisely when the analyst's participation is presumed beyond question *not* to be an enactment, but rather to be securely "neutral," that the relationship is, in fact, in the greatest jeopardy of being a counterproductive enactment. It has been argued that it is precisely at those moments when the analyst most fully believes his or her clinical judgment to be most objective, rather than subjectively based, that there is the greatest danger of self-deception and departure from sound technique (Renik, 1993a).

As I discuss in the following chapters, open and collaborative scrutiny of what is going on in the interaction, including the patient's scrutiny of the analyst's participation, often is the best protection against counterproductive enactments, especially because it may help to alert the analyst to preconscious forms of participation of his or her own, and thus clarify the patient's participation.

In this way, enactments—seen in this instance as a resistance in action—become the servants of progress. Looking at only one side of an enactment, however—either the analyst's or patient's, in isolation or emphasizing only detrimental effects—is not fully satisfactory. Both partners are participant-observers in the relationship. As enactments are cocreated, so is their clarification or "resolution" cocreated through collaborative technique.

CHAPTER 5

THE MANY MEANINGS OF NEW RELATIONAL EXPERIENCE

*I*t has been observed that if Freud was the father of psychoanalysis, then certainly Sándor Ferenczi was its mother (Hoffer, 1993, p. 75). Following Ferenczi's untimely death at the height of his creative powers, psychoanalysis was left to develop as Freud's "one-parent child." If Ferenczi's impact had been greater, then the importance of new relational experience might have been recognized long before it was. Ferenczi (1931), who challenged the Freudian ideal of analytic detachment as "professional hypocrisy," advocated creating a loving analytic relationship that would enable the patient to "feel the contrast between our behavior [analysts'] and that which he experienced in his real family—knowing himself safe from the repetition of such situations" (p. 132). Many of Ferenczi's seminal ideas, the precursors to contemporary views of new relational experience, were introduced by his followers (Michael Balint and Clara Thompson, for example) into different psychoanalytic schools. Therefore, although most analysts now have come to agree that new relational experience ranks as a major factor in the therapeutic action, there is a range of understandings of it.

Diverse Forms of New Relational Experience

Maintaining the primacy of advancing insight, analysts following the one-person model have understood the role of the psychoanalytic relationship primarily through "alliance" concepts. Recently, however, the analytic relationship has received attention in very different ways. Relational theorists as a group have asserted that something salutary occurs in the interaction itself, something that is new, different, and better than the analysand's past relationships—and something that is crucial in inducing personality change. For relational analysts, it is not interpretation alone that is crucial in change, and thus not just the analyst's role in maintaining an alliance to advance insight. The analyst interprets, but it is the quality of the object (or selfobject) relationship that develops around such interventions that is seen as central. Although relational analysts may agree on its significance, however, they have conceptualized new relational experience in a multiplicity of ways—the analyst's neutrality, empathy, the provision of developmental experience, intimacy, authenticity, even indulgence, for example. Thus there is little agreement on the actual nature of new relational experience or its role in the therapeutic action.

While the many meanings of new relational experience might be interpreted as commentary on how little we know about the therapeutic action in psychoanalysis, we may more accurately view this multiplicity as a reflection of the complexity of the therapeutic action and how much we actually do understand about it. It is only when practitioners subscribe to a single significant aspect of new relational experience and, like the blind men with the elephant, interpret it as the whole that a lack of appreciation of the real complexity of the psychoanalytic process is revealed.

What do common elements tell us? In exploring this topic and attempting to show what is unique in each and yet common to all, I reduce the views of new relational experience to four. The following perspectives are summarized: 1) one-person "alliance" views; 2) "corrective emotional experience" (Alexander and French's, 1946, "flexible" approach); 3) the analyst's provision of developmentally reparative experiences; and 4) an enrichment model.

The One-Person Model: The Nontransference Relationship as an Alliance

Although Freud never described the role of new relational experience with the analyst as a direct therapeutic factor, he did see the need to cultivate mutative interpretation within a facilitating relationship. Freud (1917) observed, for instance, that "what turns the scale in his [the patient's] struggle [against repression and repetitions of earlier outcomes] is not his intellectual insight—which is neither strong enough nor free enough for such an achievement—but simply and solely his relation to the doctor" (p. 445). Overall, Freud's early ideas about the relationship were taken as forerunners to later "alliance" concepts (e.g., Zetzel, 1956; Greenson, 1965). To explain how the relationship might best facilitate the development of insight, these ideas embraced aspects of the "real" relationship while nevertheless segregating it from transference.

Although a few contemporary orthodox analysts (e.g., Arlow and Brenner, 1990) continue to minimize the role that relational factors of any sort might play in psychoanalysis, on the whole a trend has developed recognizing the importance of the quality of the analytic relationship itself and the characteristics of the analyst as a new object. Strachey's (1934) early formulations emphasizing the therapeutic importance of the analyst's benign participation laid the groundwork for recognizing relational factors in the therapeutic action. Loewald (1960) described the treatment relationship as a "new object-relationship" and a "real" one (p. 32). Kanzer and Blum (1967) also noted that the analyst, more than a transference object and an interpreter, was also "a participant in reliving experiences that revise the personality" (p. 125). Dewald (1976) emphasizes the importance of the regressed patient's experience of the analyst's respect, recognition, exclusive focus, and empathy. In stating a position that speaks directly to the role of new relational experience, Dewald asserted that this positive response of the analyst is "*new* and *real* and *experienced by the patient for the first time.*" He also noted that it was only *after* the new experience that "the patient's cognitive appreciation of the difference between the original objects and the analyst [can] be interpreted and grasped" (p. 227). Many classical analysts (e.g., Pine, 1993) now take the position that the analyst's neutrality and commitment to the analytic task of interpreting provides the new relational experience.

Let us consider the position of Pine (1993), which is both explicit with regard to the relationship between insight and new relational experience and also fairly representative of contemporary classical analysts. Pine asserts that interpretive and relationship factors are inseparably linked and that each requires the other for analysis to be effective. His main thrust, supported by quotes from the staunchly classical views of Arlow and Brenner (1990), is that "analyzing" forms the essence of the psychoanalytic process and that insight holds the key to the therapeutic action. Thus he concurs in large measure with those authors, who acknowledged that there might be superficial individual elements in the analyst or in the analytic setting that might evoke and intensify the nature of the transference—physical appearance, national or social background, professional positions, for example; but these characteristics, quite superficial, are not considered an essential part of the course of psychoanalytic treatment.

Pine goes on to explain nonetheless that, in his view, there are certain relationship factors that are "part of the very essence" of the psychoanalytic process and are essential for change. These are the "forms of relationship" that flow from the defining features of the psychoanalytic situation itself. In addition to those features which support the asymmetrical structure of the psychoanalytic situation, they are, specifically, the analyst's neutrality, abstinence, relative anonymity, and, Pine adds, general reliability—all contributing to a context of safety. This context of safety is thought to facilitate the reintegration, following destabilization resulting from the analyst's properly timed interpretations.

Pine emphasizes the role of the analyst's benignity, as revealed in a noninteractive stance at the particular moment "when it counts. . . . By contradicting the patient's wish, fantasy, or expectation at the moment of interpretation of drive or superego derivatives, they [the aforementioned forms of relationship] add a direct experiential impact to the already affectively laden cognitive impact of interpretation" (p. 196). He states, epigrammatically, that interpretation and the analytic relationship are both necessary but insufficient for change; together, however, at specified moments, they are both necessary and sufficient to bring about change.

Classical Views and the Two-Person Model

One might reason that constructive interactions that patients live through when their analysts interpret repetitive old experiences and contrast them with transferential expectations themselves provide a form of mutative, new relational experience. But, emphasizing the role of insight, many classical analysts such as Pine have belittled the idea that any specific actions be undertaken to enhance the quality of the relationship—actions disparagingly framed as "self-conscious role-playing," "interactive efforts," or "trying to be nice." Such actions, these analysts seem to fear, promote relational factors at the expense of sound interpretive work. Thus, interaction processes remain understood primarily at the level of their ability to potentiate interpretations and insight into the analysand's mental functioning.

In fact, many traditional analysts still only grudgingly acknowledge the therapeutic significance of the analysand's new relational experience, as such, with the analyst (e.g., Sandler and Sandler, 1984). Their formulations highlight new relational experience not as lived experience that itself can be directly mutative but as a relational background that supports insight-oriented work with the patient. One way of representing this difference between the two models is to reverse the figure-and-ground configuration: in the classical view, the relationship forms a background through which insight, seen as primary, can be realized; in relational approaches, constructive interactions, including interpretations, result in relational processes that are held in the foreground and that themselves are seen as bringing about change. It has been increasingly realized, however, that the therapeutic action encompasses both insight and new relational experience.

From a two-person perspective, it is not difficult to criticize the staunchly classical position. The ubiquity of the interplay of individualities, of mutual influence, of the very real impact of the analyst's individuality, involvement, and perspective, of the specific role of the analysand's awareness of the analyst's personal contribution and thus the importance of the actual (versus transferential) relationship—all are neglected in strict classical methodologies. When the particulars of an individual analyst's personality and responses are viewed as an inevitable but *nonessential* part of the psychoanalytic situation, even as a kind of analytic "noise" that interferes with optimal technique, then an intensive application of two-person insights, and a profound appreciation of the role of new experience, simply cannot be realized.

I agree with Pine that one of the reasons interpretations have their optimal therapeutic impact is that the analyst does not respond *in kind*. In the light of what has been learned about enactments, it is extremely important that analysts not simply respond automatically in the fashion that patients' interactional pressures might demand. Further, it can be a compelling experience for patients to discover how "wrong" they have been in their expectations of their analysts. Many patients, however, trace their difficulties to parental reserve or lack of response; in such cases, the analyst's neutrality and abstinence, manifested in impassive ways, raises the possibility of destructive retraumatization rather than a "benign" presence. I further disagree with Pine that what is therapeutic is that the patient comes to learn that "nothing happens" through observation of the analyst's "matter-of-fact" response and "reserved" listening and interpretive stance. A great deal actually happens, and it is inauthentic to pose as if that were not the case. In fact, that tactic is every bit as inauthentic as attempting to offer a corrective emotional experience, Alexander and French's (1946) idea, which classical analysts have criticized, because it, too, fails to acknowledge with the patient what really is going on. Efficacy may not be attributable to the analyst's active "role-playing," as Pine pointed out, but neither is it the result of the analyst's impassivity, another sort of role. The patient's feeling of safety in relation to the expression of threatening, unacceptable impulses toward the analyst is very important; but it is far from the whole story, and there is something both mystifying and potentially anxiety provoking about a view that consistently obscures the analyst's reactivity. I believe it can be shown that the patient's feeling of safety is as much the result of the analyst's self-defining actions as it is of his or her concealment.

One-person conceptualizations that dichotomize the analytic relationship into components of "transference" (distortion) and "non-transference" (reality) ultimately are limited. They fail to recognize the intersubjective idea that patients' and therapists' reactions to one another are embedded in the here-and-now interaction and are constantly shaped by and resonate with one another. Concepts that dichotomize distortive (analysand) and realistic (analyst) relational processes further fail to recognize that the patient's subjectivity can be analyzed in relation to the analyst's real contribution (as an instance of perspectival realism) and that the analyst's subjectivity is shaped, and thus his or her authority compromised, by the analysand's influence. One-person views also minimize the role of ongoing mutual transactions, or negotiations, that advance the analysis over time and that from a two-person perspective are seen as therapeutically integral and highly significant in providing forms of new relational experience.

In summary, new relational experience remains a debatable concept when applied to classical psychoanalysis. To achieve it, no particular actions of the analyst are required—only analyzing the patient while maintaining a strict standard of so-called benevolent neutrality. The patient's new relational experience with the analyst is truncated; benign aspects of the analyst's neutrality are less something uniquely positive than the absence of something negative. As Rangell (1981b) pointed out, corrective emotional experiences play a part in classical analysis but more in terms of what the analyst does not do, rather than what he or she does.

Alexander and French's "Corrective Emotional Experience"

The concept of "corrective emotional experience" and the therapeutic strategy for achieving it were first presented by Alexander and French (1946). This discussion is intended to clarify the similarities and differences between "new relational experience" and "corrective emotional experience." Corrective emotional experience is a very particular sort of new relational experience, and pervasive confusion of the two has formed the historical basis for analysts' appraising negatively the more general analytic contribution of new relational experience.

Collaborating with 23 other psychoanalysts at the Chicago Institute for Psychoanalysis, Alexander and French searched for a "shorter and more efficient means of psychotherapy" (p. iii). The team arrived at what they called a "flexible" approach, which included a number of essential revisions of the standard psychoanalytic technique, among them the corrective emotional experience. Basically, these authors took the position, radical at the time, that a patient's corrective emotional experience—and *not necessarily insight* into it—was primary in the therapeutic action. They wrote:

> The main *therapeutic* result of our work is the conclusion that, in order to be relieved of his neurotic ways of feeling and acting, the patient must undergo new emotional experiences suited to undo the morbid effects of the emotional experiences of his earlier life. Other therapeutic factors . . . [including insight] are all subordinated to this central therapeutic principle [p. 338].

According to these authors, "reexperiencing the old, unsettled conflict *but with a new ending* is the secret of every penetrating therapeutic result" (p. 338).

This approach to the therapeutic relationship, which self-consciously aims at achieving a specific kind of corrective emotional experience, or new relational experience, is fundamentally different from the classical approach. In fact, because therapists' *actions* with patients were regarded as more important than interpretations, and because it mattered little to these theorists whether corrective emotional experiences actually were achieved with the analyst or with other people, this position was exceedingly provocative to analysts operating from the traditional perspective. Dissenting from the classical commitment to neutrality and interpretation, a position that at the time was thought to avoid the analyst's personal contamination of transference developments, the authors advised analysts to deliberately manipulate the interpersonal climate of the therapy. Alexander (1956) later clarified that the analyst must assume an attitude different from the decisive historical personage who dominated the transference and replace spontaneous countertransference reactions with attitudes "which are consciously planned and adopted according to the dynamic exigencies of the therapeutic situation" (p. 93), thereby provoking the sort of emotional experiences that were thought to undo the pathogenic influence of earlier parental attitudes. This required that the analyst become aware of, and control, spontaneous countertransference reactions and substitute for them responses thought to be conducive to correcting the pathogenic emotional influences in the patient's life. The psychotherapeutic formula was straightforward: what was psychologically mutative and reparative was the analyst's ability to overcome pathologic repetitions by deliberately administering experiences that *opposed* them.

Corrective Emotional Experience and Current Views of New Relational Experience

Let us now turn to a two-person model and consider Alexander's corrective emotional experience.[1] When it was first introduced to the American Psychoanalytic Association, the idea of corrective emotional experience created a furor among American psychoanalysts. Those emphasizing neutrality and interpretation took umbrage at formulations that so blatantly manipulated the psychoanalytic situation while emphasizing change mechanisms that were not directly related to the interpretation of transference phenomena. Wallerstein (1990) recently observed that had Alexander and French not made the claim that their approach was in some ways superior to standard psychoanalysis, it is possible that the controversy that erupted might not have set off so heated a territorial dispute. Instead, mainstream psychoanalysts criticized the approach as nonanalytic—rightly, in my view—but then attempted to demarcate pure psychoanalysis (interpretation) from psychoanalytic psychotherapy (new experience) (Eissler, 1953; Gill, 1954; Stone, 1954). If psychoanalysts had not been so determined to set psychoanalysis apart from other modalities, such as

---

1. Interested readers may wish to refer to *Psychoanalytic Inquiry* (Volume 10, No. 3, 1990). The entire issue was devoted to this topic.

Alexander's, then these ideas might have led to an understanding of what analysis has in common with other modalities and might have expanded the understanding of broad psychotherapeutic principles. The actual outcome delivered a devastating blow to American psychoanalysis and retarded for many years further acknowledgment and investigation into the role of experiential and relational factors in the therapeutic action.

Today, with virtually all psychoanalysts appreciating the significance of experiential and relational factors in personality change, the importance of the quality of the analytic relationship has come to equal, and for many theorists to exceed, that of insight in the analytic endeavor. These developments, while challenging the earlier dichotomy between psychoanalysis and psychoanalytic psychotherapy, tend to cast a more favorable light on some of Alexander and French's early contributions. What may prove most important about their approach over the long run is that, historically, theirs was the first *American* approach to underscore the therapeutic value of directly experiential and relational factors in psychoanalysis. (Ferenczi, whose work went unappreciated in America, had long before described related phenomena in Europe.)

I evaluate the contribution of the corrective emotional experience differently, and somewhat more favorably, than did Wallerstein (1990), who in his earlier reexamination of the concept concluded that "the corrective emotional experience is not a part of psychoanalysis, as either a concept or a technical manuever" (p. 322). Although Wallerstein's critique is both thoughtful and comprehensive, I disagree with aspects of his conclusion. I believe that conclusion follows from the author's purpose of understanding the growing concern with the importance of "affective relationship factors" (p. 289) within the analytic situation and the countertransference coloring of the analytic work. It was not Wallerstein's intention, as it is mine, to extend the reach of two-person ideas. Following that reasoning, I distinguish *conceptual/strategic* aspects of Alexander and French's approach from the *specific techniques* they recommended.

In some respects, the disparity between the corrective emotional experience that Alexander and French described and the more recent views of new relational experience is a matter of degree. Alexander and French did seem to grasp the ubiquity of interaction, but they applied that insight into the psychoanalytic situation nonanalytically, through manipulation of the transference. Thus, while many of the specific techniques that the authors recommended remain objectionable, certain conceptual and strategic elements of the approach are similar to contemporary ones. Consider a statement made by Alexander (1961) 15 years after he first introduced his radical idea, which, I think, shows movement in his thinking: "The corrective—or 'reconstructive' value of the therapeutic experience is enhanced if the analyst's spontaneous reactions, the specific nature of his countertransference attitudes, or his studied attitudes are quite different from the original parental responses" (p. 330). If, by "studied attitudes" Alexander had in mind the elements of analytic discipline that are today so familiar (Hoffman, 1992a, for example), then his position might not fall that far from those of many contemporary relational practitioners. But, highlighting his willingness to manipulate the situation, he continued, "I fully recognize the fact that the analyst cannot change himself and not every analyst is a *good enough actor* to create, convincingly, an atmosphere he wants" (p. 331; italics added).

Still, the overall strategy of the corrective emotional experience—and I use that term very specifically here, as Alexander and French did, as reexperiencing the old, unsettled conflict but with a new ending, but certainly not the therapist's manipulative technique to achieve it!—is a far less radical proposition today than it was when introduced by Alexander years ago. That is because of the extensive subsequent impact of the ideas of Ferenczi, Fairbairn, Kohut, Winnicott, and other relational analysts on American psychoanalysis. Kohut (1984) addressed this matter quite directly when he wrote, "To my mind, the concept of 'corrective emotional experience' is valuable so long as, in referring to it, we point to but a single aspect of the multi-faceted body of the psychoanalytic cure" (p. 78).

It seems reasonable to say that contemporary relational analysts do adopt a corrective interpersonal orientation of sorts to their patients and their patients' relational difficulties. It operates something like this: as the pathogenic past is enacted and becomes more fully in evidence, formulated, and understood in and through the analytic work, the analyst adjusts his or her behavior; there is a progressive movement—spontaneous or deliberate—away from salient, counterproductive enactments that are articulated and related to other destructive interactions, past and present. If analytic treatment is to succeed, the analyst *must* become progressively less likely to enact these patterns with the patient and more likely to analyze or to interact in other constructive ways, rather than actualize the patient's unconscious wishes, fears, and expectancies. The consequence of this behavior, congruent with Alexander's intentions, is that the patient will "reexperienc[e] the old, unsettled conflict *but with a new ending*" (Alexander and French, 1946, p. 338).

The corrective emotional experience has been singled out and criticized as contrived and manipulative—quite correctly, in my view. But *all* therapist stances are subject to that same criticism. By deliberately following any single psychoanalytic ideology or strategy over another—and every analyst must—the analyst adopts a particular mental set that predisposes him or her to respond in certain ways to certain patient behaviors but not to others. Indeed, Alexander (1956) himself pointed out that the customary neutral, abstinent stance of the Freudian analyst is itself a studied, practiced, and unnatural one, rather than one that calls for spontaneity or authenticity on the part of the analyst.

Corrective emotional experience is not unique in its embodiment of strategy when compared with contemporary views. For example, Greenberg's (1986) relational view of neutrality, which is broadly recognized by relationists as having value, involves a dynamic understanding that recognizes the necessity that analysts make adjustments in their participation in order to facilitate an optimal balance of old and new experience with patients. These maneuvers are not necessarily discussed or shared openly. The work of the Mount Zion Group also deserves special consideration here. Weiss and Sampson (Weiss and Sampson, 1986; Weiss, 1988, 1990, 1993; Sampson, 1992) have shown that people come to therapy not only with conflicts and difficulties, but also with conscious and unconscious desires and plans to master them. According to this view, they set out to find, or to establish with their analysts, the conditions of safety necessary to implement their unconscious plans. Most similar to Alexander's strategy is Weiss and Sampson's (1986) observation that direct experiences with the analyst sometimes may lead to significant analytic progress—even *without* interpretation; "a patient may, by unconscious testing alone, gradually disconfirm a pathogenic belief and make it conscious" (p. 84).

These authors' observations now confirm Alexander's basic idea while providing specificity as to what is mutative about the corrective emotional experience. It now can be seen that, as it was originally described, this idea combined many active, complex, largely intuitive patient processes, both conscious and preconscious, such as presenting tests to therapists, assessing their outcomes, determining whether the conditions of safety are present, and deciding whether or not to reveal warded-off material. We see that in addition to, or even in ways that supersede, spoken interventions, interactions reflecting therapists' attitudes and feelings may be important in refuting (or confirming) pathogenic beliefs that the patient is addressing. It seems an important complement to traditional psychoanalytic theorizing to highlight the therapeutic importance of what is done (or not done), in addition to what is said. Doing so enables us to understand why the issue of therapist–patient "fit" can be so important and how, inadvertently, enactments might occur that are, under the right circumstances, therapeutic.

In my opinion, there is a great deal that is flawed, from a psycho-analytic point of view, in this early attempt to introduce the mutative impact of new relational experience. Articulating and emerging from problematic interactions that the patient and therapist mutually estab-lish, to the extent possible, are quite different from a therapist's iden-tifying, formulating, and then assuming an opposing stance that is presumed to "correct" a single transference theme, as Alexander rec-ommended. That idea is simplistic, we now realize, and fails to address the complexity of the multilayered self–other configurations that may develop throughout an analysis. It also overlooks what we now see as the essence of the intersubjective idea, related to the patient's psychic reality, assuming that what the analyst intends as "corrective" in his or her behavior actually will be experienced by the patient in that way. For instance, I may wish to behave warmly toward a patient who has been treated coldly by his parent; I may even authentically *feel* warmly and believe that I am acting so toward him. But I am not surprised to learn that he finds coldness and even exploitation in what I am experiencing as my authentic expression of warmth toward him.

Thus it seems impossible to translate the corrective emotional experience into practical terms that fully grasp the complexity of psy-chodynamic functioning and the role of interaction. Through what form of attentiveness am I to "correct" for a patient's "emotionally absent" father—by simply listening empathically, encouraging the patient, actively involving myself in the patient's life, directing him, or confronting his refusal to acknowledge my attentiveness? Even if it were possible to prescribe a specific corrective course of action with a patient beforehand, it is unrealistic to assume that therapists can deliberately overcome the "grip of the field" (Stern, 1997) or be able to set aside personal issues in order to follow such a course.

There are further flaws in the approach. The technique *substituted* the analyst's "corrective" actions for analyzing and in so doing depended on contrived forms of relating. A major flaw of the corrective emotional experience is its special vulnerability to criticism of the analyst's *inauthenticity*. By playing the particular strategic role that Alexander described, analysts were constrained to systematically represent themselves to patients in ways that deviated from their actual experience. I think it is safe to say that analyst inauthenticity always diminishes efficacy. And it is difficult to imagine that the patient would not sense that inauthenticity in the analyst's self-conscious persona, especially when it involved a shift to a "corrective" role that was established following an initial evaluation. (I will focus on the analyst's authenticity in chapter 7.)

It is more than an interesting theoretical sidelight that, despite its very significant differences from the classical position in fundamental respects, the corrective emotional experience aligned with it in others. Like the classical approach, it was rooted in a fundamentally objectivist epistemological attitude that took for granted the therapist's ability to implement the treatment objectively from outside the two-person field while paradoxically claiming to have therapeutic effects through the therapist's participation within it. Alexander's objectivist position was, in fact, a sort of theoretical hybrid, not unlike that in Kohut's (1977) early work, based on the assumption that the therapist could assess the patient and then somehow participate interpersonally with him or her in a therapeutic manner *from outside the field created by the patient's relational patterns*.[2] It was not enactments per se, therefore, that held out the potential for new relational experience and change, since, by definition, enactments involve the preconscious participation of *both* participants. Rather, Alexander located the potential for change in the patient's blind, one-sided repetition and the therapist's presumed ability to observe without becoming involved. While this approach placed in relief the experiential factors that came to be recognized as crucial in an analysis, it overlooked a more profound point based on two-person insights. That point cannot be made too often: that it may be precisely when therapists are the most confident that they are not enacting that they may be most susceptible to enactments.

Providing Reparative Developmental Experiences

Another type of new relational experience involves what I will call a "provision" model. Practitioners who subscribe to this model, like

---

2. Mitchell (1997a) made a similar point.

those who offer a corrective emotional experience, propose that the analyst relate to the patient from a position that offers the possibility of a mutative interpersonal experience; in this instance, however, the analyst's role is not contrary to the patient's transferential expectations but is thought to provide crucial experiences that the patient missed during earlier developmental phases. Here, more in a manner resembling Alexander and French's view than the classical approach, but significantly different from both, new relational experience develops from the analyst's reparative actions toward the patient. In short, the analyst provides the patient with something needed but that was denied.

Winnicott (1960), whose approach embodied the provision of needed relational experiences, took the mother–child relationship as the basis of the psychotherapy relationship. He believed that pathology resulted from an unresponsive childhood environment that failed to affirm the patient's normal developmental strivings. This failure promoted the development of a "False-Self" adaptation that conformed to environmental expectations at the cost of the patient's authenticity and spontaneity. Thus the overall treatment relationship created a metaphorical "holding environment," itself a new relational experience, that sought to offer the patient growth-enhancing responsiveness through consistency, optimal timing, and empathy, all thought to contribute to an atmosphere capable of containing disruptions and releasing the patient's developmental processes and "True Self." With the provision of reparative experience as a priority, interpretation became important more as an expression of the analyst's attunement and responsiveness than as a means of advancing insight.

The other primary figure who defined new relational experience in terms of meeting developmental needs was Kohut (1971, 1977, 1984). Like Winnicott, he saw the patient's fundamental motivation as the fulfillment of intrinsic potentialities in the context of a responsive environment. He also emphasized the need to provide certain kinds of affirming responses presumed to have been deficient at crucial times in the patient's psychological development.

Key in understanding the role of new relational experience in Kohutian self psychology is the idea of *selfobject transference*. Listening empathically, Kohut first observed patients' struggles to express the need for responses that could evoke, maintain, or enhance their sense of self. He defined this need as "selfobject transference," which he believed originated from thwarted developmental needs for "mirroring," "idealizing," and "alterego" selfobject experiences. Kohut's early views of change were based on the idea of "transmuting internalization," the translation of slight frustrations associated with the analyst's unwitting empathic failures into new structure. Thus the patient was thought gradually to take over selfobject functions that formerly were experienced as being provided by the analyst.

According to Stolorow, Brandchaft, and Atwood (1987), whose intersubjective viewpoint evolved, in part, from Kohut's, what is crucial about the new experience is that the analyst respond *empathically*. Thus the therapeutic process is seen as progressively establishing the analyst as an understanding presence with whom early unmet needs can be revived and aborted developmental thrusts reinstated. It is noteworthy that Atwood and Stolorow (1984) expressly distinguish their view of new relational experience from Alexander's as from Kohut's. They write, "The process of structural transformation does not require that the analyst play out any artificial parental or 'corrective' role . . . [only] the dedication to the use of introspection and empathy to gain and provide understanding of the meaning of the patient's experiences" (p. 60). More recently, these authors also have set their work apart from Kohut's (Stolorow, 1992; Stolorow, Orange, and Atwood, 1997), distinguishing its origins and essential features from self psychology. However, many of Kohut's essential insights, including the concept of the selfobject dimension of experience, have been integrated into the broader framework of intersubjective theory.

Many others have built upon Kohut's earlier ideas and elucidated the analysand's new relational experience with the analyst. Lachmann and Beebe (1995), for example, regard the selfobject experience as "an attempt at *self-regulation* through self-strengthening, enlivening, and affect regulation" (p. 415). Rather than transmuting internalizations, Tolpin (1983) reasons that the internalization of the selfobject tie fostering cohesion is involved in the therapeutic action. Shifting from Kohut's ideas about frustration, Bacal (1985) introduced the idea of *optimal responsiveness*. An advantage of Bacal's formulation is that it moved beyond a limited conception of empathic responding. Freeing the analyst, it has expanded the range of analytic activity, calling attention to actions in addition to verbal responses, for example, that might be regarded as needed forms of new response needed at a particular moment in a treatment.

For many self psychologists, it is not empathic or optimal interaction alone that is emphasized; they emphasize the blending of this new experience with the patient's achievement of insight into repetitive experience. Thus Stolorow and Lachmann (1984/1985) see transference as always multidimensional, involving both the patient's selfobject longings for the analyst to provide missed experiences and also repetitive elements involving the patient's fears of repeated developmental failure. Indeed, Lachmann and Beebe (1992, 1995) describe these two forms of transference as existing in a figure-and-ground relationship, each providing a critical context for organizing and interpreting the other. Likewise, Lindon (1994) argues that the psychoanalytic role of abstinence ought to be replaced with the concept of "optimal provision"—"*any provision that, by meeting a mobilized developmental longing, facilitates the uncovering, illuminating, and transforming of the subjective experiences of the patient*" (p. 559). Note that the provision is explicitly subordinated to the goal of advancing insight—markedly different from Alexander's view substituting interaction for insight.

Providing Developmental Experiences and the Two-Person Model

Psychoanalytic models stressing provision are inherently limited when measured against fully developed two-person criteria. The analyst's experience and participation are restricted by his or her functioning as a caretaker and, in certain models, by the continuously empathic role the analyst is constrained to play. Adopting a pervasively empathic manner attunes the analyst to the patient's internal process but also draws attention from self-scrutiny and from important cues about the interaction. Further, the analyst is prevented from responding in certain "adult-to-adult" ways, through directness and openness, for instance, that can illuminate enactments and create more intensive two-person explorations. Moreover, since developmentally minded analysts often presume that what they are doing is best for patients and do not bring their stance under joint scrutiny, there can be an inauthentic and even manipulative element involved in the analyst's behavior and in the new relational experience it seeks to offer.

What is thought to be new about the relational experience that Kohut offered resembles Alexander's corrective emotional experience in certain ways and, in the context of a two-person model, calls up some of the same difficulties. For instance, the analyst tries to maintain a uniform role—not a contrary one, but an empathic one thought capable of releasing the patient's thwarted development.

This role, like Alexander's prescriptive, can be criticized on the basis of its ultimately positivist assumption that the therapist can operate beyond the grip of intersubjective influence in order to provide the patient with what he or she "really" needs. Kohut also failed in his early studies to take full account of the range of ways in which the patient's transference, including selfobject needs, may be shaped by the analyst's individuality and countertransference. For instance, the analysand may have a sense of the analyst's attributes and what he or she may actually be capable of in the relationship, and that sense may play a role in shaping what the patient requires of the analyst. A current trend among self psychologists counters the earlier tendency and emphasizes an intersubjective view, two-person phenomena, and interaction (Bacal and Newman, 1990; Fosshage, 1992).

Fosshage (1995), among others, has sought to broaden the listening perspective of self psychologists to address this limitation. He has delineated two principal listening orientations that affect the analyst's experience of the patient. The first, the "*subject*-centered listening perspective," is the usual sustained empathic mode of inquiry of self psychologists; it involves listening from within the analysand's perspective. This empathic mode remains the analyst's primary listening mode. The second orientation Fosshage calls the "other-centered listening perspective." Fosshage suggests that the patient's experience of "self-with-other" can be more fully illuminated if the analyst listens, in an oscillating way, both from without and from within, that is, in the "other-centered" as well as the empathic (or "subject-centered") mode of experiencing the patient. To supplement empathy, the other-centered mode is thought to provide the analyst with insight into the patient's ways of experiencing and relating to others.

From a two-person point of view, this conceptualization is useful in that it extends the empathic self psychologists' listening perspective. Listening "as-the-other," as Fosshage puts it, potentially enables the analyst to tune in to the patient's relational patterns. (It also permits "decentering" from personal feelings and places the patient's responses in a nonpersonal, *generic* framework.) Yet, as Fosshage (personal communication) agrees, that is precisely where a potential danger lies; if the therapist takes the idea of other-centered listening too literally and processes the patient's reactions as the *generic* "other," that misses a crucial issue—the patient's responses to the "*me*" of the individual analyst in the relationship. Although the approach helps the therapist zero in on the patient's relational patterns, we need to remain aware of the continuous influence of the analyst's actual personality and actions and the singular nature of the relationship between therapist and patient. Recognizing that the analyst is not a generic other, but a unique individual, and integrating that recognition into the work, is, in fact, sine qua non in the two-person model approach I am advocating.

Enrichment Models

Although other forms may come into play, a staunch two-person interpretation of the psychoanalytic situation favors the final view that has been called an "enrichment" model of new relational experience (Hirsch, 1994). In this model it is intended that the patient's internalized as well as external object relationships will be enhanced by the new relational experience with the analyst, which involves forms of new experience based on the patient's and the therapist's authentic contact as individuals. The role of the analyst as an actual, separate person is most fully recognized in this model of the therapeutic action. As a true second person, the analyst cannot possibly remain outside of the interaction (drive-conflict model), successfully oppose the patient's transferential proclivities (corrective emotional experience), or selflessly provide missed developmental experience (developmental-arrest model). Rather, because the analyst's individual responses become shaped within the two-person field, and in part by the patient's internalized world, it is essential that the analyst use his or her separate experience of self, perhaps openly and directly, to identify, understand, and transcend the developments within the field. There are two interrelated strategies. One, the more familiar, involves analyzing and thereby transcending enactments; the other I call "realistic interpersonal contact."

Transcending Enactments

According to some theorists, such as Fairbairn (1952, 1958) and Guntrip (1968, 1971), what is mutative in the analytic relationship results from attempts to overcome, by analyzing, enactments that are intrinsic in the analytic interaction. In the process of transcending enactments—and it is doubtful, of course, that that ever can be accomplished completely—the analyst works with the patient so that each can find an authentic voice that transcends the constraints imposed by preexisting relational configurations that are integrated into the relationship. As that new relational experience develops, the pair approaches the *ideal* of authentic relatedness, involving open-system, flexible ways of relating to one another that are more fully responsive to the realities of the two individuals and their interaction, rather than prepatterned modes of relating.

Fairbairn (1958), anticipating more recent views of the transference-countertransference interaction, assigned the greatest importance to the new experience that is inherent in the *actual* ("real," "total," or "open-system") relationship with the analyst. He stated, "In my own opinion, the really decisive [therapeutic] factor is the relationship of the patient to the analyst . . . not just the relationship involved in the transference, but the total relationship existing between the patient and the analyst as persons" (p. 379). In addition to the repetition of old and often self-defeating patterns, the therapeutic experience with the "reliable" and "beneficent" analyst allowed the patient to transcend the old parameters of relationship that were rigidly maintained because of anxiety and old object attachments. Successful analysis of the patient's transference caused the closed-system way of relating gradually to be replaced by an open system involving "a true relationship between patient and analyst as persons in outer reality." For Fairbairn, genuine emotional contact occurred with the analyst as a *realistic* object—not just a good one.

That feature is similar to Guntrip's (1968) characterization of psychotherapy as "a progress out of fantasy and into reality, a process of transcending the transference" (p. 354). Guntrip's thinking, which reflects the influence of Winnicott as well as of Fairbairn, also offered explicit ideas about the role of the analyst's authenticity. He wrote about the therapeutic importance of a relationship that is "on the level," meaning one in which the analyst acted without deception. In a widely quoted statement acknowledging the importance of the uniquely authentic elements in the analytic relationship, Guntrip wrote, "What is therapeutic, when it is achieved, is 'the moment of real meeting' of two persons as a new transforming experience for one of them, which is, as Laing said (1965), 'Not what happened before [i.e., transference] but what has never happened before [i.e., a new experience of relationship]'" (p. 353). Guntrip's definition of transference analysis follows from that statement. He saw it as "the slow and painful experience of clearing the ground of left-overs from past experience, both in transference and countertransference, so that therapist and patient can at last meet 'mentally face to face' and know that they know each other as two human beings" (p. 353). This development occurs, according to Guntrip, as both the therapist and the patient reach the persons behind their defenses.

Guntrip, like Fairbairn, did not discuss enactments as such but believed that the real or personal relationship not only emerged more strongly from analyzing these "left-overs" but simultaneously provided leverage for overcoming the patient's closed-system or transferential patterns of relating. In other words, he emphasized the dialectical interplay between realistic interpersonal contact and enactment; accordingly, transference analysis became the path to progressively achieving mutual authenticity and realistic interpersonal contact as the goal of treatment. This mutual appreciation of self and other as separate subjects implies the achievement of mutual recognition (Aron, 1996).

Realistic Interpersonal Contact

A second strategy of therapists following enrichment models more directly stresses the significance of realistic interpersonal contact. I include Levenson, Wolstein, and to an extent, Ehrenberg as representatives of this group. One of the major differences between Levenson and Wolstein (if not Ehrenberg) and the authors just discussed is that the others incorporate restitutive functions, with the analyst aiming at achieving a better experience than the patient previously has had in life. Except for Ehrenberg, the "realistic interpersonal contact" group, operates without that explicit objective, in undertaking a detailed inquiry of the patient–therapist relationship. Although restitution is not sought after directly, as by self psychologists, for example, when it is achieved it is desirable. Deemphasizing the asymmetries of the analytic relationship while seeking to make explicit what is hidden, these practitioners stress the realistic interpersonal contact that occurs between the analyst and the analysand. This contact carries the therapeutic action.

If new relational experience is not deliberately sought after, it may likely develop as a byproduct of the collaborative interpersonal exploration. In this view, the analyst focuses on the *real* matrix of events and the expressions of the patient's and analyst's individual personalities within the psychoanalytic setting. There is no implication that enactments are any less authentic than open-system ways of relating; indeed, what could be more authentic, or real, than that which the patient needs to enact? What is sought after is an increasing clarity about what is actually happening. An analyst's profound assumptions about the therapy process, rather than being encouraged as therapeutic, are seen as his or her contribution to the patient's mystification.

For Levenson, a successful outcome of therapy is the patient's developing interpersonal competence based on semiotic skills that enable the patient to make distinctions among the nuances of interaction. Interpersonal competence, synonymous with mental health, is held to be the critical form of enrichment of the self. To achieve this goal, as Levenson (1983) puts it, "psychoanalysis becomes a communication between two real people engaging in a real way out of their own experience and personality (p. 35) . . . [and] the therapist must actualize his variables, not exclude them—the latter, a patent impossibility" (p. 57). To be real with the analysand, to be oneself, to be authentic is more important than offering one's "best" through contrived forms of relating.

In a related view, Wolstein (1981) saw the analytic relationship as a collaborative attempt to explore all the developments that might come into existence within the two-person analytic field. Describing an analytic paradigm that perhaps comes the closest to a truly "mutual" analysis, Wolstein described his perspective as "psychic realism." It is an approach in which the psychoanalyst and patient choose confidentially to share an undertaking of mutual therapeutic inquiry and to "immerse themselves in a shared stream of consciousness" (p. 400) in order to explore the unique, concrete clinical reality that develops between them. The patient and the therapist thus aim for the fullest exploration of whatever that experience contains, as far as either one can.

For Ehrenberg (1992), authenticity, self-expression, and interpersonal intimacy go hand in hand. She focuses on engaging and microanalyzing live experience at the interface of the analyst–patient interaction—the nature of the integration, the quality of contact, what goes on between the participants, including what is enacted and communicated affectively and unconsciously. Ehrenberg has defined new relational experience in terms of the "intimate edge"—the point in the interaction process, at the boundary of self and other, through which the patient can become more intimately connected with his or her own experience through the evolving relationship. An interactive creation, the intimate edge is a dynamic construct; it reflects the participants' sensibilities and subjective sense of what is most crucial or compelling about their interaction at any particular moment. Accordingly, "What is achieved is not simply greater insight into what is or was, but a new kind of experience" (p. 34). Ehrenberg sees acknowledgment and explicitness as the keys to increasing the moment's dimensions and changing the nature of one's experiences of it, while protecting against intrusion or violation. Thus the intimate edge of the analytic relationship, while identifying the point of developing intimacy and interpersonal possibility, also is the patient's "growing edge," the boundary of expanding self-discovery. Learning that one is able to handle aspects of experience that have been avoided but that come alive at the intimate edge provides additional forms of new experience.

Is Synthesis Possible?

When analytic therapy is successful, the patient typically has a new relational experience with the analyst that is, in important ways, different and better than in his or her previous experience. Although the new experience may manifest itself in many ways, a favorable outcome usually depends on that salutary context. However, more than being merely divergent, some of the alternative understandings of new relational experience seem actually opposing. There are vast differences, for example, between the new experiences that develop from an analyst's detachment, or benevolent neutrality, and new experiences that develop from expecting oneself to be drawn into enactments in order to find one's way out, or that develop from meticulously examining the realities that exist in the two-person field. Distinctions also can be drawn between classical practitioners who reject, as opposed to those who attempt to integrate, the idea that new relational experience may play a significant role in the therapeutic action. And there also are fundamental differences between the methods of relational analysts who see new relational experience as the byproduct of the analyst's activity and those who make deliberate efforts to bring it about.

Can views so diverse possibly be synthesized in practice? Gill (1994) suggested that perhaps some day the several prominent views and the systems of which they are part would find a place in a more comprehensive system of psychoanalysis, with room for hierarchical differences among the several major emphases on the basis of individual instances. Meanwhile, in actual practice, I believe, many clinicians informally and intuitively integrate, both consciously and unconsciously, the various forms of new relational experience that I have considered.

When we examine what individual analysts actually do, we see that most of the modes of new relational experience play a role at some time or other, probably with every patient, as the analytic pair moves through the complex, ambiguous psychoanalytic process. Here I agree with Pine (1985), whom I cited earlier in disagreement. He takes the integrative position that differences in the ways analysts respond in terms of drive, ego, object, and self, rather than being mutually exclusive, are a matter of hierarchical organization. Lichtenberg, Lachmann, and Fosshage (1992) also have asserted that different patient motives, requiring different sorts of therapeutic responses, act in ascendancy at different times. But this is a point of debate (Goldberg, 1988; Schafer, 1993) and many analysts claim that integrative positions of this kind avoid a commitment to a particular approach.

Although some of the formulations we have considered—Levenson's, Wolstein's and Ehrenberg's, for example—are similar in certain respects in ideology and therefore more easily synthesized, the differences between their ideas and those of others such as Pine and Alexander seem so extreme as to be clinically incompatible. When we take each of these views and its own metapsychology as a whole, the perception of incompatibility undoubtedly is confirmed. But in examining real-life clinical interactions, we can tease out forms of analytic interaction corresponding to each of these modes, even though analysts remain fundamentally committed to one or the other. It is tempting to polarize the different views—to *replace* ideas about corrective experience with those of analysts' spontaneous authenticity, for example; but in practice, I believe, we, consciously and unconsciously, find ways to synthesize apparently opposing orientations—counterbalancing the analyst's spontaneous reactions with deliberately corrective actions, for example.

In questioning the possibility of synthesis we must be concerned with two issues: *what* analysts are doing and *why* they are doing it. Sometimes analysts' actions may appear to be similar, although the basis for these actions may be understood very differently. If an analyst tends to be reserved with a particular patient, for example, it does not mean that he or she is necessarily following classical notions of neutrality; rather, a relational analyst may be thinking about new relational experience with a patient whose family acted falsely effusively or intrusively. As another example, analysts operating from both one-person and two-person models may recognize, fundamentally, the dangers inherent in responding "in kind" to a patient. That tenet, originally stressed by classical analysts, has found confirmation, on very different theoretical grounds (those of projective identification [Tansey and Burke, 1989], for example), in recent two-person thinking about interaction and enactments. Thus it becomes integrated into, and applied differently in, relational analysts' thinking about what constitutes useful analytic experience. The point is that practitioners sometimes behave in similar ways but for very different reasons.

Consider how, clinically, the threads of these diverse approaches might become interwoven. As we grasp the pervasive nature of enactments, we recognize how the needs of patients are served by analysts' interpersonal attitudes that are intended to be *corrective*, similar, in certain respects, to Alexander and French's (1946) earlier advice. The analyst does not operate in deliberately opposing ways, as in Alexander's preset, rigid method, but does seek to provide a "new ending" and to avoid falling in with enactments that come to light, working instead with the tensions created by the dialectical relationship between old experience and new. Thus, as the analytic process develops, a corrective attitude can be expressed in a variety of different ways, prospective as well as retrospective, through analysts' actions as well as words.

In accord with the clinical/developmental implications of the provision model, all competent clinical analysts—not only the disciples of Kohut, and without ever formulating in terms of "selfobject" transferences—proceed with a sensitivity to their patients' specific vulnerabilities, needs for support, self-esteem, and developing self-articulation and self-cohesiveness. Although they may not necessarily emphasize developmental insights, all competent analysts also are fully aware of the potential for retraumatization that these insights may point to. Empathy is the basic listening mode of *all* psychoanalysts. It cannot be claimed with exclusivity by self psychologists, nor, for that matter, is it most usefully taken up as the sole listening perspective of analysts operating within that modality. There are certain patients—actually a minority of those who seek analysts' help—for whom the analyst's mere presence as a separate person is too threatening; the analyst's empathic responding, attempting to reflect the patient's personal experience, is thus the most the patient can tolerate. But, if the analyst settles for that medium of therapy alone, too little may be asked of the patient, and thus gained. A singularly empathic stance—and there are those analysts who feel that that alone is enough to sustain the process of analytic growth from beginning to end—encourages solipsism and fails to appreciate and tap the many other forms of new relational experience and modes of constructive analytic relating. It is here, harking back to the interpersonal tradition, that we recognize the need for clarifying interactions and for helping patients to grasp their impact on the experience of others, including the analyst.

The staunch classical analyst is doomed to fail the patient whose growth depends on gratification and a caring responsiveness, just as the analyst too strictly committed to realistic interpersonal contact will be unable to keep a severely narcissistic patient in treatment for very long. The same can be said of the analyst's traditional anonymity, abstinence, and neutrality, of confrontation, or of any single analytic stance that is maintained at the price of clinical flexibility. Granted—and this is something that is reflected in referral practices all the time—certain approaches, rather than others seem more promising for particular patients, when they are administered in the hands of competent practitioners. But the multiplicity of forms of new relational experience all have value and come into play as creative clinical contributions, as the practitioner, concentrating on one predominant clinical mode, moves through treatment with different patients.

New Relational Experience, Negotiation, and "Righting" the Relationship

Margaret Little (1951) wrote:

> We often hear of the mirror which the analyst holds up to the patient, but the patient holds one up to the analyst, too, and there is a whole series of reflections in each, repetitive in kind, and subject to continual modification. The mirror in each case should become progressively clearer as the analysis goes on, for patient and analyst respond to each other in a reverberative kind of way, and increasing clearness in one mirror will bring the need for a corresponding clearing in the other [p. 37].

A patient's motivations and functioning never are simply pathogenic, never just an effort to engage the analyst in maladaptive enactments, and never simply a distortion. They are simultaneously realistic and adaptive, reflecting a striving to achieve healthy and reparative forms of relatedness. To overcome difficulties and to achieve a new relational experience, *the patient must work with the reality of the analyst.* The patient's constructive relating includes perceptiveness about the analyst—what the analyst is doing and, beyond that, what the analyst actually is capable of—mediated by the patient's own need for the analyst's constructive participation. This striving of the patient is used to help the analyst and the patient make constructive adjustments in their mutual participation. It permits forms of collaboration and negotiation that enable the analyst to recognize and provide what will benefit the patient.

I call this process, based on constructive processes of mutual accommodation, "righting the relationship." Like Little's description, righting the relationship plays an integral role in maintaining the context for productive analytic work and for achieving new relational experience. *Each* participant becomes aware of the other's personal and emotional capacities as well as limitations, and through ongoing sequences of negotiation both mutually adjust their expressions and expectations, consciously and unconsciously, tacitly and explicitly, in order to advance the analytic task. Accordingly, the relationship progresses toward an ideal atmosphere of analytic intimacy in which both individuals can authentically respond and be responded to and in which the experience of both becomes accepted. A related process has been described by Pizer (1998) who observed that "the very substance and nature of truth and reality—as embodied both in transference-countertransference constructions and in narrative reconstructions—are being negotiated toward consensus in the analytic dyad" (p. 4).

A range of the analyst's and patient's mutual responsivity makes possible a "holding" environment within which the patient feels his or her transferences can be safely expressed, explored, and understood. If the analyst takes a position beyond that range, one that is perhaps too individually expressive in either direction—that is, either too overbearing or too remote—then the analyst's responsivity (or lack of it) may feel disruptive to the patient. Such a position makes the work more difficult or even impossible. The patient signals, and the analyst must somehow respond by reshaping what he or she is attempting to accomplish or by adjusting the means used to accomplish it. Much of this process, involving mutual regulation and recognition, goes on subtly and tacitly; sometimes, however, it may occur through open negotiation. In either case, both participants, and not the analyst alone, cocreate the atmosphere of safety that is essential for the progress of the analysis.

I am describing something more fundamental than merely clearing away temporary, superficial counterresistances. Righting the relationship participates directly in the therapeutic action; the patient helps the analyst to repair problematic responses, or countertransferences, ones that often are induced through unconscious communication, including affect-laden projective identifications—and therefore are rich in especially meaningful mutative opportunities— to "right" childhood failures. The analyst, too, has limitations and requirements that permit him or her to operate more effectively, and they, too, need to be respected.

In a two-person model, we refer not to a neutral, immovable analyst who analyzes transferences at a remove but to both participants' mutually accommodating to each other so as to advance analytic objectives through their interactions and the new relational experience that can be inherent in and result from them. There are times when the individualities of the two participants clash countertherapeutically—defined as "empathic failures," "enactments," or moments of "discordance." When handled effectively, these developments can hold enormous therapeutic potential, especially when the participants are able to delineate personal contributions. Ferenczi (1928), speaking of the "elasticity" of the analyst's technique, suggested that the analyst, like an elastic band, not yield to the patient's pull without ceasing to pull in his or her own direction until one position or the other has been shown to be untenable. This idea is a precursor to more recent ones about the two individuals negotiating transference-countertransference tensions and dialectical ways of understanding the change process.

Because the analyst is always subjectively involved and is sometimes lost in the countertransference, there can be preconscious aspects of the analyst's participation over which he or she has little control. The idea that the analyst can recover from and work out of analytic entanglements independently has been increasingly recognized as an illusion. With the analyst reflectively open to the patient's observations about the analyst's experience, however, the two may together illuminate enactments that have become integrated in counterproductive ways and act to recover an alignment that is more therapeutically productive. The process of recovery is itself therapeutic. It involves transcending enactments and, in the process of expanding relational possibilities, achieving new relational experience. It is not preparatory work for an analysis; it is the real analytic work.

Scrutiny of the role of righting the relationship highlights the observation that at times the analysand acts as therapist to the analyst. The analyst's loss of a grounded analytic perspective is a situation to be avoided; yet it can potentially have important therapeutic benefits. So potentially significant for the outcome of treatment is the deep involvement of the analyst that, according to Searles (1986), "the time will come, in our work with neurotic patients, when, just as we now use, as a criterion for analyzability, the patient's capability for developing a transference neurosis, we may use as an additional criterion, of earlier predictive significance in our work with the patient, his capability in fostering a countertransference neurosis, so to speak, in the analyst" (p. 207). It is in this extreme form of therapist involvement that we see the importance of what Searles (1979) has called the analysand's role as therapist to the analyst.

The central interactive axis called righting the relationship, involving the therapist's and the patient's negotiating accommodations to one another, forms a dialectical basis for analyzing transferences, that is, for understanding the ways the participants assimilate the elements of the analytic relationship into structures based on past figures. It is not a matter of the analyst's reality versus the patient's fantasy, accuracy versus distortion, or right versus wrong. It is a matter of the experience and perspective of each, in relation to the other, what the therapist actually can give, and what that pair negotiates and agrees can be helpful. Consider the example of a patient's criticizing the analyst for a lack of response. It must be considered by the analyst, in this view, that this patient is reacting not just to a transference fantasy that has been frustrated but possibly to something real about the analyst and what the analysand may most constructively need. Such complaints may also reflect what the analysand senses the analyst is actually capable of becoming. Analysts must continually assess the meanings of patients' transference against their own self-perceptions, rather than assuming that their baseline participation is appropriate, or that their readings are correct. Critical adjustments are made, unique to each analytic pair, that enable the two to work effectively together.

Righting the relationship is different from dealing with empathic failures, in which the analyst is thought to make unilateral and private accommodations to the patient. It is different, too, from Langs's (1982) "rectification," in which the analyst's accommodations must be made secretly, without acknowledging or collaboratively exploring their sources or effects. Righting the relationship is different, as well, from the more traditional forms of mastering the countertransference, such as Racker (1968) describes, where the analyst's experience, individually processed, provides a source of information about the inner world of the patient. Analysts do not look to themselves alone to understand their countertransferences, nor, for that matter, do they subordinate their own personalities in order to make empathic adjustments in their participation. Righting the relationship is mutual, dialectical and collaborative and often can become a part of the open dialogue between analyst and patient as the two negotiate more productive ways of being together. Here is where the "elasticity" of the analyst's technique comes in. The analyst must hold ground if he or she believes that is best for the patient but also must hear and evaluate the patient's demand for a different sort of response. Mitchell (1993) made a similar point when he discussed considerations related to gratifying a patient's relational needs. Essentially, he distinguished what I am calling counterproductive (countertransference) enactments and constructive or therapeutic ones. Mitchell wrote: "What may be most crucial is neither gratification nor frustration, but the process of negotiation itself, in which the analyst finds his own particular way to confirm and participate in the patient's subjective experience yet slowly, over time, establishes his own presence and perspective in a way that the patient can find enriching rather than demolishing" (p. 196).

Everything that occurs between analyst and analysand—interpretation, the holding environment, even regression—involves mutual transactions that regulate the participation of both analyst and analysand (Aron and Bushra, 1998; Pizer, 1988). New relational experience is no exception. When we consider righting the relationship, we also can see why new relational experience is best regarded as an interpersonal *achievement*. The insight provided into counterproductive transference-countertransference interactions creates a pathway to new relational experience. As the pathogenic past comes alive in the relationship through maladaptive interactions and is analyzed, and as specific details and historic meanings become incrementally clarified and worked through, thus helping both individuals to distinguish present from past, new from old, real from symbolic, the advancing clarification of the meanings of transference and enactments forms the cutting edge of the new relational experience.

Within the asymmetrical analytic structure, the major responsibility for keeping the relationship on track, and for seeing that developments favor the patient's emotional growth, lies with the analyst, of course. But that task cannot be beneficially exercised without the analysand's conscious and unconscious participation in it. Usually, the analyst, through critical self-reflection and openness to the patient, can participate more effectively once he or she is able, with the patient's help, to identify nonfacilitating transference-counter-transferences alignments. Searles (1975) gave the example of a patient chiding his inaccessible, obsessing therapist to "come off it." But if the analyst truly cannot bring to the situation what the patient realistically needs—indeed, cannot even hear it—or cannot make accommodations as the patient's needs progress and change, then the patient must leave and find elsewhere what is required for his or her growth.

As disturbing as entanglements sometimes may feel, emergence from these states can feel as rewarding to both participants. The goal is to assist the patient; yet the shared sense of reaching a new thera-peutic plane, and of having learned and grown from the interaction, is personally meaningful for the analyst as well as the patient and includes the restoration of the analyst's own feelings of efficacy and hopefulness. Enhanced self-awareness results for the analyst, along with an experience of new relational possibilities, so that the analyst, like the patient, may achieve new and strengthened capacities that transcend the therapeutic situation.

One final point before ending this section. The collaborative emphasis of the approach I am describing should not be a burden to patients. Certain patients may have been called on to assist their care-takers in excessive ways that felt overwhelming and were damaging to their psychological development. One must trust the intrinsic self-corrective capacity that exists in a responsive, open system. A patient who needs an atmosphere in which he or she can more fully regress can help the open analyst to become aware of ways in which the ana-lyst has asked too much. The analyst responds by making adjustments. That too is a form of righting the relationship.

Examples of Righting the Relationship

The patient in the following case, was treated by an experienced col-league who discussed his work intensively with me. The patient had seen another therapist (whom my colleague had heard of) for many years, and when she first began treatment she complained relentlessly about her new therapist and constantly compared him with her pre-vious therapist. Her behavior was alternately critical and seductive. Despite the negative ending of the prior relationship, she described how the other therapist had offered her a great deal of praise and affection, and she insisted that the current therapist's predecessor was a warmer, more generous, and more giving person. Internally, the therapist felt angry, competitive, and discouraged by these comments and resented the negative comparisons, especially since he had heard about the other practitioner in a far less flattering way; indeed, he believed himself to be far more capable than her former therapist.

In the interests of illuminating the sources of what he experienced as the patient's excessive need and criticisms, the therapist sought to clarify what it was that the patient really wanted from him and to locate its sources in her history. He tried to identify with her what she felt was missing from his actions toward her, which she was all too willing to focus on. As the two worked to illuminate the patient's experience, the therapist continued to feel bullied, devalued, and under a great deal of pressure to respond to her in demonstrative ways that seemed excessive, inappropriate, and inauthentic to him. For instance, she criticized him for not making his home telephone number available to her, seeing that as a symbol of his selfishness and lack of professionalism, even though she had little real need for it clinically. Complaining about his lack of warmth, she repeatedly threatened to leave treatment and at one point, infuriated by his moderated responses to her, she did in fact leave for several months and made a failed attempt with another therapist. She returned, however, "reluctantly." Subsequently, a great deal was clarified about the patient's feelings of maternal rejection, especially in relation to an apparently preferred male sibling, and a compensatory, sexualized attachment to the father, which, it seemed, the patient wished to duplicate with the therapist. Gradually, the pair became able to see that she equated the therapist's moderated responses to her, which were not sexualized, with her mother's bland response, lack of interest, and preference for the patient's brother. They also understood her negative comparisons of him to the other therapist in the light of her mother's comparisons of the patient with the preferred brother.

As she gradually owned the historical origins of her devaluing response and relented in her need to attack the therapist, he was able to recognize elements of his own defensiveness in dealing with her. He became able to engage in a form of self-examination that her previous attacks, and his resulting defensiveness, had foreclosed. Thus he began to question his own inability to respond to her more warmly and openly—ways more familiar to him in the clinical setting. With clarification of his own withholding from her, which her complaining had exaggerated but which was nevertheless a very real aspect of his reaction to her, the emotional tone of the treatment relationship continued to warm. His softening toward her as she began to grasp the excesses of her demands, and their origins, diminished the urgency of her need for a response from him that he felt as inappropriate. Over time, the therapist became aware of a growing appreciation of the patient, especially as he came to understand more fully and grow more sensitive to the emotional pain that had been involved in her very rejecting personal past. The therapist gradually became aware of developing fond feelings toward his analysand that seemed less a reaction formation than an authentic, shared achievement. A mutual accommodation was being worked through, a form of "righting," with changes in each in relation to the other.

As his view and feelings toward her softened, the therapist became more receptive to the patient's efforts to elicit his warmth, and one day she was able to reach him quite definitively by contrasting his reserve with the warmth of a very open, relaxed, and endearing person, a public figure known to both of them, who stimulated warmth in him as in her. He began more clearly to sense, in contrast, his own pulling back from her. He now came to focus on this response as a characterological issue of his own, as well as a reaction to her provocations, and understood that it might also be associated with the expressly sexual threat of her fantasized seduction of him. This, too, he realized, had caused him to adopt a generally withholding attitude toward her, which, in turn, had intensified her need for his affirming response and had contributed to her self-protective attacks. Thus he was able to acknowledge that the patient's criticisms of his own withholding were, in part, valid, and he was freed by this understanding to be more openly responsive to her. To "loosen up" and to be less "uptight" was not, he realized, necessarily to be manipulated or seduced, which, he had come to recognize, was one reason he had been resisting her pressure to be more responsive. Rather than seeing her behavior as an assault on his integrity, as it had formerly been to him, he recognized a defensiveness on his own part. He thus responded more generously with the greater warmth that gradually had come to be a part of his authentic response to her. At a later date, the therapist shared his understanding of what had occurred between them and tried to spell out how the pair had reworked the interaction in terms of the cyclical elements of their psychodynamics and what he saw as both their parts. From a new, shared vantage point, they discussed elements in the behavior of each that had perpetuated the old experience and also had gradually enabled the pair to work out of it.

Thus, progressive, negotiated new experience had been created from a dialectical tension between the new and realistic experience with the analyst, on one hand, and the old or maladaptive pattern, on the other, that their own issues had defined. Beyond their conflicts, they had been able to find what she needed constructively from him. Over time, an insightful, mutual accommodation had been achieved—one that made possible the clarification and modification of the parties' joint participation—and that represented mutually insightful new relational experience. As their intimacy within an open system replaced closed-system ways of relating, the treatment, now characterized by an atmosphere of increased safety, became a very powerful one.

It is often important that there be insight not only into the developmental ramifications of old experience, but also into the ways that the new experience with the analyst differs from the old. (By old, I refer here not only to the similarities to figures from the past but also to the earlier experience with the analyst.) Mitchell (1988) has noted that "the [analyst's] . . . struggle is to find an authentic voice in which to speak to the analysand, a voice more fully one's own, less shaped by the configurations and limited options of the analysand's relational matrix, and, in so doing, offering the analysand a chance to broaden and expand that matrix" (p. 295). I suggest that this is the analysand's and analyst's shared struggle; each struggles to find a voice that can be heard and to hear the voice of the other as the two realize a new and positive relationship.

While these mutual adjustments usually are subtle, even elusive, at other times they can be usefully explored openly and directly, as in the brief example to follow. A long-term patient seemed to his analyst to have become aloof and uncommitted during a phase of treatment. The analyst took up this development directly with the patient. The analyst's directly opening up the interaction to scrutiny was first experienced by the patient as the analyst's attempt to influence him, which resembled early parental domination. A power struggle ensued. (Questioning a patient's detachment from the analyst in the treatment context might well be experienced as an attempt to deepen the patient's involvement.) As this development was further explored and clarified, it became apparent that the analysand was also experiencing profound gratitude to the analyst and was struggling to maintain his own autonomy and the confidence that he eventually would be able to leave the analyst and maintain his gains. So charged was the issue, however, that he was unable to introduce the idea of termination directly. His maneuvering to achieve a feeling of safety through aloofness aggravated the analyst's own anxieties about separation. The analyst reflected on his own behavior and concluded that, because of personal issues exacerbated by a major separation he was experiencing, he might well have been exerting subtle pressure on the patient to remain committed to treatment and to him, rather than exploring the analysand's behavior with adequate respect for the patient's autonomy. It was helpful to both to elucidate the basis for the analysand's need to keep the door ajar, as well as the threat the analyst found in those actions, and especially his resulting impulse to slam the door tight. Having these aspects of the interaction out in the open (both parties' responses) facilitated a mutual repositioning (what I am here calling a righting of the relationship). Through their insight into the interaction, both were subsequently able to relax their self-protective efforts and to reflect on them, enabling them to deal with one another openly, directly, and in a manner that was ultimately therapeutically beneficial. The resulting discussion led to an open exploration of termination possibilities. This was a new experience for the patient, who, not surprisingly, had been held too close in important relationships, as well as for the analyst, who had to deal with reciprocal difficulties of his own.

Without mutually accommodative participation of the kind involved in righting the relationship, which is clarified and made understandable within a two-person model, it is difficult to imagine how a change process, with emergent new experience playing an integral role in it, could occur. (If the analysts in the examples had maintained their initial positions, it only would have led to a polarization and either the patient's inability to move or acting out and leaving in a state of resistance.) I believe the process of mutual negotiation that I have outlined is an integral part of all analyses—classical and relational—although some analysts, especially those conforming to the classical model, may accommodate within narrower limits and are certainly less inclined to make their own participation explicit with patients. In a relational medium in which safety has been established through such negotiations, there develops an overall movement toward authentic relatedness, mutuality, and intimacy that can occur only as both parties' constructions are made explicit and, to the extent possible, constructively modified through negotiation. These negotiations, which involve a progressive expansion and deepening of mutual understanding, do more than simply make analytic collaboration possible, or "set the stage" for it; they represent a critical element in achieving new relational experience and in the therapeutic action of analysis.

CHAPTER 6

THE HISTORICAL TREND TOWARD
SELF-DISCLOSURE

I doubt there exists a psychoanalyst who has not had the experience of disclosing personal experience or information to a patient, spontaneously and authentically, with the impression that that sharing had critical therapeutic impact and yet a nagging self-doubt for having gone too far. The relational psychoanalytic shift and its acknowledgment of the healing potential of the psychotherapeutic relationship itself has brought a growing interest in the constructive applications of the analyst's participation through self-revelation. Yet, since the traditional perspective and the basic model technique provide virtually no justification for a therapist's disclosing personal reactions and information, it is readily understandable that a great deal of theoretical and technical ambiguity and controversy have resulted from that expressive trend. Needless to say, these shifts have made life extremely difficult for contemporary practitioners, many of whom feel uncomfortable abandoning time-tested methods that carry the imprimatur of authority for more innovative methods based on the newer relational technical ideas.

Because expressive uses of countertransference represent a radical turning point in the practice of psychoanalysis, disclosure remains a controversial technique even among contemporary relational analysts. We need not search far to discover a negative attitude toward analysts' revealing their experience to patients. Analysts' self-concealment, embodied by the idea of an *incognito*, has been integral in the psychoanalytic tradition. Until recently, for instance, many authors, even relational authors such as Hoffman (1983), Gill (1983), and Greenberg (1991), who have given self-revelation a fair hearing and selectively sanctioned it, earlier referred to the analyst's self-revelations as "confessions." That term obviously connotes culpability on the part of the analyst and implies that, by expressing countertransference, the analyst necessarily commits a breach.

Heimann (1950) first used the term confessions years ago to condemn disclosure. This judgmental term, while perhaps compatible with the monadic technique, reflected a negative view that in the light of two-person insights can be judged a bias. It is related to concerns that the analyst might too readily confess or "plead guilty to lesser charges" of countertransference, as it were, in order to ward off further attacks or criticisms rather than fully exploring transference developments. That negative emphasis inhibited exploration of the constructive therapeutic uses of the analyst's self-disclosure and, placing the burden of proof on the disclosing analyst, eliminated the analyst's free choice of disclosure, even when it was being considered as a potentially constructive therapeutic option.

Within the classical tradition, the analyst's self-revelations always have been treated as a technique of last resort, and its difficulties have been selectively emphasized. The movement toward an intersubjective definition of the treatment relationship has done a great deal to diminish the resulting inhibition, "normalizing" both transference and especially countertransference experience and viewing them as each individual's own experience rather than as distortion or psychopathology. But pressures rooted in the one-person model still act against analysts' revealing their experience to patients. Thus, rather than weighing the pros and cons of specific opportunities for sharing their experience, analysts continue to adopt concealment as a rule of thumb. In my opinion, what has been prevented by the traditional position on disclosure is not an impeded inquiry into the patient's experience, as many traditional analysts may have interpreted, but the many benefits associated with more active forms of psychoanalytic participation.

Recent conceptualizations and techniques involving analysts' expression of their individuality, both deliberate and inadvertent, have proven highly productive. For instance, working through the effects of empathic failures comprises a central aspect of the therapeutic action as it is understood by self psychologists. Yet what are these empathic failures of the analyst if not individually self-revealing expressions? Here the inadvertent expressions of the analyst, seen as "lapses" in technique, become therapeutically beneficial. Enactments, as another example, might be understood in the same way—as involving personal expressions of the analyst that are induced by the interaction and can be included in an analysis of interactions with patients in ways that can be highly beneficial. Individual differences also define those "discordant" instances when the analytic pair falls out of sync, creating moments when interpretation becomes viable (Greenberg, 1995a). Thus important aspects of theory implicitly recognize and incorporate the therapeutic value of the analyst's inadvertent introduction of spontaneous and induced experience, and yet many practitioners still disparage the *deliberate* use of such revelations. Rather than being grounded in the assumptions of a two-person model, I see this position as a detrimental carryover from the standard technique. Many practitioners' methods have not kept pace with the relational theories on which those analysts base their understandings. Instead, torn between established and innovative approaches, these practitioners continue to carry over the more restrictive elements from the one-person model—sometimes inappropriately, in my view.

In this chapter, I elucidate the historical, expressive trend toward the analyst's fuller participation through self-revelation. I characterize the attitudes of several major contemporary psychoanalytic schools here—the classical, object relations, self-psychological, and interpersonal—toward countertransference disclosure.[1]

The Classical View: Disclosure as Faulty Technique

Let us first briefly consider the evolution of transference theory itself in classical views before we move on to consider attitudes toward disclosure. Freud (1910) originally emphasized that the analyst's countertransference reactions, like the transferences of the patient, originated in unresolved, unconscious, infantile conflicts. As transferences were thought to block the patient's associations, so was countertransference thought to obstruct the analyst's efficient functioning.

---

1. This format has certain limitations. A major one is that diversity within any single orientation may be lost. Schafer (1983) pointed out that practitioners identified as "classical Freudian analysts," for example, may actually vary widely in their conceptions of what is "classical," what is "Freudian," and what is "analysis." Another problem is that assigning theorists to separate categories inevitably involves a loss of information and does not effectively accommodate the inclusion of the "hybrid" features of many approaches.

Freud (1912a, 1915, 1931, 1937) often referred to the limitations created by the analyst's own "blindspots." To "overcome" the difficulties countertransference might cause, Freud (1910, 1915) repeatedly encouraged analysts to remain objectively detached from patients. After Freud, some analysts argued that the term countertransference should be used as a source of interference, as Freud had used it, but others reasoned that countertransference should be limited even more narrowly to the analyst's transference to the patient as an earlier object. Both of these formulations, termed "narrow" definitions, remain influential to this day.

Heimann (1950) is usually credited with recognizing that countertransference, more than an obstacle to understanding, might be used to help the analyst understand the meanings of the patient's material.[2] She defined countertransference as "*all* the feelings which the analyst experiences toward his patient" (p. 81, italics added), not just the pathological ones in the prevailing definitions. Heimann pointed out that her approach introduced a way of understanding the analyst's responses that embodied a "relationship between two persons" (p. 81). Eventually, such developments led to the "totalist" understanding of countertransference (see Tyson, 1986, and Tansey and Burke, 1989, for reviews), which included not only interfering reactivations of the analyst's conflictual areas but also the total response of the analyst to the patient, thought potentially to furnish the analyst with important data about the patient's psychic life and the therapeutic interaction.

An integration of the narrow and totalist viewpoints later developed (Sandler, Dare, and Holder, 1973). Accordingly, the most useful view of countertransference referred to the analyst's specific emotional reactions to the patient aroused by the patient's specific qualities. In this more differentiated "specifist" view, the patient's influence was thought to be present always in the countertransference. Throughout treatment, the analyst's countertransference reactions might be detrimental if not recognized and handled effectively but also could provide information about the patient's internal processes.

As we saw in the last chapter, yet another wave of countertransference opinion followed. Analysts began to emphasize the *transfer-*

---

2. Fromm-Reichmann (1950) also had the idea of a totalist view of countertransference when she described "the therapist's share in the reciprocal transference reactions . . . [that] may furnish an important guide in conducting the psychotherapeutic process" (p. 6).

ence responses of the analyst, a distinction that recognized the analyst's involvement and individual contribution to the psychoanalytic situation. While narrow countertransference was regarded as a signal affect and used to *control* departures from neutrality, these newer developments introduced the assumption that transference to the patient inevitably alters the analyst's understanding and even actions; only after countertransference has affected the analyst's actual behavior will it lead to insight into countertransference and new interpretations. In this broader view, the analyst not only is responding to the analysand's transferences (countertransference), but also is contributing something that arises from his or her own personality, or idiosyncrasies.

Turning to analyst self-disclosure, Freud (1912b) wrote, "Experience does not speak in favor of an affective technique of this kind. Nor is it hard to see that it involves a departure from psycho-analytic principles and verges upon treatment by suggestion. . . . This technique . . . makes him [the patient] even more incapable of overcoming his deeper resistances" (p. 118). Hence Freud's familiar recommendation that the analyst should "be opaque to his patients and, like a mirror, should show them nothing but what is shown to him" (p. 118).

Over the years, the interpretive goal of classical analysis has changed relatively little. Interpretation has remained the analyst's "decisive instrument" (Levy and Interbitzen, 1992) and continues to organize the analyst's participation. Many Freudians still articulate a view of transference similar to Freud's (1923)—that they "develop inevitably, *irrespective* of the persons who are their object" (p. 45, italics added). Thus Greenson (1967) emphasized that the analyst "must mute his own responses" in order to remain neutral and anonymous to the patient. "Only in this way can the patient's transference reactions come into clear focus so that they can be singled out and distinguished from more realistic reactions" (p. 272). More recently, Arlow (1985), urging analysts to minimize their personal impact, has encouraged them to try to act the same with all patients; he explained that the analyst in the psychoanalytic situation should provide "a standard, experimental set of conditions" (p. 76). This structure attempts to assure that what emerges into the patient's consciousness is as far as possible endogenously determined.

The less the analyst contributes personally, and the less the patient knows about the analyst as a person, the better, since that makes it easier for the analyst to convince the patient, and for the patient to develop conviction, that his or her transference actually involves displacements and projections having to do with past figures. Thus the analyst must always "safeguard" the developing transference from the danger of contamination by his or her own expressions (Greenacre, 1954). What is critical in distinguishing this from the two-person view of transference as cocreated, as Arlow (1984) asserts, is that "the analytic situation does not create the transference. . . . What can be revived in the transference is only that which is persistently active as a dynamic force in the patient's mind" (p. 26).

Following this reasoning, disclosures are uniformly contraindicated. Techniques of last resort, they continue to be seen as potentially dangerous methods that compromise the predominantly interpretive goals of the analyst. They must be employed minimally, and their detrimental effects are to be eliminated through their analysis. Moreover, a pessimistic view is taken with regard to the analyzability of interventions that are employed as parameters. In short, as pertains to analyst disclosure, the classical view has changed very little over the years; active participation, and self-revelation specifically, are taboo. Countertransference disclosure, if not calculated carefully as a parameter, is acting out.

Relational Views of Countertransference Disclosure: Preliminary Considerations

Most practitioners of virtually all orientations have come to recognize the value of silent application of their subjective experience. But from the earliest introduction of the uses of countertransference for understanding, warnings were issued about expressive uses. For example, Heimann (1950), who was influenced by Kleinian thought, stressed that the analyst must "sustain" the feelings that are stirred up but not "confess" them. Nevertheless, over the years, an increasing number of analysts has gradually discovered value in the active technical possibilities that result from the broadened definition and detoxification of the analyst's countertransference experience. Thus, today there is a discernible trend with analysts reevaluating their hesitancy to use their countertransference actively through its disclosure. The gradual shift to an understanding of the analyst's participation as occurring within an interactive field further encourages expressive uses of countertransference, or countertransference disclosure.

Historically, Ferenczi (1933) was the first to promote an interactive approach to the psychoanalytic situation in which therapeutic benefits were thought to be advanced through the analyst's counter-transference disclosures. Ferenczi openly acknowledged the analysand's real impact, rather than operating with detachment, and proposed that patient and analyst "come to a radical understanding through mutual analysis" (Dupont, 1988, p. 131). This was an egali-tarian, interactive approach that, in Ferenczi's view, avoided retrau-matizing patients through abstinence. In a "mutual" analysis, the analyst could reveal countertransferences to the patient, including his or her own felt weaknesses and feelings. Although Freud initially was disposed positively toward Ferenczi's work, he and his disciples later withdrew their support. Ferenczi finally noted many of the prac-tical difficulties associated with his technique—patients' resistively deflecting attention to the analyst, analysts' susceptibility to overin-volvement, empathic failures, enactments, breaches of confidential-ity (Dupont, 1988). That outcome seemed to shut off further study of transference and especially its disclosure for many years.

The 1950s brought a resurgence of interest in countertransfer-ence theory (Epstein and Feiner, 1979; Tansey and Burke, 1989). Gradually, countertransference analysis became the means by which analysts attempted to understand and make therapeutic use of their specific responses to their patients—not merely to "get through," "fil-ter out," or "overcome" what they recognized as inappropriate reflec-tions of their own personalities but to determine how one's experience was uniquely shaped and colored by the therapy experi-ence with a patient, and in particular by the specific qualities of the patient's predominant transferences to the analyst (Ogden, 1982).

By that time, polarized views of disclosure associated within two distinct psychoanalytic traditions could be identified. The restrictive, basic model technique maintained the need for the analyst to be a blank screen; countertransference disclosure was condemned as a form of "acting out" that inevitably interfered with the fundamental task of analysis—interpretation (Reich, 1951, 1960). Concurrently, the American interpersonal tradition, which saw the analyst as a participant-observer and the interpersonal relationship between ana-lyst and analysand as the crucible of change, was becoming estab-lished in the United States. That view had been influenced by Clara Thompson, an analysand of Ferenczi. Some proponents of this view approached disclosure actively (Tauber, 1954, for example).

An act of disclosure has decidedly different meanings in these alternative perspectives. Based on the one-person model, although silent uses can be appreciated, the disclosure of countertransference violates the analyst's crucial positioning outside of the patient's psychological reality. In the strictest sense, the narrow view defines countertransference as information about the analyst's own difficulties and no more; accordingly, there is *never* justification for putting countertransference disclosures actively into play in the analytic process. Even though few classical analysts today accept this very staunch view, still, other fundamentals of the one-person model cause them to approach the idea of disclosure extremely cautiously.

Consequently, there exist today two opposing yet strongly held conceptions of countertransference—the narrow and the broader, totalist/specifist—each being associated with very different attitudes toward disclosure and the latter grounded in the two-person model. The rationales for and against disclosure that emanate from these different traditions embody clashing theoretical convictions that are crucial to the ways in which the different analysts view themselves and their specific therapeutic roles with their patients. Ultimately, they address whether the analyst is to operate as a veiled persona whose individuality, being of little constructive significance, is to be shrouded in order to facilitate interpreting the patient's inner world (one-person model); or whether, as an involved, active participant, the analyst ought to operate more openly, as an individual in a two-person field. In order to demonstrate the trend that has developed, let us trace the historical progression of countertransference disclosure within the evolution of the three relational schools of thought, self psychology, object relations theory, and interpersonal psychoanalysis.

Psychoanalytic Self Psychology and Disclosure

Within psychoanalytic self psychology, Kohut and his followers all have acknowledged the superordinate importance of the structure and subjective experience of the self, selfobject transferences, the empathic mode of observation, and the value of the new and positive experience with the analyst. By initially conceptualizing the development of the self and object relations separately, Kohut created a model that carefully attempted to preserve a one-person psychoanalytic psychology. Wolf (1988), a close collaborator of Kohut, observed that "clearly, Kohutian self psychology is an individual psychology, not a social psychology" (p. 47). Diverse streams have developed within and from self psychology, and attitudes toward countertransference disclosure vary among therapists according to their specific orientations. Notwithstanding its origins in a one-person psychology, self psychology gradually has moved toward a two-person model, with an increasing role for the analyst's disclosure.

Kohut originally emphasized the crucial curative role of the analyst's availability through empathic responsiveness. Accordingly, the analyst was to convey attunement, understanding, and empathy through "vicarious introspection . . . the capacity to think and feel oneself into the inner life of another person" (Kohut, 1984, p. 82). However, empathy depended on the analyst's ability to remove himself or herself as an individual from the analytic interaction. Thus countertransference (and its disclosure) were at first viewed in a manner similar to the classical position, that is, as representing the interference of the analyst's own dynamics with an optimal therapeutic responsiveness.

Kohut shifted in his thinking. He first discussed countertransference as "the tendency of some analysts . . . to respond with erroneous or premature or otherwise faulty interpretations when they are idealized by their patients" (Kohut, 1971, p. 138). In 1984, in his final statement about countertransference, his understanding continued to echo the blank screen view, with countertransference seen as harmful. He wrote: "If we want to see clearly, we must keep the lenses of our magnifying glasses clean; we must, in particular, recognize our countertransferences and thus minimize the influence of factors that distort our perception of the analysand's communications and of his personality" (p. 37). Thus, even late in his work, Kohut emphasized countertransference as the analyst's "shortcomings as an observing instrument" (p. 38).

Kohut reasoned that the development of psychic structure through "transmuting internalization" played a central therapeutic role and was a consequence of the analyst's inevitable "empathic failures" and the analytic work that followed them. Empathic failures came to be defined as "the analyst's failures as manifested by his erroneous, inaccurate, ill-timed, or unfeelingly blunt interpretations" (Kohut, 1984, p. 66). Kohut further reasoned that even a correct and accurate interpretation could be flawed if the patient sensed that the analyst offered it in an emotionally flat, preoccupied, or disinterested way.

Although empathic failures were understood as being countertransference-mediated, Kohut emphasized the analyst's personal psychology but not the role that the patient's actions played in leading up to these reactions; the role of interaction was not at first considered by Kohut. It came to be the mainstream opinion among self psychologists that the patient's subjective experience should be held in the foreground; and the analyst's empathically derived subjective reactions, potentially nonempathic, were to be scrutinized but not shared with the patient (Atwood and Stolorow, 1984; Stolorow and Lachmann, 1984/1985; Goldberg, 1986; Stolorow et al., 1987). As the Freudian analyst was to scrutinize countertransference in order to screen that which compromised objectivity, the self psychologist was similarly to screen that which distorted empathy.

The central relational concept of self psychology, empathic failure, was interactional in the sense that it embraced the psychologies of both patient and analyst, but it was to be dealt with in a way that followed the reasoning of a one-person model. Disclosure of countertransference, by introducing a perspective external to the patient's own, was seen as countertherapeutic within Kohut's early framework and was tantamount to an empathic failure. In his later writings, however, Kohut (1984) described a somewhat more interactive technique, one that actually broached the topic of disclosure and suggested a fuller recognition of a two-person model. Now the analyst was to take note of the analysand's retreat following empathic failures, search for any mistakes the analyst might have made, "nondefensively acknowledge them after he has recognized them (often with the help of the analysand)" (p. 67), and then give the analysand a noncritical interpretation of the dynamics of his retreat.

Without actually proscribing countertransference disclosure, Goldberg (1986), a disciple of Kohut, seems clearly negative about this technique. He charges that, although confrontations such as disclosures often are rationalized as being in a patient's best interests, they are, in fact, empathic failures and are actually for the analyst's benefit. Such techniques, he asserts, represent narcissistic injuries to patients and are experienced as such: "The analyst serves as selfobject to the patient and interprets these heterogeneous functions rather than the patient serving as selfobject to the analyst and thus substituting action for interpretation"(p. 387). Echoing the earlier, censorious classical position of Reich (1951, 1960), Goldberg emphasizes the dangers of disclosing and sees it as tantamount to acting out.

Stolorow and his associates (Atwood and Stolorow, 1984; Stolorow and Lachmann, 1984/1985; Stolorow et al., 1987; Stolorow and Atwood, 1992), who are intersubjective theorists, see their work as "a development and expansion of psychoanalytic self psychology" (Stolorow, Brandchaft, and Atwood, 1987). They have extensively incorporated two-person insights into their articulation of the psychoanalytic situation. They have stated that psychoanalysis is neither "a science of the intrapsychic, focused on events presumed to occur within one isolated 'mental apparatus.' Nor is it a social science, investigating the 'behavioral facts' of the therapeutic interaction as seen from a point of observation outside the field under study. . . . Rather, psychoanalysis is . . . a science of the intersubjective, focused on the interplay between the differently organized subjective worlds of the observer and the observed" (Atwood and Stolorow, 1984, p. 41). The analyst's empathic, observational stance is always from within, rather than outside the intersubjective field being observed, a fact that guarantees the centrality of introspection and empathy as the methods of observation. These authors believe that, since the patient's experience of the therapeutic relationship is "codetermined" by the organizing activities of both participants in the therapeutic dialogue, analytic investigation must encompass the entire intersubjective field created by the interplay between the subjective worlds of patient and therapist. Yet, when analysts are accustomed to treating countertransference as a problem, they may have difficulty seeing themselves as part of the field and working with their own contribution, which may become lost to them in any event if they are working hard to remain aligned with the analysand's experience.

Expressing limited interest in the role of the analyst's self-disclosures, Stolorow and Lachmann (1984/1985) have articulated the position that "the actuality of the patient's perceptions of the analyst is neither debated nor confirmed [but] serve as points of departure for an exploration of the meanings and organizing principles that structure the patient's psychic reality" (pp. 32–33). The analyst may influence the shape of the transference, but is exploring the patient's experience empathically. In that sense, the individual reality of the analyst and the analyst's actual contribution matter relatively little.

In contrast with Kohut's early views, more recent publications have evidenced an appreciation of the value of selective countertransference disclosure within this area of theorizing. For example, Stolorow and his collaborators (Atwood, Stolorow, and Trop, 1989; Stolorow and Atwood, 1992) have described therapeutic impasses that became resolved when analysts reflectively disclosed to patients interfering aspects of their own psychological world. The analysts disclosed experience in a limited sense, confessing, as it were, to their detrimental personal contributions. Similar to narrow views of countertransference, the analyst's experience is viewed as an interference with the developing therapeutic process and the disclosure therefore represents an acknowledgment of, to rectify, the pathological intrusion of the analyst's defensive operations. Stolorow and his collaborators have remained less than enthusiastic about the value of analysts' self-disclosures. In a recent paper devoted to deconstructing the myth of the neutral analyst, Stolorow and Atwood (1997) emphasize that the mode of "empathic-introspective inquiry" that they now recommend, extending the former empathic mode, "is sharply distinguished from the prescribing of self-expressive behavior on the part of analysts" (p. 431).

As the intersubjective theoretical formulations of Stolorow and his collaborators might lead one to anticipate more disclosure than is actually encouraged in clinical practice, the theoretical formulations of Wolf, who argued for the one-person nature of psychoanalysis, might lead one to expect fewer such interventions. Emphasizing his commitment to a one-person psychological model, Wolf (1988) reiterated that "self psychology, like Freudian theory, is focused on the intrapsychic experience of individuals" (p. 32). Yet, while attempting to preserve his one-person model commitment, Wolf nevertheless formulated a technique in which countertransference had to be shared. Wolf defined countertransference broadly, rather than narrowly, as "the analyst's experience of the relationship" (p. 137). He saw it as ubiquitous and capable of either impeding or facilitating the analytic process. Wolf aligned himself with Atwood and Stolorow's (1984) intersubjective conceptual framework and viewed transference and countertransference as "a dialectic of subjectivities" (p. 137), but he developed the two-person technical implications of that theory for disclosure. Wolf advocated, through a focus on the *discrepancies* between the two participants' experiences of the analytic relationship, an exploration of the interpersonal interaction. According to Wolf, the analyst creates a setting in which "the discrepancies of differing subjectivities can become discernible, understandable, and explainable—in other words, analyzable" (p. 154). Understanding the discrepancies between the two versions of reality as inevitable differences in meaning derived from the participants' different experiences allows them to accept each other's interpretations as appropriate within their individually different contexts. In this view, both participants benefit from new perceptions that become part of the construction of a new analytic reality.

Unlike earlier self-psychological formulations, Wolf's ideas emphasize the central importance of analysts' disclosing their experience of the relationship (countertransference) to the patient. In fact, in this respect Wolf's approach seems similar to the "realistic interpersonal contact" described in chapter 5 as part of the therapeutic action. It is unclear how Wolf's technical departure is reconciled with other features of his ostensible one-person model commitment. Nor is it clear how openly the interaction, and especially the sources of the analyst's contribution, may be examined to determine how interactions come into play to mutually shape the experience and behavior of the participants. What is clear, though, is that the analyst's disclosures of countertransference, through a focus on the discrepancies of differing subjectivities and guided by an emphasis on empathic concern for the patient, occupy a central technical role. In fact, this approach is similar, in spirit at least, to the one Ferenczi (1928) eventually settled on so many years ago; he saw the need for a mutual analysis tempered by the "empathy rule" and by "the imperative need to respect the patient's sensibilities" (Dupont, 1988, p. xxi).

Nowadays, we find a diverse group of practitioners gathered under the rubric of self psychology, and many of them have moved away from the original one-person model's emphasis on the experience of the patient alone and toward a relational view of treatment as occurring in a two-person, or self-selfobject, field (Bacal, 1990; Bacal and Newman, 1990; Fosshage, 1990). Among such theorists, the therapeutic benefits of countertransference disclosure have begun to find fuller recognition. Fosshage (1992), for example, in considering the vicissitudes of the self in a relational field, has observed that direct, appropriately timed sharing of the analyst's experience, as garnered from both empathic and relational listening perspectives, can facilitate the analytic process. From an intersubjective point of view Fosshage argues that disclosures can be employed to create an open ambiance, to provide needed validation of the patient's perceptions, to repair empathic failures, to illuminate schemas, and to implicitly provide alternative ways of organizing self and "self-with-other" organizations related to new relational experience.

Object Relations Approaches and Countertransference Disclosure

Now let us consider how, within object relations approaches, too, there has been a progressive trend toward increasing countertransference disclosure. Those following this approach include a diverse group of theorists who conceptualize psychic structure and motivation on the basis of the internalization of early relationships and the interactions among them. While some object relations theorists, such as Kernberg (1976), integrate an emphasis on internalized objects with instinct theory, others, such as Fairbairn (1952, 1958), stressed the individual's object-seeking motivation and rejected Freudian instinct theory.

One might conceptualize a continuum expressing the extent to which commitments to one-person and two-person models find full expression in technique among different psychoanalytic orientations. Along such a continuum, the classical and interpersonal perspectives would form one- and two-person extremes, respectively, with their radically different views of the participatory role of the individual analyst, while diverse object relations points of view (and self-psychological, too) span a range of positions along that continuum.

From an object relations point of view, an interest in representational psychological phenomena—fantasies, wishes, and dreams, for example—is combined with attention to such relational phenomena as enactments and new relational experience. Despite their use of two-person *conceptualizations*, however, many object relations analysts operate with a *methodology* drawn from a one-person model. That is, interpersonal processes can be significantly, even centrally, acknowledged on a conceptual level, and yet the focus of treatment remains on the patient's (and the analyst's own) internal experience of these relationships rather than on the real analytic interaction. Accordingly, many object relations practitioners remain cautious in approaching countertransference disclosures.

Thus far this exploration has contrasted two conceptualizations of the analyst in the psychoanalytic situation—the blank screen and interactional views. In considering object relations approaches, a third view of the analyst might be mentioned, sometimes termed the "empty container" (Spillius, 1988). The empty container view, first elaborated by Bion (1959), organizes the stance of many contemporary Kleinians and has broadly influenced object relations analysts, particularly through its understanding of countertransference. It derives from Klein's (1946) intrapsychic concept of projective identification. The empty container differs from the blank screen view in that countertransference reactions generally are seen as externalizations of the patient's self- and object representations *into*, rather than onto, the analyst. Through the patient's projective identifications, the analyst is thought enabled to experience directly elements of the patient's inner world. Accordingly, the analyst's subjective experience, influenced by the patient's, may be used in the service of understanding the patient's mental states. Countertransference experience, held to be ongoing in the empty container view, is construed not as a sign of the analyst's dysfunction but, rather, as a potentially valid source of psychoanalytic data. Although it is processed by the analyst as the basis for interpretations, countertransference is not directly disclosed.

Recent reformulations of projective identification illustrate the theoretical and technical ambiguity inherent in disclosure from an object relations point of view. Several theorists have attempted to extend the more strictly intrapsychic conceptualization originally outlined by Klein (1946) to emphasize how the patient's interpersonal actions induce the analyst's corresponding experience without the participants' awareness. Encompassing interactions between patient and analyst, this reformulation of projective identification appears compatible with a two-person model of the psychoanalytic situation. Ogden (1982), for example, has synthesized intrapsychic processes such as the patient's "getting rid of an unwanted or endangered part of himself" with interactional ones such as the patient pursuing the therapist "to think, feel, and behave in a manner congruent with the ejected feelings in the projective fantasy" (p. 2). Ogden describes how pressure on the therapist leads to actual expressions that are congruent with the patient's unconscious fantasy: "The task of the therapist is not simply to eliminate errors or deprivations, but to formulate the nature of the specific psychological and interpersonal meanings that have led the therapist to feel and behave in this particular fashion" (p. 6). Tansey and Burke (1989) have applied this interactive idea very specifically to the issue of countertransference disclosure.

Although Ogden and Tansey and Burke have attempted to show the analyst's active role through introjective identification, other theorists, rather than describing an *inter*action, sometimes describe formulations that seem ultimately to concentrate on the action of the patient on the analyst. It is as though the concrete experience of the patient were telepathically deposited into the analyst. When analysts minimize the role of real interactions or their own contribution to what are called the patient's projective identifications—how they are both shaped and processed by analysts' own psychodynamics—these formulations fail to fully develop a two-person model.

Tansey and Burke (1989) have devised a very specific and useful schema to help analysts sort out their own contribution to projective identifications. They use that schema to show how projective identifications might be employed to guide analysts' disclosures primarily to clarify patients' internal experience. On the basis of a thorough-going two-person model recognizing the role of action in psycho-analysis, one might argue for the advantages of collaboratively examining the interactive behavioral processes through which such experiences are cocreated. From such a vantage point, disclosures might be employed more liberally than has been customary among such analysts.

Let us consider countertransference disclosure within the frameworks proposed by some of the more influential object relations theorists. We have seen that Sandler (1976a,b, 1981) went to great lengths to develop a framework that integrates object relations formulations into a psychoanalytic theory of interpersonal behavior. Seeing the analyst's involvement as inevitable, he described transference and countertransference in terms of a complicated system of unconscious cues, both given and received, not unlike the ordinary process involved in object choice. Sandler (1976a) suggested that the analyst's responses in the psychoanalytic situation might best be viewed as a "compromise between his own propensities and the role-relationship which the patient is unconsciously seeking to establish" (p. 47). Likewise, he saw the analyst's *behavior* toward the patient, similar to evenly hovering attention, as a source of psychoanalytic data and noted that often interactions can be understood only after the analyst has taken action. In this view, the analyst implicitly is a separate person who experiences the influence of the patient and whose unique personality, involving his or her own need for role responsiveness, has an impact on the patient, the transference, and the treatment. Yet Sandler (1981) explicitly aligned himself with an "essentially intrapsychic psychoanalytic psychology" (p. 195). In a statement related to countertransference disclosure, he cautions that knowledge of the analyst "be kept to a minimum. . . . There are, of course, times when the reality of one or another aspect of the analyst's behavior or attitudes has to be pointed out, but we would counsel caution in this regard" (Sandler and Sandler, 1984, pp. 386–387).

Fairbairn's (1952) formulations show many consistencies with a two-person model. He observed:

> The basic unit of study is not the individual as a separate entity whose desires clash with an external reality, but an interactional field within which the individual arises and struggles to make contact and to articulate himself. . . . Mind is composed of rela-

tional configurations. . . . Experience is understood as structured through interactions [pp. 3–4].

Since Fairbairn never commented directly on countertransference disclosure, however, it is necessary to infer his position—an uncertain undertaking. Expressing a loyalty to a one-person psychology, Fairbairn placed heavy psychodynamic emphasis on endopsychic structure related to the vicissitudes of internalized object relationships. Yet he also assigned prime therapeutic importance to the actual relationship between patient and analyst. Technically, Fairbairn (1958) went so far as to acknowledge the personal interests of *both* parties in the relationship. He advised, "If it is felt necessary to impose restrictions in the interests of the analyst, this fact should be explicitly acknowledged (p. 378). Because he recommended that the analyst's personal contribution be openly acknowledged in this respect, one might assume that Fairbairn was inclined at times to disclose countertransference to the patient. But since he did not directly address this subject, that is not altogether clear. In fact, such an understanding receives little support from Guntrip's (1975) account of his personal analysis with Fairbairn, whom he described as "the intellectually precise interpreting analyst" (p. 52) and as "becoming more *orthodox in practice* than in theory" (pp. 51–52).

I see Fairbairn's ideas, like Kohut's, as transitional in the evolution of personality theory, and that is why some commentators have noted the one-person elements in his approach while others have emphasized the two-person. Hirsch (1987) has suggested that Fairbairn believed it possible to conduct treatment from outside of the relational matrix. In Hirsch's analysis, such remnants of a one-person technical stance would certainly preclude the use of disclosure. Yet Rubens (1996) suggests that it is fully in keeping with Fairbairn's beliefs for analysts to be totally self-expressive. Rubens asserts that Fairbairn's thinking is discomfortingly radical. He comments: "To recognize, as Fairbairn did all those many years ago, that we are essentially full 'co-participants' with our patients in the psychoanalytic process in a way that opens us to being known as profoundly and completely as they are is frightening to many of us" (p. 434). Likening Fairbairn's position to those taken by Searles and Wolstein, Rubens reads Fairbairn as requiring the analyst's open and direct dealing with his or her personhood in an analysis. From that reading of Fairbairn's work, self-disclosure would seem *essential.*

Identifying Winnicott's position on countertransference disclosure is less problematic because he addressed disclosure explicitly. Placing strong emphasis on external object relationships, Winnicott attempted to bring the analyst into the process as another person, acting in ways that were responsive to patients' developmental needs while limiting the potential impact of the analyst's eccentricities and negative emotional reactions. From his work with seriously disturbed patients, Winnicott introduced a distinction that is still employed by many analysts, that between "objective" and "subjective" aspects of countertransference. Subjective countertransference refers to "neurotic features" thought to spoil the professional attitude and disturb the course of the analytic process as determined by the patient. Objective countertransference, in contrast, was thought to be "in reaction to the actual personality and behavior of the patient, based on objective observation" (Winnicott, 1949, p. 70). Accordingly, Winnicott wrote, "If the patient seeks objective or justified hate he must be able to reach it, else he cannot feel he can reach objective love" (p. 72). The analyst's claim on this objective-subjective distinction is questionable from a more current two-person point of view, since in that view all countertransference, as cocreated within a particular relationship, is necessarily intersubjective.

For Winnicott, it was the cautious disclosure of "objective" countertransference that was therapeutic, and he recognized a need to reflectively disclose countertransference experience only when it was believed to be in the interests of the patient. He also noted that the analyst at times needed to ventilate his or her countertransference in order to "bear the strain" of the treatment relationship, thereby diminishing more subtle and indirect forms of countertransference interference. He stressed, crucially, that in expressing countertransference reactions the analyst had to moderate intense feelings and protect the patient from them.

Further evidence of the radical trend toward self-disclosure is found in the more recent contributions of Bollas (1983, 1987, 1989, 1992), who cultivated some of Winnicott's insights in ways that promote a more intensive sharing of the analyst's subjective experience. Like Winnicott, Bollas emphasized the analyst's role as a "facilitating environment." The analyst places his or her ideas in the "potential space" between the analyst and patient. The analyst becomes a "transformational object" who helps the patient like the mother who aids her infant by transforming preverbal utterances into some form of representation. In formulations suggesting the role of projective identification, Bollas asserted that the analyst's experience may represent the patient's "truly" free associative process. Analysts can thus free associate with patients in order to stimulate their free associative process and help them recover and own aspects of self. In tentatively disclosing some of their "musings" as objects with which patients might "play," analysts thus make available to patients certain freely associated states, feelings, or positions that the analysts believe are sponsored by some part of the patients. Even though clinicians may not know what the ultimate meaning will be, they can offer these subjective experiences to patients so long as it is clear to patients that such disclosures are intended in the overall interests of the analysis. Bollas also emphasized the need to analyze patients' unconscious reactions to such disclosure. He thus encouraged analysts to establish themselves as subjects as well as objects in the analytic field—to describe the internal process through which they came to an interpretation, for example. They must disclose experience that is congruent with their own character, that is, in Bollas's view, authentic. They might also share ways in which they differ with themselves—over time—thus bringing into the work their own psychic reality and even neutralized conflicts, through "the dialectics of difference."

When they do not combine the importance of external as well as internalized relationships, object relations approaches offer a limited expression of a two-person model. Technically, many contemporary object relations analysts emphasize intrapsychic exploration but not the real contribution of the analyst, self-revelation, the new relational experience, or the value of illuminating interpersonal influence processes that are centrally involved in their theoretical formulations. In contrast, Bollas, through a willingness to introduce himself as a subject in the analytic field, to include his associations, psychic reality, and even conflicts, and an openness to analyzing his own experience with the patient, leans strongly in the direction of a fully expressed two-person articulation of the psychoanalytic situation. Disclosure is most compatible with an approach that recognizes the significance of external object relations in intrapsychic exploration, or interpersonal inquiry.

Disclosure and the Interpersonal Tradition

If the classical analyst is the most restricted with regard to self disclosure, the interpersonal analyst applies the techniques of disclosure most intensively. Diverging from the classical view from its beginnings, interpersonal psychoanalysis recognized the analyst as a participant in a relationship, rather than an observer (Sullivan, 1953). The compatibility of countertransference disclosure with the interpersonal approach is attributable to its use of active, collaborative inquiry rather than working strictly with patients' free associations, and to its emphasis on the exploration of patient–therapist interactions rather than interpretation. Thus, Levenson (1972) described the analyst's "extended participation with the patient—his or her ability to be trapped, immersed and participating in the system and then to work his way out" (p. 174).

Sullivan did not address countertransference theory per se, but he, Fromm-Reichmann (1950), and Fromm (Bacciagaluppi, 1989), all seminal figures in the interpersonal movement, described the significant role of the analyst as a real person. Accordingly, they and other theorists operating in the interpersonal tradition have played a significant historical role in reformulating the narrow definition of countertransference. Stressing the mutual influence of both patient and therapist on one another, interpersonal analysts have for many years given wide berth to countertransference disclosure. Tauber (1954), a contemporary of Heimann, offered a counterpoint to the latter's warnings concerning disclosure. He wrote, "By discussing some of the countertransference fragments, both the analyst and the patient may find out that the analyst has a richer understanding of the patient which can be put to good use in the exploratory process of analysis" (p. 331).

Arguing against the view of the impenetrable mirror analyst, Wolstein (1959) was among the first contemporary analysts to make the radical case for a dyadic, transactional view of transference and countertransference in a two-person field. Wolstein noted that the procedure and attitude taken toward countertransference were doomed to confusion, because it was simply impossible for analysts simultaneously to view their experience as a self-enclosed system and to reach out to patients also construed as self-enclosed systems. He advised that characteristic transference processes become the central focus of study within a two-person experiential field, as they interweave with and are assimilated by the analyst's countertransference. As Wolstein saw it, the processes in one participant, whether patient or analyst, tended to produce the very experiential conditions they require in the other for ongoing relatedness. Transference analysis was to take place in an experiential field that was coconstrued by the analyst and in which, for better or for worse, the analyst actively participated. It included the analyst's particular personality traits and foibles, his or her characteristic modes of response, conditioned by his own past experience, and, ultimately, his very being as a person.

Interpersonal analysts have recognized that they implicitly and inevitably convey a great deal about themselves through their interventions. For example, Singer (1977) has stated quite compellingly: "I am convinced that the whole notion of analytic anonymity is fictitious. . . . It seems to me that this anonymity is an artifact carefully maintained by an analytic folie a deux" (p. 188). Singer emphasized that the analyst's interpretations were *first and foremost* self-revealing statements. Likewise, Levenson (1983) has argued that "regardless of the therapist's ostensible intent, he cannot help but react to the patient. . . . He can try to minimize revealing this to the patient in an effort to keep his participation neutral. [But] one might debate the feasibility and even honesty of that effort" (p. 52). The analytic process, in Levenson's view, results "not by interpreting the patient's resistance to one's truth but by reporting one's *own* experience of the transaction" (quoted in Gill, 1983, p. 228). Similarly, Chrzanowski (1980) described a therapeutic atmosphere of "exchanging and documenting mutual impressions, emotions, and observations" (p. 354). And in contrasting the interpersonal and self-psychological approaches, Bromberg (1986) has noted that the work of interpersonal psychoanalysis proceeds on the basis of the self psychologist's empathic failures. He notes, "It is in the clashes, the narcissistic wounds, the confrontations, the inaccurate interpretations, the analyst's appropriate need to respond as a person in his own right, that the potential for growth in the patient exists—if the analyst can use these so-called 'failures' in the right way" (p. 380).

Wachtel (1983) has pointed out that it is joint participation with the "crucial difference" of reflectiveness that enables the patient to achieve interpersonal insight and thus learn what is necessary in order to change. If the analyst hides behind a so-called neutral self-presentation, according to Wachtel, obscuring his or her own participation in the session's events and not making it a part of the focus of what is discussed with the patient, it is difficult for the patient to understand how he goes about creating and re-creating the same experiences in his or her daily life.

Searles (1975, 1986, 1987) has for many years been an ardent spokesperson for the value of countertransference disclosure, especially though not exclusively in treating more severely disturbed patients. He (1986) has written, "I have become increasingly able to appreciate the richness and accuracy of the information, at times no less than amazing, which flows from the patient to oneself, largely by nonverbal avenues, and which is made available by largely unconscious empathic processes" (p. 365). Searles sees it as crucial that analysts not react to such personal responses with self-condemnation but by regarding them—until they are proved more properly a function of the analyst's own unanalyzed childhood history—as inherent and priceless data for *mutual exploration*—well timed, of course—on the part of both patient and analyst, and eminently deserving of inclusion in any subsequently published account of the analysis.

Ehrenberg's position involves a recognition that "what is structured in the interactional process by both patient and analyst must be analytically addressed" (1982, p. 536). She suggests that the analytic focus be shifted from content to context, elevating the analytic transaction ("all of the transactions in the immediate field of experience") to the position of primary analytic data. Ehrenberg (1984) has noted that "attempting to make the implicit transactions [in the analytic relationship] explicit requires monitoring the slightest ambiguities of one's own experience in a painstaking way, as well as monitoring the impact of each participant on the other"(p. 564). For Ehrenberg, the analyst's active, affective participation goes far beyond traditional levels of countertransference disclosure. In case after case, she (1992) illustrates her conviction that analytic participation, including acknowledging details about oneself, one's participation, personal limitations, struggle, and investment, all can open up significant new dimensions of exploration and growth.

For these interpersonal analysts, countertransference disclosure plays a continuous and central role. Analysis is not focused on the patient's inner life alone, as in the one-person model, but, significantly, on the interaction, including an examination of behaviors that may occur between the co-participants. Here it is not the analyst's ongoing maintenance of a neutral impassivity with regard to the patient's experienced impact (that is, silent uses of countertransference) that results in change; it is the skillful, collaborative analysis of the origins and implications of that impact once it has been constructively disclosed to the patient. When the exploration of mutuality in its many forms is seen as the crucible of change, countertransference disclosure becomes indispensable.

We have observed an overall trend among postclassical psychoanalysts toward more expressive forms of participation. That trend, with its earliest origins traced to the long suppressed work of Ferenczi, has progressively gained momentum in the broader field of psychoanalysis over the past half century. It reflects the growing awareness, long supported by analysts working in the interpersonal tradition, that analysts' sharing subjective and personal experiences can at times be highly rewarding rather than detrimental to treatment. While the voices of those who entirely forbid disclosure now belong to a shrinking minority, other, cautioning voices remain strong (e.g., Epstein, 1995; Greenberg, 1995b; Stolorow and Atwood, 1997). These voices, reminding analysts to consider their openness carefully, have served to moderate the participatory trend.

Some of the considerations we have addressed—specifically, enactments and new relational experience—contribute to the backdrop against which analysts make clinical decisions about revealing themselves to patients. Beyond these variables, many other very difficult and complex questions arise relating to the questions of why, when, and how analysts might optimally share their personal experience with patients. These decisions, rather than being clearly prescribed by one's preferred theoretical position, are perhaps best understood as highly personal matters—that is, as related to personality factors in both analyst and patient, and the specifics of particular moments that develop in the analyst–patient interaction. In the following chapters, to advance a framework for making these decisions, we will examine additional considerations related to self-disclosure. First let us anchor the discussion in an exploration of the analyst's authenticity.

CHAPTER 7

THE ANALYST'S AUTHENTICITY

*A*s analysts participate more fully in analytic interactions and become increasingly more self-expressive, traditional technical guidelines such as anonymity and abstinence are of little value. There is, however, value in considering the analyst's participation from the viewpoint of authenticity. To illustrate the complexity of the concept of authenticity in the analyst, especially as it pertains to technique, I will begin this discussion with a clinical vignette.

There is a lump in my throat as I listen to my patient describe her feelings of nostalgia and how hard it was for her to sit through a video of her family's celebration of her grandmother's 90th birthday. It always had been so very hard to read or keep a diary, she explained, to end an extended summer vacation, to view photographs, even to take them.

My thoughts turn to our approaching ending. (We had worked together for nearly a year. She was an exchange student and would remain in therapy—in this country, for that matter—for only a few more months.) I think about "authenticity," a topic I am writing about. What is authentic here? Is this feeling of mine—of sadness, of being touched, of being moved—my own, that is, something primarily about me? Lord knows, I too avoid looking back. And, like her, I am a historian of sorts. (She was a graduate student of world history.) I wonder, can this feeling of mine be understood as a "concordant identification" or an "intersubjective conjunction" facilitated by my own sensibilities and a way that we are similar? As she speaks, she does not seem at all sad. Perhaps it is a "complementary identification," a preconscious experience of hers that I am holding. Should I share it?

That would be a risk, given all I understand about her. Or should I hold it for her? I recall the many times she has been put off and reproached me for trying to make myself, and our relationship, an active part of the work.

She continues speaking, now of her childhood therapy, and recalls an observation offered at that time by the therapist, that her problem of dread as a child coincided with her stopping sucking her thumb. We mull over the meaning of her giving up her thumb—an ending. Time passes through one's hands like grains of sand, she says. You simply can't hold on to them, stop them. It is like bailing a boat that is sinking, she adds. "Time the Destroyer," I echo Richard Wright, whom I have read. She has grown more available, I observe in silence. Would it be going too far to tell her what I feel—that I am sad about our ending? Is it my feeling to share with this woman who has been so locked up in herself? A woman who never achieved a meaningful, close relationship with either a man or a woman and is even uncertain as to her sexual orientation? To share my feeling with her could be a very positive experience, very powerful, authentic. Certainly it would model something she would like for herself, albeit conflicted, something to internalize, to become. But would that behavior negatively echo the past? She has made clear to me her aversion to my, and others', intruding, imposing themselves on her. That seems to be a key dynamic, what her avoiding closeness, intimacy, is ultimately about. Perhaps it would be more valuable right now to hold this feeling for her, let her find it in me herself. But can she if I say nothing? And if she does not find it with me now, will she later? She does plan to continue with analysis. Which of these courses is the more "authentic?" I wonder. I test a formulation of my authenticity: remain "in touch"; try to follow, identify, to "know" your experience, as well as the patient's, as fully as possible; if you share it—depending on the particulars of the moment—try to share it truthfully, as you experience it.

As is her custom, she notes that she has come to the end of this topic, closes it off, and asks if I have any thoughts. Plenty, I think to myself. But what to share? I pause, think for a moment, consider a way of sharing my sadness—or is it hers—with her. Then I put out a feeler, testing her receptivity: "You won't like my thoughts." After a silent pause, I add, "Are you sure you want to hear them?" She says, "No," sternly, emphatically, and then looks away, at the clock. I say nothing, waiting attentively. She knows she has made me aware that she doesn't like to talk about "us." There is no "us"; we have no relationship; there are no feelings between us. I am merely her doctor. Rather than letting the moment die, I decide to speak indirectly from my feeling. Following up on an earlier session about avoiding closeness, I suggest that that might be a reason to hold back from attachments—the knowledge of the pain at ending. I am now very aware, very sad, that the end of the year of our work together is coming. Is she aware of that, that indirectly we are discussing her feelings about ending and the need to avoid them? My eyes have become watery, I become aware, although she now smiles. I wonder if she's noticed my tears. I believe I feel sad, that my sadness is heightened because we cannot acknowledge feelings about our ending, put them into words. For me, there is a tragic sense to all this. And I know it is at the heart of her difficulties. With a sense of urgency I think, isn't there any way we can use this experience to connect?

In this moment, although frustrated, I feel there has been something very important about our work. She insisted at first that we talk only about her academic and work difficulties but not about relationships. Now, at least, we broach these feelings about an "us." I suggest to her in a way that intimates the possibility that something positive may have happened between us, that this is a year she might look back on and remember favorably. My attempt feels feeble to me, however. She tells me she has thought about celebrating this year, having completed it on her feet, having grown following last year's collapse. But now she considers, in a way that seems highly intellectual, the possibility that that might be a way of avoiding the sad part of ending the year—a year of building herself up, advancing her career, creating a brighter future. No mention of therapy, of me. I feel deflated; the moment of potential intimate contact seems lost. "It's the final two minutes," she announces. She continues, "I might talk about the ending with you. I'm not accustomed to talking about these feelings, having them be real with other people. Only in the abstract. I'm not able to discuss feeling sad over you." *She* ends the session punctually, smiling. "We'll continue on Wednesday."

Defining Authenticity

There is no consensus as to the meaning of authenticity in the analyst, and many questions about it need to be addressed. I will consider some of these questions here and then propose that we think about analytic authenticity in terms of an *attitude* that helps us grapple with the complexities of a thoroughgoing two-person model of the psychoanalytic situation. I have come to think that an authentic analytic attitude, properly defined, is a useful replacement for the one-person model-analyst's principle of anonymity.

Until recently, the role of the analyst's authenticity received relatively little explicit attention from analysts. That omission can be interpreted as an outgrowth of the classical tradition, with its suppression of the analyst's individuality and its concentration on the patient's distortions of the psychoanalytic situation. The principle of anonymity that guides analysts' behavior in that model fails to offer much guidance to participatory analysts following a two-person model.

It is not widely recognized that Freud, in developing his ideas on technique, was very concerned about elements related to analysts' authenticity. He wrote:

> If the doctor is to be in a position to use his unconscious . . . as an instrument of the analysis he must himself fulfill one psychological condition to a high degree. He may not tolerate any resistances in himself which hold back from his consciousness what has been perceived by his unconscious [Freud, 1912b, p. 116].

In that passage, in which Freud stressed the need for analysts' self-awareness, he also noted the problem of blind spots, the idea that normal self-scrutiny was not enough but that analysts' self-observation skills needed to be enhanced through a training analysis. Highly sensitive to themselves, analysts were nevertheless to remain "opaque" to their patients and were not to "bring their own individuality freely into the discussion" (p. 117).

Freud (1915) also was concerned with analysts falsifying their feelings to patients so as to achieve favorable outcomes:

> Psychoanalytic treatment is founded on truthfulness. In this fact lies a great part of its educative effect and its ethical value. It is dangerous to depart from this foundation. . . . Since we demand strict truthfulness from our patients, we jeopardize our whole authority if we let ourselves be caught out by them in a departure from the truth [p. 164].

Freud's major purpose in emphasizing self-scrutiny and awareness was to enable analysts to read patients' unconscious processes and then to control and master their own reactions so they could maintain an attitude of detached objectivity. Thus, although Freud never commented on the analyst's authenticity directly, clearly he believed analysts had to remain true to their own experience with their patients.

As analysts grapple with a psychoanalytic technique that is based on a two-person model, it becomes increasingly important to reach a systematic understanding of how the analyst's individuality actually contributes to, and can be integrated into, analytic work. Here Freud's concerns with the analyst's self-scrutiny and truthfulness, elements of the very complicated issue of the analyst's authenticity, acquire considerable importance. The analyst's authenticity is germane not only to the suppression of the analyst's individuality, as Freud emphasized, but at least equally to its expression. And, as we have seen, many analysts have come to realize that expressions of their individuality, both deliberate and inadvertent, not only cannot be overlooked but also profoundly influence the course of an analysis.

There is little agreement among psychoanalysts regarding the meaning of their authenticity. In common usage, authenticity is related to genuineness, to a truthfulness (rather than falseness) with which an individual responds and represents himself or herself to another; it is related to directness as opposed to manipulation. Little (1951) equated authenticity with the analyst's "sincerity" and stressed the need, at times, for an "honest recognition" of essential feelings. Levenson (1983) stressed "the interpersonal effort to be, with others, oneself" (p. 104). He emphasizes that the authentic analyst responds in a way that is "in touch . . . with one's experience of the situation" (1991, p. 108). Bollas (1989) speaks of authentic self-disclosures as those which are congruent with the analyst's character. Ehrenberg (1992) stresses therapists' authenticity in relation to the need to avoid denying or resisting awareness of countertransference experience. Both Ehrenberg and Levenson tend to conflate self-awareness and openness, an equation I discuss later. Mitchell (1993) discusses authenticity in relation to the analyst's attempts to be "true to himself". Fosshage (1994) sees authenticity as a "nondefensive presence." Bader (1995) frames it as "a view that cherishes surprise, an appreciation of ambiguity, spontaneous responsiveness, and an acceptance of the free play of the analyst's unconscious" (p. 287). Hoffman (1996) and Renik (1996) both equate authenticity with spontaneity and contrast it with the analyst's adherence to any technical formulas or deliberate techniques.

The analyst's authenticity is a highly complex attribute and must not be understood simply as an invariant expression of a static self. Thus Mitchell (1993) redirects analysts' concerns with their authenticity to their momentary experience rather than to a "true" or "core" self. In part, authenticity is related to what Carl Rogers (1961) long ago called congruence when he emphasized the need for therapists to be dependably real and to act in a manner that corresponded with the feelings and attitudes they actually were experiencing. Rogers contrasted congruence, or authenticity, with a stereotyped demeanor, one of loving acceptance, for example, that was rigidly maintained no matter what was occurring within and between patient and therapist. Relatedly, Mitchell (1992) has pointed out that an assessment of authenticity based on an internal reference alone is insufficient. He states, "Authenticity derives from the use of what has been *socially negotiated* to represent and express myself; inauthenticity derives from the use of what has been socially negotiated to create and manage impressions of me in others" (p. 16). These observations call our attention to the role of context in understanding authenticity.

Authenticity and Context

In elaborating the dialectical relationship between internality and externality, Mitchell (1992) writes, "The self operates in the subtle and intricate dialectic between spontaneous vitality and self-expression on the one hand and the requirement, crucial for survival, to preserve secure and familiar connections with others, on the other" (p. 11). Accordingly, what feels authentic to the analyst harmonizes both internal experience and the external, interpersonal context. Bader (1995) further clarifies the ambiguity of the analyst's authenticity when he, too, notes the value of thinking about our authenticity contextually. Like Mitchell, Bader reasons that the analyst's authenticity can usefully be understood dialectically in relation to the analyst's theory of technique.

Aron (1996), too, emphasizes that it is the personal elements contained in an intervention—specifically, the emotionally responsive aspects of the analyst's subjectivity that are communicated—that lead to an intervention's effectiveness. According to Aron, "It is, however, precisely because the subjective element is contained within a technical intervention that it is transformed from being simply an idiosyncratic emotional response on the analyst's part into an analytic intervention carrying a sense of dialectical objectivity . . . and it is this mix of the personal and the technical that potentially generates its transformative analytic power" (p. 93).

Closely held theories form a part of the context that shape an analyst's experience and actions. They determine which aspects of the analyst's full repertory of experiences are "authentically" called forth—not only in terms of how the analyst might act and what he or she might interpret or express, but the actual experiences that the analyst becomes aware of. Accordingly, the analyst's theory, often acting preconsciously, predisposes him or her to organize and react to certain aspects of the psychoanalytic situation and the analysand's responses in particular ways but differently to others.

Some authors, such as Weiss (1993), have emphasized the value of operating very deliberately, with the express objective of giving patients what they need in words and action, that is, of providing mutative forms of new relational experience. Others, like Renik (1996), have emphasized the new aspects of the analytic experience that result when patient and analyst inadvertently "stumble on" developments based on their unconscious motivations and then analyze them retrospectively. Far less is prospective in the latter view; rather, it is the reparative effects of a full and authentic engagement of the partners in the clinical encounter, combined with retrospective analysis, that carries the therapeutic action. In considering these two approaches, analysts do well to regard their experience dialectically, attending both to the importance of what they *intend* to do and to the subtlest cues about what they may be spontaneously expressing and unconsciously *enacting*.

When we approach authenticity contextually, we see that there are many authentic shapes of the self and that we, as individuals and as analysts, have many authentic faces. Authenticity cannot be understood simply in terms of thematic personal organizations and behaviors that find direct and uniform expression across the entire range of a person's conduct and relationships. Authentic expressions are elaborated differently, depending on the context in which they are experienced and expressed. Thus, while in fundamental ways we may remain very much the same in all our interactions, we are nevertheless differently authentic, say, as friends rather than as parents, teachers, or therapists. We also are differently authentic with each of our friends, children, students, or patients. These differences are based on specific interpretations of roles, on the perception of others' particular sensitivities, needs, and intentions, on the momentary receptivity that is perceived in others, and on the influence individuals may wish to have or not have, to name but a few variables that shape one's authentic participation. A clinician's theory of technique, itself a very personal expression, plays a major role in defining the relational context and, in turn, the ways in which the analyst's individual personality and authenticity play out.

There is a story about a meeting between classical and jazz musicians. The classical musician has witnessed an improvisational performance given by the jazz artist and, impressed, asks him how he prepared for his gig. The jazz player responds, "Just as you do—I practice scales and play sheet music. But then I just forget about all that crap!" To describe the dialectical interplay between the analyst's authenticity and theoretical commitments, Bader (1995) has offered a related, compelling analogy about jazz improvisation:

> Jazz musicians, for instance, are able to improvise without appearing to think about it in advance or without having to interpose any conscious framework of musical theory. Because they understand the abstract relationships among chords, keys, and harmonies in great complexity, on some level, they can take the scaffolding for granted and respond and improvise "spontaneously." There is a dialectical relationship between theory and spontaneity, between conscious intentions and unconscious playfulness and creativity. The knowledge of theory makes spontaneity possible. Similarly, in the analytic interaction, the analyst's deliberate intentions and theoretical understanding provide the scaffolding, within which a great deal of spontaneous interpretive and affective improvisation can occur [p. 297].

Authenticity and Role Playing

Thus we see how spontaneity and discipline can combine constructively, authentically. But do theory, strategy, and theoretically prescribed roles always combine with spontaneity, creativity, and unconscious playfulness in ways that potentiate the analyst's work, or is it possible for these elements to interact in detrimental ways?

Recall that when Alexander and French (1946) first introduced their idea of corrective emotional experience, it was intensely criticized as contrived and manipulative—correctly, in my view. Yet a dialectical understanding of authenticity that takes into account one's clinical theory of technique clarifies that Alexander's approach is not unique in its reliance on strategy and, at least in that sense, manipulation. In chapter 5 we considered that *any* analytic stance is necessarily strategic to some degree; for in subscribing to any single psychoanalytic ideology over another—and every analyst does, implicitly and explicitly—the analyst adopts a particular mental set and with it a disposition to respond to certain developments in certain ways. Moreover, many practitioners are unwilling to openly discuss their strategies with their patients, which implies another element of manipulation. As Gill (1994) pointed out, any position that is taken, including silence, without exploring the patient's experience of it, manipulates the transference.

Thus, when analysts such as Pine (1993) refer disparagingly to non-Freudian forms of "self-conscious role playing," one wonders how they reconcile this criticism with the neutral, anonymous, and abstinent *role* of the classical analysts. And it seems to me not unreasonable to describe that stance as no more authentic but another form of just the role playing Pine is criticizing. There simply are no exemptions. Every version of psychoanalysis casts the analyst in one analytic role or another. Thereby, all tend to shape the analyst's participation in ways that predispose certain forms of responsiveness, allow certain of the analyst's intentions to remain tacit, and may require that still others be actively obscured, as part of an influence process.

When Strategies Collide

Are all practitioners who are authentically committed to one approach or another equally authentic in their analytic roles? Does the playing of analytic roles exert comparable influence across all approaches? Are personal and analytic authenticity the same?

Consider the following as an example in which strategies collide. One practitioner, emphasizing developmental considerations, suggests the need to allow the patient to idealize the analyst; but another suggests that that is a charade and that in knowingly going along with such developments analysts are being inauthentic. One might ask, following Bader, how could it possibly be inauthentic to act on deeply held convictions about the value of idealization (or even anonymity or any stance, for that matter) in psychological growth? The analyst's actions accord with his or her own convictions (internality) and the patient's needs as the pair has come to understand them (externality).

Yet, operating from similar conviction, another relational analyst might observe that it is precisely those areas in which the patient's vision of the analyst is incongruent with the analyst's own (including a patient's idealization of the analyst) that define what needs to be analyzed. According to that analyst, to go along with the patient's idealization, or to role play in that instance and not to engage that disparity, is more than inauthentic; it is indulging the patient's problem.

Seeing the first practitioner's actions as disingenuous, dissembling, or inauthentic, the second practitioner doubts that the first's actions can be profoundly helpful to patients, at least over the long term. The first therapist in this instance is aware of the patient's gross exaggeration of his abilities, resources, or personal attractiveness and yet sees advantages in allowing the patient's idealized construction to remain unchallenged. On the basis of his own theoretical commitment, predisposing psychodynamics, and experience, he authentically believes in the value of idealization and gives it a higher therapeutic priority than a reconciliation of the two views of him. The therapist who believes that idealization facilitates emotional growth also has doubts about his colleague's very different, more confrontational methods. He believes that the other therapist proceeds with a lack of empathy and fails to appreciate the fragility of many patients' articulations and emerging changes. He might reason, further, that the colleague operates too intrusively, even self-centeredly and without adequate regard for his patient's developmental needs.

So where are we left with regard to analytic authenticity? Is one of these analysts more authentic than the other? Operating most skillfully, analysts seem able to blend their particular analytic strategies, to which they (and their patients, apparently) are personally well suited—whether they be Freudian, Kohutian, Winnicottian, or what have you—seamlessly and even synergistically with their spontaneous self-expressions. As in the example of the jazz musician, it seems that the more profoundly and coherently integrated is an analyst's grasp of transference, countertransference, resistance, and other analytic principles, as understood within any particular theoretical system, the more imaginatively and effectively can the analyst operate within that particular framework with authentic and spontaneous creativity.

But strategy, while unavoidable and capable of providing a framework that shapes and sponsors an analyst's spontaneous participation also may curb creativity and limit analytic authenticity, and ultimately the analyst's efficacy. When analysts follow strategies too rigidly, in ways that constrict their personal freedom and spontaneous expressiveness, as when they attempt to play roles that are at odds with their fundamental philosophical (including theoretical) beliefs, then, rather than synergistically combining spontaneity with intention, the combination can be detrimental. Further, when analysts hold their methods, whatever they might be, sacrosanct, refusing to welcome questioning of them and thus holding them exempt from joint scrutiny, that, too, represents a manipulative form of analytic role playing that compromises analytic authenticity and truthfulness. In such responses we see how strategy and an adherence to analytic roles may act to keep analysts as individuals out of the relationship, permitting them to hide, rather than bringing them authentically into it. Here is where one's analytic role threatens to become role playing. To repeat Mitchell's (1992) point, authenticity derives not from the use of what has been socially negotiated to create and manage *impressions* of oneself in others, which is inauthenticity, but from the use of what has been socially negotiated to represent and express oneself. The authentic analyst may be deeply committed to a theory, even steeped in it; but he or she must not be dominated by it.

Authenticity as an Attitude

Was I being authentic when, with the patient in the opening example, I chose to withhold my response rather than share it? There is value in considering the analyst's authenticity not so much in terms of specific interventions, moments, or states, as in terms of an *attitude* that the analyst strives to maintain toward his or her own experience of and with the patient. Here the effort is to synchronize self with context, that is, to remain "in touch" with the experience of the situation, as Levenson (1991) put it. A guiding principle is to try to avoid deception, including self-deception, in order to foster introspective, accountable psychoanalytic participation as an individual. This strategy is reminiscent of Freud's (1912b, 1915) early writings stressing the need to be sensitive to oneself but is developed here to suggest a way of thinking about our authenticity that can advance a two-person perspective across a wide range of relational approaches.

In this view, being authentic with a patient involves an active effort to remain honest through a sensitivity to one's own experience, actions, impact, and their meanings, in addition to the patient's. By trying to remain sensitive to the moment-to-moment interplay of the spoken words, physical actions, and affective expressions of both individuals, the analyst attends closely to ongoing interactions. One might ask oneself: What is happening here right now? What am I feeling? What, in addition to the words, am I hearing from the part of the patient that is endeavoring to make itself *felt*? How is this patient "using" me right now? Beyond the formal analytic agreement, what is being structured into the relationship at this moment? How am I causing, going along with, or advancing it? Attention to our "free-floating responsiveness" (Sandler, 1976a)—the actions we are inclined to take—can help us to fine-tune self-awareness and participation, and thus authenticity.

The struggle to sort out elements of the total relationship—that is, what may be new versus old, symbolic versus actual, transferential versus real, constructive versus counterproductive in the patient's experience with us, which inevitably is inconclusive—raises our consciousness of the many facets of ourselves that we and the patient may experience. Remembering that accepting patients' perceptions of us as plausible is more than a mere device to advance the inquiry; we must take up these ideas internally—and, if we wish, externally with patients—*in earnest*. Here, where there is little room for certainty, we realize that we may learn something truly new and valuable about ourselves.

Striving toward authenticity, analysts try to be as sensitive as possible to their own internal process, including what they may have *failed* to notice about themselves. This they may do, for instance, through a willingness to grant consideration to the unknown— unknown to the analysts at least—which a patient may see in the analyst's personality and actions and signal both consciously and preconsciously. Thus we allow for the "authenticity," as it were, of unconscious or unknown elements, of aspects of our experience of which we are not yet aware.

A facilitating, authentic attitude thus is advanced in many ways: struggling internally to remain attuned to ourselves as well as to our patients, while nevertheless retaining a skepticism about the ability to know and to clarify fully our personal experience and actions and their meanings; attempting to monitor patients' conscious and preconscious reactions to us to the extent possible, so as to raise awareness of our inadvertent self-revelations and their impact on the transference and to reconsider and modify our participation accordingly; exploring transference and countertransference dialectically, as when we actively and collaboratively explore, in order to clarify, our own part in interactions with patients, so we can promote transference analysis and meaningful forms of new relational experience.

To return to the question of whether I was being authentic with the patient I described in the example, I believe I was, according to these standards. I was wrestling with conflicting impulses to share and to contain my feelings of sadness. Insofar as the wish to share my feelings seemed, potentially, to be an outgrowth of my own desire to connect, and at that moment to oppose an important need of hers, it was unclear to me whether I would be sharing my experience for personally indulgent reasons or to advance her growth. That decision was further complicated by the pressure of time in the treatment; if not then, little opportunity remained to get into this material, on the one hand, and yet there would be little chance to follow up on related themes if these feelings were introduced, on the other.

Some might argue that, nevertheless, a disclosure might usefully have confronted a defense of hers. But my experience with this patient, including many past attempts to be open, had convinced me that that was not the case. In the past, I had experienced myself at the nexus of similar crosscurrents relating to distance and intimacy, dominance or submission, the negotiation of which had seemed crucial to the work. But previously, she had experienced my disclosures in attempting to work with these issues as intrusions that had caused her to pull back, rather than as cultivating the inclination to approach me that was strengthening within her. Thus, ultimately, I decided to withhold the strong reaction I might otherwise have shared, and, in retrospect, I do not think a different course—including my describing my dilemma to her—would have been significantly more useful at that point in the treatment. Of course, I cannot know that with certainty. (In fact, as I write about this experience, I get in touch with the possibility that her withholding might have involved some sadistic motivation that we might eventually have explored.)

What is important in evaluating the analyst's authenticity is not whether an intervention is "correct"; for certainly opportunities to pick up on specific themes continue to present themselves, at least in ongoing analyses. What is more important is whether, throughout the process, the analyst maintains a facilitating, authentic attitude, as described above, characterized by introspection, an openness to alternative understandings of analytic events and experiences, and a related quality of skepticism toward one's own experience. In that sense, my authenticity in this instance earns passing grades.

Making authenticity an active part of one's analytic attitude modifies the more staunchly neutral analytic attitude that Schafer (1983) has defined. He endorses Anna Freud's (1936) "equidistant" definition of neutrality and stresses that "to achieve neutrality requires a high degree of subordination of the analyst's personality to the analytic task at hand" (p. 6). Acknowledging, striving to be aware of, and monitoring one's personal experience and impact are not the same as striving to achieve an ideal of *eliminating* one's personal impact. Authenticity calls our attention to aspects of our participation that have less to do with our subordinating our personalities to essential analytic roles—maintaining an emotional detachment or sustained empathic presence, for example—than with a willingness to acknowledge, examine, and specify our inevitable personal involvement, sometimes openly, as it is expressed within those roles.

An authentic attitude strives for harmony between interiority and exteriority, between being and action. Analysts struggle together with their patients to work through mutual constructions, trying to clarify the gap between intent and impact, for example, as they negotiate what "really" is going on. Dyadic psychoanalytic views locate the therapeutic action in understanding and mastering the interface of the patient–therapist experience; in this way, analyst and analysand together connect through authentic voices, achieving an analytic intimacy that is freed from prestructured interaction patterns. Thinking about authenticity in a way that is integrated with the analyst's overall analytic attitude organizes a particular way of being with patients that can optimize work with the analyst's personal contribution and make use of one's theoretical understanding while nevertheless minimizing the potentially detrimental contribution of role playing.

Authenticity and Disclosure

Our thoughts jump reflexively to deliberate self-disclosure when we speak of authenticity. Some analysts tend to combine the two. Yet a commitment to authenticity is not exactly the same as one to verbal openness. If analysts regard authenticity as an attitude, it is recognized that the analyst who verbalizes his or her experience to the patient is not necessarily any more authentic than the silent analyst; it is no more authentic, for instance, for an analyst to discuss his or her reactions with patients than to draw a line of privacy when that is his or her more authentic inclination. What is far more relevant than disclosure is that analysts strive, internally as well as externally, not to be deceptive and, as far as possible, to avoid misrepresenting themselves and their experience, both to themselves and to their patients. Thus disclosure remains a *choice* for the authentic analyst, but not a requirement, and involves retaining a kind of autonomy, personal freedom, and integrity in the analytic relationship. I agree with Mitchell (1993) on this point—that authenticity in the analyst "has less to do with saying everything than with the genuineness of what actually is said" (p. 146).

In the example at the beginning of this chapter, I shared my internal struggle to achieve congruence between experience and expression; there we saw how complex the relationship between authenticity and self-disclosure really can be. In actual practice, it is extremely difficult to know when it will be helpful to deliberately reveal one's experience to patients, and also how best to do so. Theory offers relatively limited guidance in this respect, and while striving for authenticity in one's expressions eases the problem in some respects, it further complicates matters in others. At times an authentic attitude may suggest the value of letting a patient know why we are acting as we are, that is, our *understanding* of it.

Notwithstanding the many complexities that are involved, operating with an attitude of authenticity sometimes can be relatively straightforward. Authenticity involves the analyst's active attempt to remain aware of his or her experience and the role it is playing with the patient in the psychoanalytic situation. It further involves a willingness to consider and choose whether to openly discuss one's understanding of that subjective experience. The analyst may choose to discuss virtually anything that seems relevant to therapeutic objectives. An analyst who chooses to open up his or her reactions to the patient, attempts to do so in a way that truthfully and accurately reflects his or her internal experience.

Thus, to return again to the opening example, if an analyst felt it appropriate to talk about his or her reactions under the circumstances depicted—and, as we saw in the example, that can be a very challenging determination—then the analyst might consider saying to a patient simply, "I'm feeling very sad right now about our ending." The analyst might also describe his or her confusion about these feelings, as he or she is best able to articulate it, including specifying the dilemma about whether or not to share the feelings. Depending on the circumstances, though, it can be equally authentic to choose not to share one's experience. (Whenever we choose to share, implicitly we are selecting elements of our experience and therefore choosing also what not to share.) I, personally, would consider offering my conscious reasons for not sharing. Again, I am defining authenticity as an attitude, self-disclosure as an option.

Operating authentically, we need not hide our strategies from patients. If a therapist followed Kohut's tenets and were asked why by the patient, the patient might find it helpful if the therapist truthfully explained why. The therapist might say, for example, "It seems to me that your childhood didn't really provide you with an adequate opportunity to discover and to realize yourself. We need to be able to create that together." Or, "Yes, I do choose to phrase things with the goal of helping you clarify and strengthen your sense of yourself." In this example, disclosure may minimize any manipulation implied by such role playing. Yet, while sharing our thinking and even making interactions explicit sometimes can be extremely meaningful as expressions of authenticity, at other times talking about our experience or analyzing spontaneous developments can drain those moments of their authenticity and emotional significance.

Problems arise when analysts are experiencing, say, anger toward a patient, or a judgmental or disapproving reaction. Questions arise as to whether it can be helpful to reveal such a reaction. The analyst might wonder, especially if asked directly by a patient, wouldn't it be "authentic" to tell? Here the analyst may experience the conflict between being "honest" or "sincere," as he or she might when acting with certain good friends, and managing the more cautious, nurturing responses that we know to be so important in our role as analyst. Operating with a commitment to openness, the analyst might even act to "resolve" the conflict over openness by sharing the dilemma with the patient—but not with all patients, for such sharing sometimes asks too much. At other times, analysts may suspect that problematic reactions of this sort have more to do with themselves and with their own issues than with patients; in that case, why burden the patient with them? But how can an analyst be certain that that thinking is not false and self-protective justification for concealment? How is sound clinical judgment to be parsed from problematic countertransference?

How strictly are we to apply the principle of asymmetry? Does the idea of realistic interpersonal contact that some interpersonal analysts promote imply that analysts should reveal such problematic reactions—indeed, *all* potentially significant personal reactions to patients? Certainly there is reason to think that precisely those reactions which are the most threatening to share directly with patients are the most meaningful. That course, however, is not always prudent in an analytic context. Yet, influenced by the standard technique and models of new relational experience that caution against responding in kind and that urge careful consideration of developmental factors, most analysts are reluctant to test the therapeutic limits of openness or even to probe more actively the ramifications of their inevitable inadvertent self-revelations with patients.

Then, too, sometimes analysts can productively explore transference and countertransference dialectically by openly comparing the impressions of both members of the pair and clarifying their own inadvertent contribution; but at other times revealing too much of oneself may be problematic. Often opposing positions are resolvable in a synthesis. But Mitchell (1997b) has pointed out that that option might overwhelm certain fragile patients operating in a paranoid-schizoid mode. And yet what better way to firm up a patient's ego boundaries, at times, than to declare one's own position?

While analytic authenticity as I am defining it is not to be equated with a deliberately self-revelatory analytic orientation, still the two tend to be associated. For, if relational analysts take the idea of new relational experience seriously, then they must recognize the importance of the total, as well as the transference, relationship and that the analyst's reality with patients, understood *perspectivally*, becomes highly significant. That view connotes an interaction between the patient's transferential organizing activity and a partially independent reality of the analyst, with the deciphering of that interaction forming the basis of transference analysis. Here analysts do not act as blank screens or generic others but recognize how patients organize the particulars of what the analysts actually say and do—in that sense, who they really are—as they acknowledge the singular significance and meaning, personally and emotionally, of the analytic relationship for the patient, and for both individuals. A transference-analytic process that involves locating the reality of the analyst within the two-person field creates greater latitude than do one-person model approaches for analysts to reveal themselves to patients, while calling on them to strive for high levels of expressive authenticity.

With experience, analysts typically come to rely on self-revelation not only with greater comfort but also with increasing frequency, a phenomenon suggesting that clinical experience teaches the value of openness and directness. That observation, made at the level of individual professional development, becomes compelling when we note that it parallels the overall historical trend described in chapter 6. I question the assumption that if analysts are authentically open with patients their actions will necessarily result in a destructive expression of their eccentricities and problematic countertransference. I am suggesting precisely the opposite: the clinically competent analyst's acting with authenticity as I have defined it gains access to shared scrutiny that reinforces protections against the analyst's deleterious contribution. I suspect that it is the closed analyst, who takes for granted that his or her reserve is constructive, who more likely will be found to be participating in counterproductive ways.

CHAPTER 8

A TWO-PERSON MODEL FOR
THERAPIST SELF-DISCLOSURE

*J*ust as Freud first saw indispensable aspects of the psychoanalytic process—transference and resistance—as obstacles to that process, so can we now, based on the two-person model, appreciate and study the analyst's individuality, involvement, and participation, once regarded as analytically detrimental, as positive factors in the analytic process. A thoroughgoing articulation of the two-person model challenges the analyst to selectively illuminate many of the experiences that are inherent in the intense, intimate, analytic relationship and thereby test the constructive therapeutic limits of a process of authentic openness. In so doing, the analyst is forced to grapple with the indistinct boundaries that so often can exist between appropriate clinical judgment and self-protection, especially during intense moments, and face personal anxieties over being more fully known by the patient. This approach raises many compelling questions. Do we always choose to withhold particular reactions to our patients—such as critical or erotic ones, for example—for the patient's sake, as it might seem to us; or are we significantly motivated by our own experience of vulnerability?

Answers to such questions are not always as clear or satisfying as we might wish. The technical implications of a two-person model, when they are appreciated, are ultimately radical, complex, and anxiety provoking, and we often fail to appreciate them fully or are tempted to avoid them. Although we may disagree with the underlying theoretical tenets of a one-person model, it is all too easy to resort to the comfort offered by the model's more familiar, insulated analytic stance (Rubens, 1996). In this chapter, I propose a framework, based on a two-person model, to guide analytic therapists in thinking about sharing their personal experience with patients.

The Problem of Terminology

The term countertransference disclosure which has evolved in the psychoanalytic literature to characterize therapists' openness, certainly is an improvement on the earlier form, "confession." Still, I think it desirable to minimize the use of such terms as countertransference disclosure and certainly confession, because they have come to connote discrete interventions, sometimes in a very negative way. By characterizing acts of self-revelation as a distinct type of technique, this terminology obscures a recognition that analysts always are revealing themselves and thus disclosing to patients. Further, that terminology slows the emergence of a two-person methodology, one in which it is recognized that the analyst's personal participation is intrinsic and that the best uses of the analyst's self ideally are those that come about seamlessly in analytic work. At best these formal terms inhibit the analyst, implicitly supporting the idea that his or her anonymity is the proper baseline for participation. Sponsoring the idea that analyst openness ought to be used in specialized, occasional ways, such terms remind one of classical technique, which treats self-revelation as a parameter and discourages analysts from sharing their experience openly while closing off the possibility of judging it as potentially helpful to do so.

In writing this chapter, I have attempted to overcome my own predilection to use psychoanalytic jargon and have tried to write simply in terms of analysts' talking about, discussing, sharing, and being open with their own reactions, understandings, and experience. I have tried to avoid the use of the more formal "disclosures" and especially the condemnatory "confessions," terms that limit the analyst's participation as a fully present person. I do so in the spirit of encouraging analysts to participate more fully, openly, and authentically with their patients.

Expressing One's Experience as an Analyst; Totalist and Specifist Ideas

Countertransference represents an amalgam of levels of consciousness derived from the analyst's own personal and professional convictions, experience and history, as well as from factors that can be related more or less specifically to the experience of and with a particular patient. Clearly, as anyone who has taught or supervised analytic therapy knows, the analyst's craft is highly complex, and it is impossible to offer precise generalizations about when analysts should open up or share their experience directly with patients. Nevertheless, as we have seen, there is a growing recognition that analyst openness may decisively advance therapeutic purposes. When and how can one best share one's experience and which aspects of countertransference should be shared?

Where do totalist insights into countertransference lead us? This way of conceptualizing provides justification for decoding the meaning of the analyst's experience insofar as it shows that some part of countertransference always will be found to be "the patient's creation," as Heimann (1950) originally put it. As Ogden (1982) has further explained, "Without an understanding of this aspect of countertransference, there are no terms with which to conceptualize a process in which the therapist is pressured to *participate in* and *experience* aspects of the patient's internal object world" (p. 82). The totalist tradition casts a broad net over the analyst's reactions, covering literally *all* responses to the patient. Clearly, few if any responsible analysts would indiscriminately disclose *all* their reactions, least of all those which seem to them associated with their own difficulties. So, although the totalist position sensitizes the analyst and facilitates a full experience of the broad spectrum of internal reactions and their potential relevance to the patient's internal world and the analytic process, it encourages silent forms of internal processing rather than offering guidance about sharing those reactions openly with the patient.

Recently asked to recall the single most valuable piece of advice I had ever received from a supervisor during my training, after considerable thought I recalled the time some years ago when the idea of "complementary" identifications (Racker, 1968) was introduced. Although I now recognize additional ways of thinking about countertransference and of dealing with the analytic interaction, some of which are spelled out in this book, through that single concept and its extension to projective identification, previously inexplicable aspects of countertransference experience became for the first time understandable and thus useful in terms of identifications with unarticulated aspects of the analysand's unconscious internal object world. That development in countertransference theory, based on the idea that important developmental interactions became internalized and then shape subsequent interactions, can be enormously helpful to analysts (and, of course, patients).

In considering revealing one's experience directly, specificity becomes key. Far more usefully than totalists, specifists have encouraged analysts to attempt to understand how particular elements of their experience might be employed to illuminate the meanings of corresponding aspects of patients' psychodynamic functioning that have been expressed in the psychoanalytic interaction. These concepts do more than provide a way into the patient's experience through that of the analyst; they also provide a framework that helps the analyst determine what might meaningfully be shared. For instance, these formulations suggest that analysts may be experiencing precisely that which the patient is splitting off and needs to integrate. Further, formulations focused specifically on the *interpersonal* aspects of projective identification enable analysts to work with newer action concepts, including the potential value of elucidating enactments.

In a thoughtful application of the specifist view of countertransference to disclosure, Tansey and Burke (1989) have taken pains to outline ways analysts might process identificatory reactions containing important information in order to reveal these experiences constructively to patients. These authors, working within an object relations framework, offer a detailed, stepwise schema for preparing countertransference disclosures. They include such steps as containing and processing interactional pressures and internally formulating the potential impact of such interventions. They assert that, because countertransference disclosures have a very strong impact (especially when an analyst introduces them very selectively, I would add) the analyst always must evaluate them thoughtfully. Tansey and Burke's cautious approach to self-revelation within an object relations system of understanding can be very helpful when working with certain patients, those who employ projective identification as a predominant mode of therapeutic communication. Yet most patients do not rely solely or predominantly on projective identification throughout the psychotherapeutic experience, and there are times when even those who do can most effectively shore up their boundaries through reacting to the definitively articulated responses of the other.

The Analyst's Openness and the Analytic Ambiance

As Bollas (1983, 1989) points out, a fundamental consideration that enables analysts to share their experience helpfully is the establishment of a very particular sort of analytic ambiance. Specifically, an atmosphere must be created in which the patient very clearly understands that the analyst shares "personal" reactions with the purpose of advancing the analytic task, which ultimately clarifies and modifies *the patient's* maladaptive relational patterns. With such an understanding firmly in place, the introduction of the analyst's experience can become far more common in psychoanalytic dialogue, rather than a special class of intervention, such as when dealing with impasses. Unless a patient is able to fully grasp this important point, however, the analyst's openness may become misconstrued and problematic in treatment. It must be consistently and firmly conveyed that the analyst's experience is being shared within the boundaries of the psychoanalytic situation with analytic objectives in mind but that the feelings and impulses that are discussed, often intimately, will not otherwise be acted on.

The purpose of the analyst's overall participation, including sharing personal experience with the patient, is guided always by the superordinate goal of advancing the patient's psychological growth. This goal relates to the patient's enhanced self-awareness, achieved in a context of experiencing something profoundly new, emotionally meaningful, and personally significant with the analyst. Growth includes new ways of experiencing the self and others—both in internalized relational patterns and in actual relationships. Implicitly, it involves constructive new actions taken, including those undertaken in extraanalytic experience, an aspect of technique that we consider in later chapters.

An egalitarian atmosphere of humility (versus authority) fosters a therapeutic climate that is most compatible with the effective sharing of the analyst's experience. Within such an atmosphere, the analyst's experience, including thoughts about what is going on, can be introduced as nothing more than his or her personal (although expert) "take," offered in the hope of furthering the aforementioned goals. The analyst's experience in many respects is similar to that of other people with the patient, and to that extent, analyzing the patient-analyst interaction has applicability to patterns that pervade the patient's extraanalytic world. Indeed, the analyst usually comes to concentrate on the patient's most salient and maladaptive reaction patterns, the amelioration of which is considered to be the most helpful to the patient. The analyst's insights may, however, turn out to be jointly evaluated as highly idiosyncratic and thus may have limited applicability to the patient's broader functioning. Even then, though, working through the interface of transference and countertransference often enables the patient to achieve fuller self-articulation, self-awareness, and flexibility. Thus the patient can learn about his or her own patterns in relation to qualities of the individual analyst.

In opening up one's experience to the patient, the analyst cannot know, for certain, the extent to which his or her own reactions involve insight that has relatively broad applicability or is more idiosyncratic. In the strictest sense, because two persons are involved, these reactions probably are both. Consider the following clinical illustration: A female patient called to cancel an appointment with her male therapist just minutes before the session was to begin. Her brief message, left on his answering machine, stated that she had a bad cold and chose to remain at home. But when the therapist returned the call shortly afterward, the patient was unavailable to receive it. The therapist, feeling somehow angry and mistreated, left a brief message. Resentfully, he began to fantasize that the patient had chosen a lovemaking session with her new boyfriend rather than coming to the session with him.

This fantasy enabled the therapist to become aware of his own wishes for the patient's admiration, which he had not realized so pointedly. He felt on shaky ground in making his angry reaction an active part of the treatment. He chose to go ahead and do so, however, noting to the patient that his reaction might be idiosyncratic ("related to his own issues"). The patient, it turned out, had indeed been ill but felt reluctant to "take up the space" on his answering tape to explain just how bad she felt about missing the meeting with the therapist and that she had been eagerly anticipating the session in order to discuss recent developments. This was found to be a pattern in her dealings with others generally—her difficulty accepting that she was entitled to define herself—and relating it specifically to a concurrent situation in her outside life had value for the patient. Further, the therapist's overcoming his discomfort in discussing his own "issues" in this instance also helped the patient to see the value of such openness and provided a model for achieving it. The exchange also defined another important aspect of the therapeutic interaction—the patient's actively downplaying the importance the therapy and the therapist had to her, and the therapist's reciprocal need to win her attentions, which had become a covert theme that now opened.

An appropriate recognition of the complexity and ambiguity of the analytic interaction and a respect for the patient's insights into it call attention to the need to explore the patient's conscious and unconscious reactions to what the analyst shares of his or her experience. Although estimations of the analysand's reactions, both before and after the moment of action, can be useful in guiding the analyst, only an actual follow-up can ascertain how any intervention actually was taken by the patient. What the analyst chooses to share and the analysand's reactions to it thus may become one more of the many interactional events that may be analyzed. Further, these reactions of the patient may become elaborated and undergo change long after the analyst's act of sharing.

How Much to Reveal: Setting a Different Standard

An important aspect of the two-person model is that it extends the possibility of participating—say, through sharing one's experience or through exploring the patient's perception of the analyst's contribution, without requiring it. Ultimately, such decisions have a great deal to do with analysts' own personalities and personal preferences. Yet I am advocating a more balanced standard than is familiar—that, to the extent that technical choices are deliberate, *the analyst ought to have good reasons for choosing not to deal in an open and direct manner as well as for choosing to do so. Tradition itself is not reason enough to conceal one's reactions.* The analyst's sharing thus becomes an important option in a broad repertoire of technique.

To date, the burden of proof has been placed on the self-revealing analyst. Yet an ambiguous but *safe* analytic atmosphere is created not by the analyst's self-concealment alone but through an appropriate blend of restraint and participation. Because self-revelation and self-containment can be employed by analysts to modulate the expression of interpersonal and intrapsychic concerns in analyses, both play important roles. Further, an analyst's prolonged concealment can be as threatening and ultimately damaging to a patient as excesses in the analyst's self-expressiveness. Traditional guidelines stressing such behaviors as abstinence and anonymity, however, are less concerned with the many active and expressive uses of the analyst's experience, so crucial in the two-person model, than with the one-person model's emphasis on obscuring the analyst.

The Analyst's Openness, Asymmetry, and Mutuality

As analysts shift from strict prohibitions against revealing themselves to a more balanced appreciation of the many creative forms for doing so, they must attempt to find ways of balancing the dynamic tension between self-expression and self-containment. There can be no categorical guidelines governing such participation; only clinical judgment in response to the particulars of the developing analytic process can be the analyst's guide. However, the dimensions of *symmetry–asymmetry* and *mutuality–lack of mutuality* provide analysts with ways of thinking about how to balance their participation.

Aron (1992), elaborating Burke's (1992) work, has broken down the mutuality–asymmetry continuum into two very distinct dimensions of the psychoanalytic process—"symmetry–asymmetry" and "mutuality–lack of mutuality." He defined symmetry–asymmetry as "a dimension referring to the similarity or dissimilarity of the patient's and analyst's roles and functions in the analytic process" (p. 482). In general, both one-person and two-person psychoanalytic models create asymmetrical treatment models, but the one-person model, more extreme in its asymmetry, implements a set of very different analytic functions. In the one-person model, each member of the analytic pair has a distinctly different role: basically, the patient, through associations, provides the raw data, and the analyst, through interpretation, organizes the meanings of the material. Asymmetry in this model is based on the classical triumvirate of anonymity, abstinence, and neutrality, which suppresses the analyst's participation; the low profile of the analyst makes it possible to convince the patient that his or her perceptions of the analyst are created by internal processes rather than by what is occurring with the analyst in reality.

Analytic restraint in the two-person model reflects an asymmetry that is understood very differently. It is intended pragmatically to create relational conditions that will make possible both the expression and the elucidation of the patient's psychodynamics and relational patterns. The relative asymmetry of the analytic relationship, involving the participants' different forms of participation, is crucially important for the success of the analytic process; but, unlike the pronounced asymmetry of the classical setting, the relationship in the two-person analytic model that I am advocating tends to be more symmetrical. The goal of asymmetry is not just to support intrapsychic explorations; it is to facilitate an exploration within the analytic relationship of how the patient operates in the world and the role of his or her psychodynamics in that functioning. Excesses in the analyst's expressions can be problematic, overwhelming or inhibiting the patient through a counterproductive concentration on the analyst's own dynamics, for example; but so can deficiencies in the analyst's self-expression become detrimental, as when the analyst's behavior resembles that of an early, neglectful figure or when the analyst's responses are so atypical as to make generalizations to ordinary life difficult.

One way of viewing the advantages of an asymmetrical analytic structure is that, unlike the ordering of ordinary social relationships, asymmetries create a setting that reveals the patient's experience and patterns while providing the analyst with an opportunity for internal processing that facilitates understanding, protects against problematic forms of involvement, and thus advances technique. The asymmetrical structure provides the analyst with an opportunity to examine his or her own subjectivity, understand the pull of the transference, and process the experience that develops in relation to the patient in order to determine how it might best be addressed therapeutically. The analyst may apply theoretical understandings to what is known about the analytic interaction, consider the patient's history, the analyst's own relevant issues, and other relationships. From that position, one can operate intersubjectively, cross-checking and interrelating his or her own and the patient's experience and sometimes comparing mutual reactions with the patient, in attempting to understand what each contributes while trying to avoid excessive reliance on the analyst's own subjectivity.

Asymmetry coexists with another important dimension, which Aron (and earlier Burke) have described as "mutuality." A recognition of the role of mutuality attenuates the asymmetry of the psychoanalytic relationship and also equalizes the authority of the participants. Mutuality was first defined by Aron (1992) as

> a dimension referring to how reciprocal the interaction and the experience of the interaction are; that is, do the two participants mutually and reciprocally influence each other and experience that they influence each other bidirectionally? Mutuality–lack of mutuality refers not so much to behaviors as to the way in which the relationship is conceptualized [p. 482].

In his more recent work, Aron (1996; Aron and Bushra, 1998) shows that virtually every psychoanalytic process is affected by mutuality—empathy, interpretation, even regression. He has expanded the concept, distinguishing three forms. *Mutual regulation* involves the way the analyst and analysand create a unique, bidirectional system that regulates the affects, subjectivity, and behavior of one another; *mutual recognition* involves the process whereby both analyst and analysand come to see one another as individuals, each with a separate subjectivity; and *mutual data generation* is concerned with the way patient and analyst coparticipate in generating and interpreting data together, as compared with the more asymmetrical monadic mode.

We can observe at least three distinct levels on which the mutuality/interactional dimension applies: conceptual, experiential, and technical. (Symmetry–asymmetry is most related to the technical dimension.) It is advantageous to distinguish clearly among these levels when we discuss mutuality, since that which is recognized on a conceptual or theoretical level may be reflected in varying degrees in the awareness of the participants and may or may not be reflected at all in technique. Recall that Sandler's object relations theorizing provides the analyst with ways of *thinking about* what is going on, such as "role-responsiveness," that are intensively interactive, or mutual, but these ideas shape the analyst's understanding of the material without affecting technique very much, which for Sandler remains relatively asymmetrical.

Contrast Ehrenberg's (1992) relatively symmetrical approach. She not only conceptualizes the analytic relationship in terms of its mutuality but also taps all the technical and experiential aspects of mutuality that we have discussed. Examining the awareness of the manifestations of mutual regulation and recognition through mutual data generation forms the heart of analytic work in this approach. Patient and analyst share not only the task of interpretation but also, through the analyst's self-revelations, data generation. Thus while Sandler's view, intensively mutual on a conceptual level, preserves an intrapsychic technical focus on the patient's experience, Ehrenberg's work also provides a bold instance of the ways mutuality can be applied to technique by experientially focusing on and clarifying the specifics of mutual influence through examining actual interactions.

Renik's Complete Epistemological Symmetry

Thinking in terms of the symmetry–asymmetry of the psychoanalytic situation enables analysts to participate in optimal ways. Renik (1995) has pursued that goal further by tilting the balance from analysts' traditional self-concealment to openness. He defines the psychoanalytic situation as one of "complete epistemological symmetry." Here, according to Renik, the "analyst and analysand are equally subjective, and both are responsible for full disclosure of their thinking, as they see it relevant to the reality of the psychoanalytic endeavor" (p. 486).

Renik thus defines a structural asymmetry compatible with the two-person model I am advancing, in that each of the participants is subjective (and subject to mutual influence) and can be open and direct, but only on the basis of their different roles in the clinical setting: *the analysand's task is to increase self-awareness: the analyst's to increase the awareness of the analysand.* I would add that *analysts also must consider potential enactments and the conditions of positive new relational experience in defining their task* and thus in deciding what to discuss about their own experience. Renik clarifies that "symmetry is not *identity.* . . . The difference between the self-disclosure of the analyst and the self-disclosure of the patient is not *how much,* but *according to what principle*" (p. 487). This position shifts the analyst's technical concerns from excesses to the reasons for disclosing. Now the analyst can be more fully expressive, analyzing in a more consistently self-revelatory way.

Following this thinking, the idea of analytic anonymity, obviously, becomes obsolete. Now analysts aim for comprehensibility rather than inscrutability and should try to articulate and communicate anything that, in the analyst's view, will help patients understand their analysts' modus operandi, including how analysts understand where they are coming from and trying to go with each patient. This position enables analysts, acting as subjects, to define themselves more fully, including the reasoning that guides their interventions. In this view, analysts try to make sure that their analytic activity is understood by their patients and that a clear picture of analysts' conscious view of their purposes and methods, including those in sharing their experience, is presented. As Renik emphasizes, making one's thinking available is not the same as imposing one's thinking on a patient. Rather, the analyst's position emerges from and enters into the complex, ongoing negotiations between patient and analyst. In an open exchange of this sort, acting with the patient's assistance, the analyst finds ways of expressing his or her position that are sensitive to, and enrich, the patient's subjective experience. Analysts remain attuned to patients' reactions to them, titrating their openness, as it were, and extending or toning it down responsively, as a part of the delicate process of negotiation (Pizer, 1988). In an open analytic atmosphere of this sort the patient cues, or even advises, the analyst about how direct and open the analyst can be. The analyst then evaluates this information in negotiating how to proceed.

An analyst's willingness to show his or her hand, as it were, can help the patient understand the sources of the analyst's behavior and thinking. It allows the pair to work to clarify transferences and countertransferences dialectically—for instance, to search out intent from impact and to clarify the patient's perceptions from the analyst's actual intentions and experience, to compare perspectives. In this way, the analyst's experience may be brought under collaborative, critical scrutiny as part of the analytic work. The approach is compatible with observations noted earlier that integrate the analyst's participation with efforts to clarify the organizing activity of the patient in relation to this participation, understanding it through an appreciation of perspectival realism and ways that patients assimilate analysts' qualities and actions into old structures.

I do not believe that analysts must limit their sharing to the content or process of their immediate countertransference or their theoretical reasoning or that their forms of sharing must always advance the inquiry, per se. In sharing, analysts also must be guided by their understanding of what might facilitate new relational experience, including goals of authenticity and intimacy, to foster patients' psychological growth. They might, for example, share biographical material such as relevant personal anecdotes (Menaker, 1990). I would extend this standard of openness to the discussion of the analyst's efforts to offer the patient a new relational experience. Should that subject come up, it is possible for analysts to be open with patients about their efforts to limit problematic enactments, without stripping interactions of their personal significance and emotional meaning. If a patient were to question the authenticity of the analyst's actions, for example, suggesting that the analyst might be behaving in a certain manner only because he or she thinks it to be good for the patient, and not authentically, the analyst might agree, openly and unequivocally, that he or she is guided in part by a desire to avoid the dangers inherent in repeating the traumatic interactions of the past. Such sharing is part of the analyst's authenticity.

Spontaneity in the Analyst's and the Patient's Roles

Analytic asymmetry provides a framework for understanding the differences in the functioning of the analyst and the patient with regard to the role of spontaneity. An intersubjective approach clarifies that neither person necessarily has a better hold on reality than does the other but that each has his or her own perspective on it. Patients, more than analysts, are encouraged to share their spontaneous experience immediately and in relatively uncensored ways that help to reveal their organizing activity, psychodynamics, and relational patterns for the pair to examine. More than analysts, patients are encouraged to share reactions spontaneously, freely associate, to "go with" rather than screen irrational material that might occur spontaneously—to be willing to be, only in that sense, less "realistic" than analysts in their expressions. While patients are encouraged to share their immediate thoughts, analysts wait, reflect, and evaluate what might be useful to share.

The relatively more reflective participation of the psychoanalyst is shaped by his or her way of understanding personality functioning, change, and technique and his or her knowledge of the workings of the psychoanalytic situation. Most patients are less sophisticated than analyst in traversing the psychoanalytic terrain in which analysts, acting as experienced guides, have become relatively sure-footed. Even when analysands are themselves psychoanalysts, however, as patients they are required to surrender the full advantage of the road map they possess. Indeed, analysts perhaps more than other patients know that the analytic process will be successful only in a setting of patient spontaneity and openness. Thus there is a requisite submission to the patient role. Idealization often is at play, as well, and, reinforced by the asymmetry and ritual of the psychoanalytic situation (Hoffman, 1998), it fosters compliance with the patient role. The asymmetry of spontaneity supports developments in the patient that we might refer to as immature, such as regression and idealization. The patient is encouraged to diminish self-monitoring and to reveal himself or herself as fully as possible. However, while patients are rewarded thereby for expressing and giving play to their irrational thoughts and feelings, the analyst, no matter how authentically self-revealing, nevertheless monitors and disciplines spontaneity and is rewarded for expertise, that is, for bringing to bear reflective responses. The couch, when it is used, underscores this asymmetry.

The analyst's participation, including his or her spontaneity, is thus structured very differently from the patient's in specialized ways based on an understanding of the self, the other, and the analytic interaction, all integrated around what the analyst believes is required for the patient's psychological growth. These differences shape the analyst's very different perspective and functions, related to the different *principle* defining how the analyst, distinct from the patient, operates. It is because of this unique structure that the analyst's perspective is apt to be more "objective," authoritative, and constructive. But the patient is, from his or her perspective, capable of seeing much that might be called realistic that the analyst in the analytic setting is unable to recognize.

The Limits of Analysts' Openness

Martin Buber's I-and-Thou relationship often has been cited by humanistic psychotherapists and relational analysts as a model for the analytic relationship (Farber, 1967; Silberstein, 1989; Ehrenberg, 1992; Friedman, 1994; Aron, 1996). That model highlights the differences between the natural science, positivist (I-it) mode and the fully authentic meeting of two people (I-and-Thou). Thus it affirms the ideal of the highest forms of human relatedness. Interestingly, and ironically, Buber's (1957) own interpretation of the psychotherapeutic process was that a therapy relationship *cannot* become an I-Thou relationship, that is, achieve full symmetry or mutuality of recognition, to use terms we have been using. As Buber stated (in somewhat broken English) in his transcribed debate with Carl Rogers (Anderson and Cissna, 1997):

> A man coming to you for help. The difference—the, the essential difference—between your role in this situation and his is obvious. He comes for help to you. You don't come to help for him. And not only this, but you are *able*, more or less, to help him. He can do different things to you, but not just help you. And not this alone. You *see* him, really. I don't mean that you cannot be mistaken, you see, but you *see* him . . . *as he is*. He cannot by far, cannot see *you*. Not only in that degree, but even eh that *kind* of seeing. Eh, you are, of course, a very important person for him. But not a person whom he wants to see and to know and is able to. . . . You are interested, you say so and you are right, in him as this person. This eh-eh kind of detached presence he cannot have and give [p. 34].

Buber recognized the asymmetrical nature of the psychotherapeutic relationship and the inherent role differences between patient and therapist. He saw the patient as incapable of empathic responses equivalent to the therapist's ("You are at your side and at his [the patient's] side at the same time. . . . He cannot be but where he is" (p. 38). It was this exchange that prompted Rogers to say, years later, that while he had thought the I-Thou relationship described the highest moments of a psychotherapy, he was surprised to find that Buber did not! (p. 43*n*).

In other words, according to Buber, complete symmetry and mutuality of recognition are impossible in the psychoanalytic situation. This observation is important as it pertains to the therapist's openness. It calls attention to the ways that the therapist's clinical (and even ethical and legal) responsibilities militate against a spontaneous openness similar to the patient's and points to the ways in which contextual factors shape both the analyst's and the patient's experience as well as authentic expressions of it. Analyst openness always must be bounded by therapeutic considerations.

The Analyst's Willingness to Be Known, the Continuing Role of Ambiguity, and the "Total" Relationship

There always exists a tension between the desire to be known and not to be known, as well as to know and not to know the other (Aron, 1997; Crastnopol, 1997). That very real and unavoidable tension lends itself to the analytic experience of ambiguity and plays out through the process of *mutual discovery* that develops as the analysand's and analyst's mutual organizing activity becomes clarified. A mutual process of discovery and the related achievements of authenticity and analytic intimacy are inherent in the new relational experience, as I have defined it. New experience can be advanced by the emboldened patient's willingness to scrutinize the analyst intensively and the resilient analyst's ability to respond to that scrutiny with candor.

In the last chapter, I proposed the value of an attitude of analytic authenticity, involving freedom from artifice and being natural and open with one's patients in the analytic role, as a replacement for the one-person-model ideal of anonymity. Within this framework, the analyst's willingness to be known, spontaneity, playfulness, and modulated openness can play a major role in advancing analytic goals and achieving insightful new relational experience. Once the analytic partners have agreed to the long-term goals of an analysis there is a great deal of leeway for analysts to be themselves and for interludes of spontaneous exchange (Hoffman, 1996). As we saw in the last chapter, such proposals do not neglect technical considerations, but recognize the dialectical relationship that exists between the personal and the technical.

A forthcoming, accessible attitude of willingness to be known advances a relational approach of the sort described here. It empowers analysts by allowing them to respond with personal as well as professional resources that they believe might advance analytic goals—common sense, personal experience, humor, wisdom, sentiment—rather than through strict principles of technique and a set clinical methodology, which, of course, continue to inform their actions. A willingness to be known not only facilitates the authentic emotional presence and empathic responsiveness that are essential to achieving a new relational experience; it also opens analysts to observations made of them and thereby enhances their ability to grasp and deal with their own contributions, enabling them to work constructively with these contributions.

I oppose the analytic strategy of making assiduous efforts to preserve ambiguity through extreme measures designed to safeguard so-called anonymity. Analysts' allowing themselves to become known and making their experience available to their patients do not eliminate the role that ambiguity plays in an analysis. The ambiguity of interpersonal experience and behavior is ubiquitous; it may be diminished but never eliminated. Unknown qualities of the analyst, or of anyone, for that matter, are a given in every relationship. That ambiguity contributes to the setting in which the analysand's organizing activity and relational patterns can become expressed and analyzed. The analyst's openness and directness do not, however, necessarily discourage analytic exploration, as has been suggested in the past. Indeed, it may stimulate, invite, and license an analysand's curiosity about his or her own, as well as the analyst's, inner life. As the analyst reveals aspects of himself or herself inadvertently as well as deliberately in the asymmetrical analytic relationship in which the primacy of exploring interactions has become established, the patient's different reactions to the person of the analyst—what is known about the analyst as well as what is not—become important transferential issues for exploration.

A willingness to be known is to be distinguished from *imposing* oneself on the patient. In fact, being authentically accessible defines an attitude that guards against imposing oneself on the patient. It involves a sensitivity to one's own impact, as well as that of the patient, and to interactive subtleties; thereby, it guards against the possibility that the analyst will become intrusive, violating the separateness or integrity of the individuals. In that sense, willingness to be known is counterbalanced by a willingness to remain "unknown"—that is, to be willing to dwell in the patient's transference, as it were, and to become the object of, and thus remain able to experience and analyze, the patient's constructions.

Rather than emphasizing the fantastic or transferential aspects of the analytic relationship and analysts' anonymity in relation to them, it can be useful for analysts to think in terms of the total relationship and moderating their personal participation in ways that can advance the overall interests of specific patients. Although this distinction may seem a matter of semantics, it is not. From a perspectivist position, understanding is based on the assumption not that the patient's (or the analyst's) perception is either actual *or* constructed but that it is only one of many possible perspectives on what has happened, one of many ways that what has occurred might be perceived or experienced. In other words, experience is treated as both realistic *and* constructed. With an awareness of themselves as very real and important persons to their patients, analysts remain cognizant that their personal contributions are at play, and they can work with those contributions to promote growth-enhancing personal relationships within which their patients' (and, potentially, the analysts') mutual constructions can be clarified. In the anonymous approach, by contrast, analysts can become lulled into operating as if their personal participation and presence as real persons are of little real consequence; they may fall back on one-person assumptions and presume to be hidden in order to advance the treatment benefits that are thought to derive from elucidating the relationship a patient is having with a fantasy figure and not a real one.

Participation and Neutrality

It has been a concern of some analysts that, if they are too open, direct, or active with their patients, they will diminish their neutrality, which they see as a precondition for analytic success. I wish to emphasize that there is no inherent incompatibility between a participatory analytic stance and an analyst's neutral attitude. An analyst can express his or her positions to a patient without *imposing* them. In fact, the goals of neutrality are often best served by openly declaring one's bias. It seems to me that the belief that participation and neutrality are incompatible confuses the concept of neutrality with the closely allied principle of abstinence, which developed at the hands of Freud's disciples.

Relational analysts do well to distinguish between a neutral *attitude* that minimizes the intrusive effects of countertransference, avoids the imposition of the analyst's personal values on the patient, and respects the analysand's autonomy, from *abstinence*, which proscribes actual therapist *behaviors* (Franklin, 1990). Attitudinal, rather than behavioral, neutrality seems most relevant in a relational view. Aron's (1996) view of neutrality epitomizes an attitudinal approach. Tying neutrality to perspectivism, he emphasizes "the analyst's openness to new perspectives, a commitment to take other perspectives seriously, and a refusal to view any interpretation as complete or any meaning as exhaustive" (p. 28). An *attitude* of neutrality emphasizes a non-judgmental orientation and introduces a check on the analyst's imposing undue personal influence; yet it does not, de facto, fore-close more intensive forms of participation that so often can be help-ful but that analytic abstinence prohibits.

Monadic views of analytic neutrality typically emphasize the impor-tance of analysts' avoiding involvement with their patients' internal conflicts. Similar to the position taken by Pine (1993), which is described in chapter 5, analysts' noninvolvement is maintained by adopting the "equidistant" stance first proposed by Anna Freud (1936). Stone (1961, 1981) and Schafer (1983), while cautioning against an excessively depriving analytic stance, are examples of monadic analysts who endorse the equidistant position. Schafer fur-ther warns that the analyst should not take sides in patients' con-flictual courses of action, while Stone recommends an avoidance of analysts' interference in the lives of their patients.

Under the influence of relational theories, reformulations of ana-lytic neutrality have tended to accommodate to the role of the ana-lyst's participation. According to Greenberg (1986, 1992), neutrality is achieved through the analyst's *striving to maintain an optimal tension* related to what might in any particular instance constitute the opti-mum of old and new experience. That view does not necessarily pro-scribe behaviors. As another example, Franklin (1990) describes "interactional neutrality" in terms of a flexible attitude in the analyst toward his selectively bringing into play any aspect of his relatedness to the patient that fosters the patient's self-expression, so that the patient can better explore and understand himself or herself. Thus analytic activity is facilitated, rather than discouraged.

Two-person model views of neutrality thus suggest that the effec-tive range of analysts' participation may be defined far more inten-sively and extensively than historically has been the case. These definitions frame the analyst's participation not by how it may sup-press the patient's analyzable transference but by how participation can facilitate the emergence and resolution of the patient's uncon-scious conflicts, extend the range of interactions in which transference can be analyzed, and can advance new relational experience. Freer to interact with the patient, the analyst nevertheless is guided by a neutral attitude that is compatible, overall, with a respect for the patient's autonomy and growth. Placing a priority on behavioral prohibitions, by contrast, actually has more to do with abstinence than with neutrality and is incompatible with a participatory, two-person treatment model.

The Ambiguous Criterion of New Relational Experience

Considering all of the analyst's behavior as falling somewhere along the continuum of old and new experience, it can be appreciated that sometimes analytic developments and the analyst's expressions can be closer to new experiences that can be afforded within the psychoanalytic situation, while others may more closely resemble pathogenic enactments, or old experience. Following that view, the analyst's sharing of experience can be guided, in part, by the intention of providing constructive new relational experiences. That goal, however, must be tempered by a recognition of the complexity of that determination and a realization that analysts never can fully overcome the influence of the past. The influence of the patient's (and the analyst's) pasts will always find expression in the interaction, even in agreed-upon terminations of treatment, after most of the work is judged to have been completed. What is therapeutic is that, additionally, there will exist something constructively new (Hoffman, 1998).

Notwithstanding its limitations, advising analysts to strive to maintain an optimal balance between old experience and new defines one useful element in a complex clinical matrix to guide informed decisions about disclosures. However, optimal is one of those words that appears throughout the psychoanalytic literature that is particularly vague—vague enough, for better and worse, that it allows individual practitioners to bring personal meanings to it. Thus my idea of an optimal balance between old and new experience may be different from that which Greenberg, or any other practitioner, has in mind, and may emphasize the role of new experience more significantly. Nevertheless, following that guide, analysts may at certain times choose to reveal aspects of their experience, and at other times not, even with the same patient. There are limitations with this idea—for instance, the two (old and new experience) exist in a dialectical relationship and each has the potential to turn into the other. As Hoffman (1996) put it, "each not only serves as ground for the other but is actually on the brink of evolving into the other [and] the prevalence of a manifestly benign atmosphere can be grounds for suspecting something latently malignant" (p. 126).

Clinical judgment is, of course, based on one's necessarily subjective assessment of an ever-changing, complex matrix of intrapsychic and interpersonal factors. Thus, an interaction that may seem to the analyst to represent a form of new relational experience at one point in treatment may, later, in the light of additional revelations, seem an enactment. Each practitioner ultimately is referred to his or her ongoing clinical judgment on a case-by-case, moment-to-moment basis, and, as it serves the interests of treatment, to subject that judgment to joint scrutiny.

Ordinarily, only that which is discordant between the analyst and the patient is interpretable (Greenberg, 1995a). The patient and therapist see the situation differently, and that difference becomes the basis for the interpretive work. Otherwise, much of the analytic exchange passes smoothly, being barely noticed by the pair, while advancing their rapport but not requiring interpretation. Undoubtedly, much of what occurs in an analytic relationship cannot and should not be analyzed, and articulating interactions at the wrong time or in ways that may dilute their authenticity and power is counterproductive. Sometimes, there may be advantages in clarifying patterns that seem primarily to constitute new relational experience. Such clarification may provide insight into what is new about them, what the patient is now doing differently, and how and why they have developed differently from other, problematic interactions. Rather than being dichotomous, interactions are always admixtures of new experience and old, and it can be helpful to patients to appreciate the nuances of difference. For example, my offering a patient an additional weekly session was based on therapeutic considerations and was raised to benefit the patient. Yet that act also was responsive to an opening in my own schedule and offered a potential source of additional income. That interaction, which involved elements of self-interest, was not the same as that with the patient's narcissistic parent whose needs had overpowered the patient in the childhood past but it may have at first seemed so to the patient. There is value in clarifying what is new, while highlighting what is old in interactions.

An Instance of Self-Expression Through Action

All analysts have had to deal with decisions about taking action—whether to phone patients, reschedule broken appointments, accept gifts, even give them. More complicated decisions must sometimes be made that have great psychological meaning for patients—referring for medication, acting to hospitalize a patient, phoning family members during a suicidal crisis. Or, on the brighter side, we must sometimes respond to invitations to outside social events that have great meaning for patients—openings, performances, lectures, weddings. Such decisions may either have therapeutic value or be detrimental. As we come to recognize the extensive communicative role that action plays in therapeutic communication, a therapist's choice of particular actions over others, in addition to words, becomes a therapeutic option rather than a taboo.

I had the unusual experience of giving a patient a hug at the end of a session during an ongoing therapy. The patient was, in my opinion, a remarkable woman who had managed through therapeutic persistence to overcome a grim personal history, including maternal physical abuse. We covered much therapeutic ground together in a long-term treatment experience and usually met once a week. Shortly before the session involving the hug, she described having seen me during the early days of her therapy as a cold, harsh, professorial figure and taskmaster who demanded too much of her in terms of her emotions and insight; now she experienced me, among other ways, as a steadfast, accepting supporter. I recall a dream we had discussed some years ago along these lines. In it, I was symbolized as a stern and frightening school teacher who conducted classes in a dark, secluded room in a land far from home, and she avoided coming to class.

One day, she returned to therapy from an encounter group weekend she had attended. During that weekend, she had chosen to submit to the anguish she felt over her personal experience with maternal abuse in order to work with it in the group. In brief, during the weekend she had felt herself in the grip of regressive memories of her childhood abuse that were pressing for resolution and felt intensely the terror and hate that characterized her feelings toward her abusive mother. As she worked with those feelings during the weekend, she became deeply saddened, so profoundly that she felt she might break into pieces. Guided by a very skillful group leader, she was encouraged to imagine the most primal terror she could, which turned out to be a memory from age four or so of being discovered while hiding in a closet by her threatening mother, who, in a frenzied state, had searched her out to beat her. My patient had replayed the memory over and over throughout the years, each time imagining herself successfully taking flight; in reality she had not been so fortunate. But as the mother opened the closet door in the weekend's visualization, instead of the patient's using her resources to run away, she stood firm, confronted her mother, and then embraced her.

The patient reported an experience of transformation following the events of the weekend. She spoke of feeling different, of being capable now of having a different impact on others and she gave examples. At first, I was skeptical and thought about hypomanic defenses and even potential decompensation, but, as the session progressed and she described her experience more thoroughly, gradually I came to sense that she truly seemed different to me, somehow less "standoffish" and more accessible. In the past, she had alluded to the need to shut off feelings and turn herself to concrete. We had both come to recognize this orientation as a way of protecting herself that thwarted her needs for contact, and over the years we had struggled together to help her break through her iciness and its impact on others.

My impulse to respond to her with a hug was not a new one, but in the past I had uncomfortably rejected it for a variety of reasons. I am conscientious about the traditional rules of psychoanalysis and am aware of the possibility, long emphasized, that the analyst's actions may prevent a thorough analysis and can even traumatize a patient. To indulge such a pull might be tantamount to new experience or old, I realized, and, being schooled in the risks of analysts' taking action, I had chosen in the past to "play it safe." To take action might represent "incorrect" technique, I feared; it might be a response emerging out of a projective identification or even be experienced as a form of abuse. Further, there were times when the patient seemed quite aloof, even with me, and her bearing sent a message to keep away. But now things seemed different. Rather than dismissing my impulse to hug her, or acting on it, I sat with it and evaluated it intermittently throughout that session. While analysts' personal satisfaction is clearly not a valid basis for making technical decisions, nor is such gratification necessarily a contraindication to taking action of a specific kind. In view of what she really might need, rather than the rigors of analytic technique, and what I might authentically offer that could be helpful, a hug might be beneficial. As I considered the possibility of offering her a hug, my very tentative understandings of it took many forms—a response to the frightened child that had just come through hell and an attempt on my part to "hold" her in a literal sense and to steady her during a very trying transitional time. Although she seemed very courageous, I knew she was feeling deeply shaken, found herself in unfamiliar psychological space, and was therefore very frightened. Most simply, a hug seemed like an affectionate expression of my concern and presence. I had a sense, too, that it offered a kind of welcoming, an acknowledgment and celebration of her new, greater accessibility. I also knew there might be many other levels of meaning that I could not reach.

The results of examining my motivations and the potential impact a hug might have were vague and impressionistic; what was clear was that it still felt like the right thing to do. I decided to ask her as she got up to leave whether she would like a hug. She consented and beamed as she participated fully in the hug. As she was leaving, she told me how deeply she appreciated that she could share this experience with me, that I could understand what she was undergoing in a way that nobody else could, and that, to her delight, I had given up my skepticism, which I then realized had been apparent to her.

Days later, as I thought about her, the session, and the hug—with some concern, by the way—it occurred to me that, over time, and in that hug, she and I had actualized the welcome and welcoming mother whom she now had connected to differently, in a new and emancipating object relationship. The changes she sensed had passed the test of time (as did our hug), and apparently the patient was strengthened by those events. What became most notable in the months that followed was her lighter, happier mood. Also, she was freer, more exploratory with people; the quality of her relationships became decidedly warmer, more open, and receptive. We did not analyze the hug in any formal sense, but months later I asked her how she had come to feel about it. A smile came over her face, and she filled with warmth as she explained to me that in retrospect it felt to her very "right" and important—welcoming, reassuring, and celebratory. I was pleased that her experience of the hug, at least consciously, resonated with my own. The hug had occurred in a long-term analytic context in which it was possible that it might later be revisited and understood differently. Yet it stood as a poignant moment in our relationship and as such one to be respected. I am glad to have chosen the unusual course of expressing my feelings, and of affirming her, through action in that way. I achieved a satisfactory, but, of course, not a complete, understanding of that important action—either before I took it or afterward. More important, I developed a certainty that my actions had been both meaningful and helpful to her.

From a two-person perspective, analysts will find it useful to recognize that a decision not to express their experience, although seeming to them like sound clinical judgment, often may originate in their own vulnerability, inhibitions, and need for safety in the relationship, which often may be reinforced by traditional analytic values. At best, such judgments are not as clear as we might wish them to be, and that is another reason that sometimes, provided we take care not to drain experiences of their authenticity, these judgments are best made together with patients and not imposed on them. That is not to say that the analyst's comfort level is unimportant. It is very important in deciding whether or not to show openly how or what one is feeling. Indeed, at times a willingness to reveal that which is difficult for the analyst may result in a like openness on the part of the patient. We all must struggle creatively and in ongoing ways to distinguish between traditional prescriptions, our personal motives in the analytic relationship, and what actually is best for our patients.

Openness, Concealment, and the Patient's False-Self Adaptation

Epstein (1995) has described a particular problem involving the analyst's disclosures: they might promote a False-Self adaptation. He illustrates this point through a personal vignette. When he was planning to undertake psychoanalytic training, he was required to change analysts. The analyst he was leaving told him that, as a result of his behavior toward her, she felt "disregarded and perhaps even held in contempt" (p. 233). On one level, Epstein had a feeling of appreciation for the analyst's authentic confrontation; but, on an underlying level, he felt punished and guilty. In anticipation of leaving on good terms, he sought to maintain the analyst's good will by expressing only his positive feelings. That is, as Winnicott (1960) put it, he made a "False-Self" adaptation in which he was "forced into a false existence" based on the belief that only through compliance could he receive needed responses" (p. 146). Epstein emphasizes the importance of analyzing the analysand's responses to being told of the analyst's experience. He asserts that it is not enough to offer disclosures simply as a means of revealing the patient's interpersonal impact on the analyst; rather they should deepen and expand the analysand's experience. It is not disclosure per se, that is the problem in Epstein's example, but a failure of sound technique—specifically, a failure to analyze the patient's reactions following a disclosure.

Analysts are less apt to consider how their *failure* to disclose may also result in a False-Self adaptation. At times, especially when an analyst encourages a patient's curiosity about the analyst's experience, the patient may correctly observe a countertransference state and inquire about that experience. If the analyst is asked, an evasiveness, a reluctance or inability to acknowledge countertransference experience that is noted by the patient, or an unwillingness to consider the possibility of it, may result in the patient's perception that the analyst is invested in maintaining a particular relational configuration. This reluctance can result in a transferential, or False-Self adaptation, to that perception of the analyst that may stifle the work. For instance, an analyst who consulted with me had the experience of working with a clergyman of a different faith. The analyst was classically trained and was trying to integrate aspects of a two-person model into his ways of thinking and working. Early in treatment the clergyman patient pressed the issue of the analyst's religious affiliation, which the analyst avoided, partly to remain "anonymous," but in part too because of his own discomfort with the topic of their religious differences. (The analyst himself was deeply conflicted over religion and his own religious identity.) Afterward, the patient made numerous subtle, indirect, and mocking comments about the religion he (correctly) believed to be the analyst's, while overall the treatment remained superficially polite and limited.

I urged the analyst to consider remaining open to discussing the topic of religion and especially to the possibility of acknowledging their religious difference (which had become obvious!) and its impact the next time it appropriately came up. It was only after the analyst did so and addressed the issue squarely that the analysand's negative sentiments and actual prejudice toward the analyst's religion could enter the work. Previously, the analysand had assumed a falsely polite, accommodating position based on his (again, correct) perception that the analyst did not wish to handle the uncomfortable issue, and that had limited his openness and progress. This tenuous defense against hostility was, in fact, a characteristic pattern of the patient's in which he sensed and avoided others' vulnerabilities and the sadistic feelings that came up in him around them. Again we see a False-Self adaptation, but this time one resulting from the analyst's *failure to disclose* and not from a disclosure.

The Inappropriately Self-Concealing Analyst

One theme of this chapter has been that excessive self-concealment can be every bit as detrimental to treatment as excessive self-revelation. Yet analysts accustomed to working in traditional ways who are asked to challenge their reluctance to reveal themselves to their patients do not do so without qualms. I am not aware, though, that there exists a valid basis for thinking that an *improperly* self-expressive analyst is any more likely to have a detrimental effect, on the whole, than an *improperly* self-concealing one is, or, for that matter, that a "holding environment" or "atmosphere of safety" can more readily be established or maintained through an analyst's self-containment than through his or her expressiveness. There are patients for whom, and moments in which, an analyst's self-expressions might be detrimental; but there are also many situations in which the analyst's reticence is equally counterproductive. The ideal, of course, is to strike the right balance in advancing a patient's psychological growth.

The transitional arena in which relational analysts think of themselves as encountering their patients is sometimes understood through Winnicott's (1958) concept of potential space. It is a realm involving emotional relationships that are thought to lie somewhere between old and new object experiences, between constructions and actualities. Gabbard (1994), in a paper specifically critical of analysts' exposing erotic countertransference, takes a position that invalidates many of the advantages of therapists sharing *any* aspect of their personal experience. He suggests that with a disclosure "a symbolic realm has been concretized, and the potential space closes rather than opens" (p. 210). He notes the very real danger that the analyst's earnest effort to provide a new object experience may result in a powerful enactment of the opposite, with the analyst acting like the old object. While acknowledging that that danger is very real, I believe that it is a mistake to emphasize too strongly the abstract nature of the transferential relationship in potential space; rather, analysts should take advantage of opportunities for engaging patients directly, openly, exploring the ramifications of the transference relationship dialectically and relating it to what is happening in reality. Patients who grow accustomed to searching for themselves in abstract intellectualizations about their transferences may grow unable to find themselves, in actuality, with the analyst, that is, in a more immediate, affectively related mode of experiencing the relationship. They are not helped in their ability to find themselves with and to relate to others outside of their analyst's office. It is often useful to ground a patient who is lost in transference fantasies by asking how those fantasies may pertain to what he or she "really" has experienced with the analyst, or to distinguish what the patient thinks the analyst might "really" be experiencing, for example.

Analysts' excessive self-concealment can inhibit patients from achieving the fullest forms of self-expression and prevent the actualization of important forms of new relational experience. It is important to note in this connection that analysts' openness and directness do not necessarily result in a superficial or facile technique as it sometimes might appear to do (see Mitchell, 1997b). To the contrary, rather than promoting a general comfort level or superficial ease of participation, this approach can create considerable difficulty and discomfort for the revealed analyst. It can, on the other hand, deepen, intensify, and make more personally meaningful a patient's analytic experience.

There are, of course, dangers of excess in analysts' self-expressions. It certainly is never advisable for an analyst to rush eagerly or compulsively to reveal his or her experience—each impulse, fantasy, accomplishment, or quirk—to the patient. Such overrevelation reflects a misunderstanding of the ways in which the analyst's openness can advance the analytic exploration. There are important reasons for preserving an awareness of the need for the asymmetry of the analytic relationship on the basis of understanding and enhancing the *patient's* patterns and promoting psychological growth. That awareness itself disciplines analytic participation and provides a useful way of subordinating analysts' self-expressions to patients' growth. Effective clinical analysts seem to develop an empathic sense of the extent to which it can be helpful to focus on their own presence and impact. Further, in addition to the possibility of openly exploring patients' reactions to revelations, competent analysts also read patients' unconscious and indirect reactions to their interventions in order to be able to make constructive adjustments to them. It is with such counterbalancing measures in mind that analysts might consider exploring the therapeutic possibilities of their self-revelations.

The Analyst's Inadvertent Self-Revelations and the Willingness to Be Known

Not only deliberate interventions but virtually all the analyst's activity, and even inactivity, is expressive and continuously communicates personal meaning to the patient. Elsewhere (Frank, 1977), I noted that there existed substantial evidence that the personality of the therapist (and therefore his or her personal contribution) was primary and that techniques could be most helpful in the hands of therapists who were inherently therapeutic. Today I realize that the personal and technical actions of the therapist are inseparable. In that volume, Singer (1977) asserted that the analyst's interpretations are *first and foremost* self-revealing remarks. According to Singer, "In their relevance [not precision or depth] the analyst's comments must willy-nilly expose him to the patient as much as the patient is exposed to him" (p. 184). He pointed out that "the structure, focus, and content of the analyst's response to the patient reveals the analyst's private religion, no matter what his pretenses to himself and others" (p. 184). Even the "deliberate" sharing of the analyst's reactions involves inadvertent elements of self-revelation, and, as with any intervention, the latter may at times have greater impact on the patient than the aspects that the analyst intended.

All interventions, even interpretations, are personal expressions of the analyst and therefore of the analyst's individuality. Note Webster's (1988) definition of the verb interpret: to conceive in the light of *individual* belief, judgment, or circumstance (italics added). Interpretations, being personal opinions, are thus self-revelations. And so the analyst's individuality, if only indirectly in the form of inadvertent self-expressions, comes inevitably to the attention of the analysand, both consciously and preconsciously. If we are to be true to the strictest assumptions of a two-person model, the role of that very personal contribution must be understood and might be openly examined with the patient.

"Meta-messages" (Wachtel, 1993b) are a prime illustration of the analyst's *inadvertent* self-revelations. These are the unintended elements of communication—the analyst's tone, rhythm, facial expression, posture, and timing—that accompany verbal communications. They grow out of the analyst's personal psychodynamics, theoretical position, and specific reactions to the patient that reflect the patient's influence. Metamessages often convey much more than the analyst's words themselves. In fact, at times they may actually communicate precisely the *opposite* of the analyst's words. A classic example is a statement containing affective and content meanings that conflict, such as a person's shouting, "I am *not* angry at you!" (We usually respond to the affect—not the words.) A more representative clinical example is when an analyst interrupts or ignores certain material or selects one aspect of a patient's communication over another and says, "Tell me more about A" (for example, transferential admiration), but conveys to the patient, "I don't wish to hear about B" (for example, criticism), which may get at the heart of the matter.

Another example is when a therapist alters the usual course of exploration to offer words of "reassurance." Paradoxically, such utterances may exacerbate the patient's anxiety; they could convey a message precisely the opposite of that intended, that the therapist is apprehensive and believes there is a real basis for the patient's alarm. Inasmuch as metamessages make it virtually impossible to conceal feelings toward a patient, they play a significant role in shaping the patient's experience of the relationship. Depending on their nature and how—and if—they are handled therapeutically, they may be therapeutic or countertherapeutic.

By definition, *inadvertent* self-revelations are unplanned. They are not a part of formal technique—that aspect of the analyst's participation that can be, to a significant degree, conscious, controlled, and deliberate. If they are called to the analyst's attention, he or she may or may not be aware of the *content* of such revelations—for example, momentary states the patient has sensed, such as irritation or a particular sensitivity, a judgmental attitude, or an avoidance of specific material—but obviously analysts are unaware of an intention to communicate them. Tacit in the analyst's every action, inadvertent self-revelations exist not only in the more obvious and superficial personal manifestations such as office decor, manner of dress, or billing practices, but also in the fundamental values, moods, attitudes, judgments, sensitivities, and other characterological qualities of the analyst that are implicitly and subtly conveyed. These are the elements that reveal the anayst's "private religion," as Singer (1977) put it. When the treatment situation is approached as a two-person model, manifestations such as these cannot but color the patient's experience of the relationship, consciously and unconsciously. To assert that they do not, that the patient's experience of them is irrelevant, and therefore to omit them from an analysis on that basis simply is invalid.

Guided by the continuing influence of the basic model technique, many analysts have tended to omit their inadvertent self-revelations from open analytic scrutiny, allowing them always to remain tacit in the interaction. If noted by the patient, they might be considered by the analyst first as potential transferential distortions and, without probing their reality, be explored in relation to their meanings for the patient. From a vantage point emphasizing perspectival realism, it is recognized that these phenomena which spontaneously develop during the course of the analytic interaction reflect both the analyst's and the patient's influence and involve analyzable referents to the interaction. Although many of the qualities and actions of the analyst that are conveyed during an analysis may not be expressed as a part of technique in a proactive sense, they are intrinsic to the analytic process, and their sources, meanings, and impact can be productively explored. Although sometimes they need not—indeed, ought not—be addressed, at other times it can be extremely useful, even crucial, to elucidate them.

Dealing Actively with the Analyst's Individuality

In a two-person model, working actively with the individual contribution of the analyst as well as the analysand's becomes integral. Helping the patient to transcend preset relational patterns that become expressed through the analytic relationship can be achieved only as both partners strive authentically to appreciate their individual contributions. There are several ways in which the analyst may take his or her individuality into account. As referred to in Langs's (1982) "rectification" (chapter 4), the most familiar is by silently taking his or her contribution into account. Here the analyst tries to understand the patient's reactions in relation to the analyst's unique contribution. Traditionally, analysts have used this approach to regulate neutrality; when the patient's responses are evaluated as potentially valid comments on the analyst's problematic countertransference responses, they form a basis for analysts' making adjustments to recover their neutral stance.

Once transference and countertransference are seen as interacting parts of a whole, analysts recognize that neither of these processes can be fully understood without an appreciation of the other. Thus the analytic pair may choose more actively to probe the meanings of their interactions collaboratively, including the analyst's inadvertent participation in them. An assumption is made that the patient's "take" on the analyst's contribution may inform and enrich the analyst's own understanding and thus lead to further clarification of the analysand's. That approach is based on a two-person model and on perspectival realism in which the patient's perceptions of, fantasies about, and reactions to the analyst are understood as transferential adaptations to, or attempts to grapple with, the individuality of the analyst. Transference analysis includes, among other activities, a joint effort to distinguish aspects of the patient's experience that result from flexible and adaptive patterns activated as he or she encounters the analyst from meanings that result from the assimilation of the analyst's actions and characteristics into old structures. Full clarity, of course, is never reached.

The Patient's Reactions as Commentary

By listening to the patient's material as potential interpretations of the analyst's contribution, the analyst can infer what his or her contribution might be and then fine tune it to advance the treatment. Greenberg (1991) has described an interesting example of this process in his supervisory work. The patient of a supervisee, before a public appearance that recognized his abilities and afforded him an opportunity to advance his career, had a series of dreams in which he was responsible for killing off his elders. Greenberg perceived that the supervisee, like the significant childhood figures of the patient, seemed uncertain and frustrated with his own level of professional achievement. This observation was confirmed by the supervisee's defensive work with one such dream; apparently feeling threatened, he offered his patient a premature, intrapsychically oriented interpretation of it. The interpretation, that the patient's ambition was tantamount to murder, avoided the essential matter that the patient was, in fact, at risk of damaging the analyst. In part, Greenberg saw the dream as the patient's commentary on the analyst's actual characteristics and suggested, consistent with the view outlined here, that the analyst might usefully have said, "Have you noticed anything in me that you take as a sign of my vulnerability to your ambition or success?" (p. 69).

Greenberg explained that he was not advocating any sort of deliberate countertransference disclosure by this statement. The dreams suggest, however, that the patient already had picked up on the analyst's inadvertent self-revelations. Therefore, the analyst's welcome comment might be seen as a point of entree into clarifying and deepening understanding of an interaction pattern, perhaps collaboratively, with the analyst willing to explore what was occurring between them and to explicate his own contribution. As Greenberg points out, that course can be very anxiety-provoking for analysts. The immediate point I wish to make is that listening to the dream or to any of the patient's material as commentary on the analyst's inadvertent self-revelations sensitizes the analyst to these self-expressions and helps the analyst to bring them, one way or another, constructively into the work. Such a course is consistent with an attitude of analytic authenticity.

As Greenberg's vignette reveals, consultation with astute colleagues offers an excellent way of identifying inadvertent self-revelations that may be playing a significant role in the analytic treatment. I am reminded of another example, which occurred during a consultation with a colleague about his treatment of a young woman. The patient had resentfully discussed with her therapist feeling pressured to play a "phony," immature role with her mother, whom she experienced as failing to acknowledge her emerging adult status. The therapist then abruptly shifted, asking the patient, "And do you sometimes find yourself pressured to play a more *adult* role at work?" Examining this interaction in supervision, the therapist was able at once to recognize his own shift as somehow self-protective and was then able to reflect on his personal investment in emphasizing the patient's immaturity. (Preliminarily, it appeared that there existed a mutual avoidance of aggression.) We wondered whether the patient had also picked up on this inadvertent aspect of this analyst's participation and what role that might be playing in the treatment, a speculation that deserved further direct exploration in the actual work with the patient.

Consider another interaction with a patient illustrating several of these points. Following a weekend vacation that the patient and her husband had taken from their two small children in order to strengthen their stressing marriage, the patient reported to her analyst that the overall quality of the time the couple had spent together that weekend was poor. Among the patient's other dissatisfactions, she felt her husband was clumsy and insensitive to her, and she felt sex was not satisfying. She finally decided to take up this matter with him. During the couple's discussion about affection, his lack of sensitivity, and their poor sexual relationship, she introduced the idea of his beginning therapy. As they discussed what it might be like for her if he were to enter treatment with a female therapist, including the patient's potentially jealous reactions, she pressured him to reveal his feelings about her ongoing therapy. He seemed neutral about it. When she asked him about feelings of jealousy, which on some level the patient sought, he assured her that he was not threatened; after all, he knew and trusted her analyst's professional reputation. She was furious with him for his response, which, she felt, revealed that he just didn't "get it." His response removed her, personally, from the equation; his trust was about the therapist—not her. She further felt that his responses reflected a failure to appreciate the complex nature of feelings generally, and especially her important emotional experience in therapy. She arrived for her session bursting to speak to the therapist, feeling that she had clarified a dimension of the marital relationship that was deeply problematic, and eager for her therapist's validation.

As the patient discussed these developments with the analyst, her anger toward her husband intensified. In the therapist's view, she was seeing her husband as "all bad," which the therapist pointed out, and as he saw it at that time, she was falling into a familiar form of splitting which the analytic pair often had discussed. The therapist felt uncomfortable with her notion that their own emotional communication was so good, while that with her husband was so poor, and he shared that reaction with her. On hearing this from the therapist, she became enraged and stormed out of the session, threatening never to come back—for reasons that, at the time, the therapist could not grasp.

One might interpret that the analyst's sharing in this instance was counterproductive. Certainly, at such moments analysts wish they had remained quiet and listened. But at the following session, the patient had regained her equanimity. The pair took up the rupture that had occurred between them, which the therapist at first continued to understand primarily in terms of *her* overreaction. But he also was interested in the patient's view that he had been the one to overreact. She expressed her fear that her affection had been too much for him to handle and had caused him to distance himself and thus to be emotionally unavailable to her. (The pair had worked on this issue, her belief that her positive feelings were basically toxic and would push others away. They explored this fear in relation to her history of paternal abandonment and longing.) In exploring the events of the prior session and why she reacted as strongly as she did, she referred to their "alliance" in describing her eagerness to share with the therapist her frustration and disappointment with her husband. It was upon hearing that word—alliance—that an insight dawned on the therapist, and he was now able to view his own behavior from a different perspective. He realized that the patient's behavior had touched on a sensitive point of his own. In brief, it was a sensitivity stemming from an early family pattern in which his mother had often sought to make him an ally against her husband, the analyst's father. This pattern had caused the therapist distressing feelings of disloyalty and guilt in relation to his parents' affections.

Based on this understanding, the therapist was then able to recognize his own part in the prior session. Despite his initial reading,
he realized that the rupture was no more the result of the patient's
overreaction than it was the therapist's own. Speaking quite openly,
he shared that based on his understanding of his own personal history he had been unable to remain sensitive to her. In the following
session, the patient expressed gratitude for the therapist's being open
with his own countertransference difficulty. His sharing his awareness
of his own contribution helped her to realize that her transferential
fears of provoking rejection with her affection, and that there was
something inherently overwhelming in her feelings, were unwar-
ranted, and thus she experienced relief. She went on to elaborate that
therapy was most helpful to her not when she examined her own
inner world and complexity, but when she was able to see how it inter-
acted with others'. (She was not a therapist, I might add.) She was
grateful that the therapist had been able to come around and to hear
her. Rather than fearing now that the pair would remain "stuck," she
took the therapist's openness as evidence of his abilities for responsibility and introspection, and thus as reassurance that he could handle his own issues as they went forward. Grasping the complexity of
the intersubjective idea, she wondered, jokingly, how do two people
ever, with all their entanglements, work out their relationship? (The
answer, of course, was a lesson being learned through their lived
experience together.) The therapist's struggle to maintain what I have
called an analytic attitude of authenticity helped him work effectively
with this situation.

Working Collaboratively with
Inadvertent Self-Revelations

It is not unreasonable to view the analyst's inadvertent actions, which
may be recognized by the patient, as unwitting or inadvertent "countertransference disclosures." When they are plausibly or even accurately (in the analyst's experience) identified by the patient, which
undoubtedly occurs more frequently than analysts formerly were
inclined to acknowledge, the question is no longer *whether* to reveal
something, but how much *more* to reveal to the patient. Here, rather
than focusing narrowly on the patient's reactions to the analyst's inadvertent expression and possibly dismissing the analyst's own contribution as something potentially real, it can be more therapeutically
productive at times to collaboratively explore mutual elements that

such an occurrence may involve. An exploration of this kind can clarify the unique, interacting roles of both participants and, crucially,
their relevance to similar, problematic experiences from the past or
that the patient may encounter in the outside world. That the analyst
may not have been ready to reveal does not make these data any less
real or valuable as a source of information about the interaction and
the patient.

Analysts' reluctance to explore their own participation openly is
related, in part, to their own feelings of vulnerability. Greenberg
(1991) recognized the analyst's vulnerability when he observed that
"countertransferential self-protectiveness is a constant, inescapable
threat to our work, and our theory itself may provide a shelter from
some of the harshest storms" (p. 72). But we may use theory either
constructively, to steady us (Shulman, 1995), or counterproductively,
to shield us. While it is more comfortable, and often more productive, to gain some mastery over our reactions before we explore and
talk about them, the ideal of mastery implied by some of the earlier
interpretations of Freud's idea of "overcoming" the countertransference is misleading. Given such traditional beliefs, it is difficult to
reorient analysts to the idea that, at those times when the analyst's
openness and directness potentially may be of significant therapeutic benefit, it can be a failure *not* to express one's experience, even
though there may be uncertainty about one's motivation.

A common subterfuge of analysts who need to conceal their participation is to interpret the patient's *investment* in having the analyst
respond in a particular way, but not to reveal that they actually have
done so. I have seen analysts twist and turn themselves inside out to
offer such interpretations while simultaneously attempting to obscure
from patients the fact that the interpretations came to them through
their own experience (irritation, for example). In the present context, such a strategy is seen as inauthentic and probably as involving
a highly transparent self-revelation. If the patient thinks the analyst
is irritated, and the analyst is aware of it, then they can explore that
development together and into a widening and deepening spiral of
other relationships, present as well as past. Discussing interactions
that involve inadvertent expressions of the analyst and the patient's
impact on the analyst thus can illuminate the patient's internal relational world as well as the subtle workings of self-perpetuating psychodynamic patterns and enactments.

The Transference Is "Correct"

For an analyst to respond consistently in the same manner, such as by
treating a patient's perceptions of him or her as plausible—whether
or not the patient's assessment corresponds with the analyst's own
experience, is questionable from the perspective I am recommending. Consider an example: A patient of mine described me, correctly
in my own view, as generally "low-keyed" with her and observed that
I preferred to avoid confrontations, yet that I did "step up" forcefully
when I felt that something important was at stake. Her unremarkable
appraisal seemed fairly obvious to me, and I offered no denials or
qualifications as we clarified how she came to this conclusion about
me. I indicated to her that her perception of my manner agreed with
my own and asked what "that quality of mine" brought up in her
toward me. In framing my question, I did not emphasize "that *experience* of me," as I might have in order to separate myself from her perception had I not seen my own responses in the way she described.
Thus I did not wish to suggest that I saw matters differently, only that
the implications of her perception of me, concordant with my own,
could be explored. "A feeling of protectiveness," she replied. Further
discussion invoked associations to her father, a timid underachiever
who was pampered by the patient's strong-minded, highly competent
mother.

Our discussion became useful in a way that I believe would not
have been possible had I not concurred but treated her perception
of me as if it were a distortion or just a possibility. That approach
might have elicited further consideration of her protectiveness, its
relation to her father, to the parents' relationship, and to how these
factors, including her identification with her mother, tended to influence her current experience—but in a more abstract way. Because I
acknowledged the relevance of that pattern, personally and to our
relationship, she was able to grapple more meaningfully in the here-
and-now with my similarities to and differences from her timid father
and to explore ways that she could then be different from her
mother. She began to make differentiations related to a split that she
had long maintained between the strong and the weak. Validating the
patient's experience of the analyst is not employed as a substitute for
analyzing, but to advance analyzing.

An analyst's directly acknowledging his or her own reactions can
heighten the immediacy, directness, and authenticity of the analytic
exchange, so crucial for the therapeutic action. That element can be

lost if one always works with analytic interactions abstractly—as representations within the patient's mind, for example. Approaching problematic interactions openly in this way also contributes to patients' attaining emotionally meaningful and personally significant new relational experience—that is, powerful new experience that is not limited simply to forms of benevolent neutrality. Through the articulation of analytic interactions in relation to outside ones, this approach further promotes insight in terms that can be grasped and applied to the actualities of the patient's everyday relational world.

Sometimes it may be better to respond openly to a patient's queries about the analyst's experience only after the patient's anticipations, wishes, and fears about that experience have been clarified. Further, the solicited reactions of the analyst may need to be presented tactfully, or in a qualified manner, of course, as in any interpersonal relationship; but such disclosures often have been withheld in the guise of protecting the interests of the patient when really they are protecting the analyst against discomfort. The traditional concern is reversed here; a failure to be open, but not openness itself, may impede the work.

Working Collaboratively with "Free-Floating Responsiveness"

Following the logical implications of Sandler's (1976a) ideas about free-floating behavioral responsiveness, rather than searching in silence while attempting to achieve an unattainable ideal of constant analytic equanimity (a process that, in any event may be traumatically experienced by certain patients as the analyst's emotional withdrawal), it can be useful at times to discuss conflicting action inclinations in order to collaboratively clarify their sources in the therapeutic interaction. The analyst might "go public" with a quandary—the impulse to influence a resistive patient to continue with treatment while acknowledging feelings of respect for the patient's sensitivity to intrusions into his or her autonomy, for example.

Another application of the idea of free-floating behavioral responsiveness is to find ways to express to patients certain *premonitions* that might occur to the therapist, identified as such, even before their sources are fully grasped—that a patient might become angry or aroused, or might withdraw, or might even wish to stop therapy following a particular intervention, for example. One need not always fully understand how or why one "knows," but trust that it *might* be a meaningful intuitive form of knowing that deserves attention and perhaps collaborative elucidation. This kind of knowing may be highly relevant, related to nonverbal and emotional cues that are sensed and processed by analysts in ways that are largely intuitive and experiential. This method is similar to an analyst's choosing to share a personal dream or dream fragment with a patient that the analyst thinks may advance an analysis. Sometimes it is wiser to contain such experiences, trying to understand them more fully while evaluating their relevance. Certainly it is never desirable to share such experiences unreflectively. But talking about one's premonitions in this way does not necessarily inhibit the exploration of relevant material; this sharing more commonly facilitates and refines the understanding of that which is revealed while encouraging like openness in the patient. With a properly established ambiance, it can be useful for analysts to talk about certain of their impulses to act, provided those impulses are described in an open and inquisitive spirit that seeks primarily to locate the sources and meanings of the impulses somewhere in patients' intrapsychic and interpersonal worlds.

One patient described feeling pleased that I had shared and been willing to explore with him my recurrent impulse to act (specifically, to rearrange our seating) in order to advance our understanding of our interaction. Formulations, he explained, were too easy to rationalize or to argue with; but the direct data of shared experience are so very "real," he noted, that one somehow has to deal with them. With his obsessive tendency to intellectualize, the direct data of my impulse offered an involving form of communication that could not be sloughed off.

Sharing Erotic Feelings: Violating a Taboo

A song from the play *Fiddler on the Roof* illustrates the transparent way in which analysts often avoid directly disclosing their experience, especially romantic or erotic feelings, to their patients. "Do You Love Me?" is sung by Tevye, the devoted husband to his wife of 25 years, Golda, as they struggle together to raise their family in a small Russian village. In the song, Tevye asks his beloved wife, simply and directly, "Do you love me?" Golda, hearing Tevye clearly, nevertheless responds, "Do I what?" Tevye repeats his question, and Golda, again acting evasively, replies in a fashion familiar to many analysts: she answers a question with a question—"Do I love you?" There are a number of other evasions in the lyric; she answers his simple question with "I'm your wife!" and "Do I love him?" In the end, acting bolder than many analysts, Golda relents, reluctantly confessing to Tevye, "I suppose I do."

Of course, there are problems with likening the analytic relationship to a marriage. Although at times it may feel so, that is certainly not my point. But because I suspect it is illustrative of what goes on in many analyses, especially in those sometimes compelling instances when romantic or erotic feelings come into play, I cite the example of Tevye and Golda here. Suppose a patient asks the analyst, directly and simply, whether the analyst has loving feelings for him or her or finds him or her sexually attractive, which is often a very difficult topic for patients to broach with their analysts. Too often we hear something from the analyst like, "Why?" "Is it important to you that I be?" "How do you imagine I feel?" "Why would I not be?" "Do you doubt that I am?" "What makes you ask that *now*?" "Am I not flesh and blood?" Something interpretive, and very possibly quite useful to the patient, might be offered. But how often are analysts comfortable in responding directly and openly?

More often than we are inclined to appreciate—and especially when the answer is positive, which is often—the best answer may be the truth. Obviously, my point here is not full disclosure but judicious disclosure employed to advance the analytic, including the relational, goals of an analysis. Nor is it my intention to reverse the prohibition of the analyst's expressions of sexual feeling with the opposite prescription—just that we consider the *possibility* of sharing such feelings, in all its complexity, in all its subtlety, as we would any other experience of the analyst. Consider a related clinical situation. A patient suspects, correctly, that he has stirred up in the analyst a wished-for/feared state, say sexual attraction, over which the patient is frightened, guilty, or ashamed. The patient's suspicion has been revealed indirectly through dream material, but convincingly to both participants. Sometimes under these circumstances a patient may be unwilling to acknowledge openly that shame-ridden perception of the analyst's experience and cannot even work productively with the resistances to doing so, since whether right or wrong about the analyst's experience, he anticipates heightened discomfort over the self-revelation and the configuration that is formed by it. Although the exploration of the resulting impasse reveals a sense that both patient and analyst are aware of what is going on, the analyst, following traditional technique, probes the development through the patient's experience, perhaps asking what the patient thinks is going on for the analyst, but abstains from directly disclosing her own experience, which the patient accurately suspects. A kind of goading by the analyst ensues, an artificial cat-and-mouse game, with the analyst's evasive questioning experienced by the patient as transparent or manipulative, attempting to expose what, in effect, both know but neither dares to reveal directly.

The authenticity of the analytic encounter is always crucially important, but it is sharply diminished by such evasive technical maneuverings. Rather than dancing around the implied development—which, not incidentally, may create the impression of the analyst's phobic avoidance that can reinforce the patient's difficulties—it may be preferable for the analyst to reveal the countertransference directly, to explore the actual relational configurations formed as a result of that disclosure and consequently those that were being avoided, as well as the associated anxiety. Otherwise, the sort of mutual avoidance I am describing, associated with nondisclosure on the part of the analyst, could act countertherapeutically to foster an identification with the analyst's perceived discomfort with his or her own and the patient's erotic feelings.

Knowing whether, when, and how to discuss sexual feelings in the analytic relationship is extremely complicated. That is why different analysts have taken a variety of positions on this form of self-revelation, with some recognizing the value of judicious expressions (Davies, 1994, 1998; Knoblauch, 1994, 1996; Slavin, Rahmani, and Pollock, 1998) and others encouraging silent uses but prohibiting direct sharing (Maroda, 1991; Gabbard, 1994, 1998). I am in strong disagreement with Gabbard (1994, 1996, 1998) on this point. He asserts, generally, that unlike analysts' feelings of anger or dismay, which can at times be shared usefully, sexual attraction (erotic countertransference) is best not revealed to patients. He (1994) generalizes, "As analysts who struggle day in and day out with the wish to be known as real persons, we must draw a line at the brink of certain kinds of self-disclosure. Sexual fantasies and feelings toward the patient reside on the other side of that line" (p. 21). Gabbard reasons that sexual feelings are fundamentally different from other countertransference feelings, that they are perilously close to violating the incest taboo and, more than other feelings, may imply some form of action, at least from the patient's point of view. Thus they are thought inevitably to compromise the crucial atmosphere of safety necessary for conducting analytic work. It is similar, according to Gabbard, with affectionate feelings. He (1996) writes that "many frank self-disclosures of love have an unconscious hostile or sadistic intent, which can be readily gleaned by the patient's devastating reaction to such disclosures" (p. 268). Drawing from his database of treatments that have broken down, he sites the example of "lovesick" male analysts who are passionately infatuated with their female patients. When these analysts' feelings of affection are penetrated, according to Gabbard, they consistently reveal underlying, split off feelings of control and hostility.

I have no doubt that Gabbard may be correct in certain instances, especially those in which treatment has broken down, which may constitute his primary data base. Depending on individual psychodynamics, however, many other analyst reactions might be equally threatening and even traumatic. Anger in the analyst often is problematic, especially when the patient was traumatized by a parent's rage. Yet the issue has become how best to deal with these feelings therapeutically, including whether to express them rather than treat them as a taboo. Depending on the dynamics of the individual patient, the analyst, and the interaction, the meanings that such a discussion might have at particular times may vary. In a position I find extreme, Gabbard (1994) likens patients' experience of their analysts' disclosures of sexual feelings to analysts' expressing wishes to physically assault patients. This observation undoubtedly is valid for some patients (and may well reflect the aggressive sexual inclinations some analysts may experience at certain times), but the withholding of mature feelings of attraction also might limit analytic potentials or represent a damaging rejection.

I would argue that erotic countertransference should *not* be treated uniquely; in fact, an analyst's ability to achieve comfort with such feelings and thus with discussing them may be especially important in helping certain patients come to terms with their own identities. Erotic countertransference represents a particularly charged area for many analysts, but talking about affectionate, attraction, or even erotic feelings that may develop is, like any other, a matter to be considered and uniquely and sensitively negotiated by individual analytic pairs in relation to the potential for new experience and growth, rather than banned summarily. As with other sensitive revelations, the context, the potential impact, and the analyst's motives in revealing such feelings require thoughtful consideration. Distinctions of degree obviously can be made, for instance, between the analyst's acknowledging the *existence* of such feelings to the patient and choosing to reveal or discuss any of the specifics. There is an enormous difference, too, between acknowledging, in a controlled way, a "feeling of attraction" and expressing a sexual fantasy involving a patient.

At times, an analyst's directly revealing affectionate feelings or those of attraction to a patient might be extremely counterproductive. It is not difficult to imagine, for example, an analyst's having counterproductive, exaggerated fantasies about the reparative, healing power of a heroic romantic love for a patient when, in the analyst's view, the patient has been unloved or otherwise abused. Other counterproductive enactments also might occur in this context, such as when analysts, motivated by an unconscious desire to guide treatment away from issues of aggression in the analytic relationship, express positive feelings. However, as we have seen, when a patient stimulates sexual feelings in the analyst that process also can be understood as part of the patient's testing of the interpersonal world in the hope of finding a new outcome (Slavin, Rahmani, and Pollock, 1998). Enactments of this sort are addressed in ways, similar to any other, that foster patients' growth. Understood in this way, enactments provide an opportunity for patients to encounter someone "new" in the analyst—that is, someone who does not respond impulsively but also does not avoid real feelings. Rather, the analyst, acting differently from past figures and as an authentic new object, is committed to experiencing these feelings and, when it is thought useful, to selectively express them as part of the analytic attempt to examine the meanings of the very real feelings that have been stirred within the relationship. Slavin, Rahmani, and Pollock (1998) describe a compelling and effective, if atypical, clinical illustration involving an analyst's sharing of sexual countertransference. They assert that what is critical is that the analyst is trying—without ever knowing fully that he or she can succeed—to avoid repeating that which is counterproductive or potentially dangerous in an enactment. The analyst strives to respond in a manner that grants priority to the patient's psychological growth, placing the patient's interests foremost. While the actual disclosure of erotic countertransference is seen as secondary to the experiencing and overall constructive management of such feelings, as these authors show, the very sort of self-disclosure that Gabbard forbids can, if managed responsibly, have effects that are capable of advancing analytic goals and psychological growth.

In a relationship in which intimate developments and authentic exchange are valued, it often becomes crucial that mutual feelings of this sort find expression, therapeutically framed by the analyst, of course. Here, as with other disclosures, I agree with Gabbard that in principle the analyst should attempt to understand, to the extent possible, the nature and sources of such responses in relation to the analysand's intrapsychic and interpersonal worlds. The limitation of that caveat obviously is that often such feelings can be clarified only after they have found expression. Understanding can be accomplished either alone, or better, with colleagues. And, of course, the analyst must monitor and, as indicated, analyze the impact of revealing such feelings. Indeed, it may be extremely valuable and useful for certain patients to grasp in a safely *boundaried* setting—and I believe the setting can remain safe for many patients—that something in their participation, and in the nature of the relationship, arouses sexual feelings. Gabbard implies that the setting cannot possibly remain safe once such feelings are acknowledged.

One of the considerations that complicates the issue of talking about erotic countertransference, it seems to me, is the incest taboo, which analysts may experience in their therapeutic roles, reinforced by the conservative influence of many senior analysts of this generation. Analysts have been further handicapped by an inability to draw dependably from a developmental model as a source of guidance, as they so often do. Adequate parents intuitively appreciate the importance of affirming, through their discreet actions, the developing gender identity and feelings of physical and sexual attractiveness of their children, as well as sensitive boundary issues, including the dangers of overstimulation and anxiety associated with direct, open, or intrusive expressions. But analysts are not parents and mature patients are not children. Nevertheless, a developmental model tells us something about the possibilities and very real potential dangers that may be involved for certain patients when analysts share erotic feelings—not with all, but with certain, and, most notably, *regressed* or immature patients. As Hirsch (1994) pointed out, "adult-to-adult" aspects of authentic relatedness are important to address in the relational model. Davies (1994) cites relational theory to point out that the two-person model leads us to an understanding of projective mechanisms that, with regard to oedipal feelings, suggest that "the analyst oftentimes must speak the dangerously charged words for the first time" (p. 168). Warning against pathologizing all such feelings, she (1998) speaks of the need, based on a developmental model of adolescence, to be sensitive to the patient's struggle to experience the self as the object of another's sexual interest. She suggests that the prototype might well be the management of desire in the oedipal period: "As adults, we can desire without the promise of satisfaction; we can want

without having to possess. Perhaps this is the true legacy of Oedipus—
the capacity to sustain desire for what we can never have" (p. 765).
She cautions that the analyst's staunch unavailability locks the patient
into, rather than freeing the patient from, idealization and incestuous desire, and can become the ultimate incestuous reenactment.

Analysts struggle day in and day out to get to know their patients
profoundly. They come to know them in an atmosphere of therapeutic intimacy and, in many ways, better than anyone else does. They
learn about patients' difficulties and shortcomings, but also come to
appreciate their very real assets and witness the courage and determination so many show in struggling to overcome their limitations.
As only otherwise with loved ones, analysts accompany patients
through the ups and downs of therapy, the painful failures, illnesses,
and personal triumphs of life. Normal, mutually loving feelings, sometimes sexual, commonly develop in this setting, but having been
encouraged to concentrate on the problematic aspects of these feelings, analysts are apt to be reluctant to discuss or even acknowledge
them. I propose that feelings of affection and attraction to our
patients are common, in fact, are the rule rather than the exception,
and their absence may constitute nothing less than a treatment crisis.
How we regard those feelings is as clinically meaningful as the feelings themselves. Moreover, as I tried to show earlier in the cat-and-
mouse example, such feelings often can be highly transparent. A
general avoidance of discussing them can send a destructive message.

There is a basis for considering that natural affectionate and erotic
feelings are among those which constitute the unobjectionable positive countertransference—a background that fosters the very best analytic work. Unlike intense or uncomfortable responses that may be
part of pathological configurations, these feelings make it possible
for analysts to endure the assaults, rejections, and other stresses of an
analytic relationship (Appelbaum, 1999). In such a view, the *absence*
of such feelings, and not their presence, and at times the failure to
share them, may be questioned. How awful for a patient who feels
himself or herself to be unattractive, who believes sexuality to be dangerous, or who has revealed his or her least "attractive" characteristics to the analyst, to find confirmation of these fears in the analyst's
lack of response—especially when the analyst does indeed have
growth-enhancing loving feelings and attraction for the patient.
Gabbard's voice is an important one in this debate; he reminds us of
our character frailties and personal vulnerabilities in a psychoanalytic
relationship. Yet, as Davies pointed out, we are all familiar with hav-

ing sexual desires on which we don't act, places in which such actions would be inappropriate and wrong. Perhaps this is an instance when we are victimized by our belief in the analytic relationship as an extraordinary place—in this instance, potentially, an extraordinarily dangerous one. That idea causes us to resort unnecessarily to inhibition and taboos. I think we can act responsibly, therapeutically, without such taboos. As with any experience of the analyst, the question is whether, when, and how to clarify and express these feelings rather than to insist that they remain tacit. That decision is always guided by the analyst's best estimate of what will further the patient's psychological growth. The decision-making process for talking about erotic feelings should be no different than for others—thoughtful, concerned above all with the analysand's psychological growth, and yet also carefully balanced against the costs of self-concealment.

Striving to Maintain an Expressive Balance

I am not suggesting that analysts respond in an open, direct, and self-revealing manner all of the time, but that they be willing, rather, to consider seriously the *possibility* of responding openly. There are many patients for whom the analyst's fuller participation can be problematic and many analysts who do not feel comfortable directly revealing themselves to patients. A complicated relationship exists between the analyst's sharing and the analysand's freedom to express himself or herself openly, for example, and we need not look far to find potential problems. Consider the example of a patient expressing something new, say anger, in a manner that represents his growth. The analyst, overemphasizing the value of letting the patient know about his interpersonal impact, responds openly and in this instance detrimentally, by sharing a negative reaction, by telling the patient that she feels demeaned by the patient's behavior. In this instance, the analyst's conveying to a patient in an ill-timed way the negative interpersonal impact of his expressions may devastate the growth-enhancing effects of a potentially new relational experience associated with overcoming old inhibitions. At a later date, timed effectively, the same disclosure might be extremely helpful.

Ehrenberg (1992), who advocates intensive forms of analytic participation through a self-expressive technique, tempers her recommendations by stressing that "active use of countertransference requires a thoughtful decision process with regard to how to use awareness of one's 'reactive' countertransference responses to inform what will then become a considered response" (p. 96). In formulating the uses of countertransference, she makes useful distinctions between the *reactive* dimension of countertransference, related to what we find ourselves feeling in reaction to the patient that is often a surprise rather than a choice, and the sort of *active* response that takes this reactive response as data and uses it to inform a considered and deliberate clinical intervention. Silence, or any other reaction, can fall into either category.

Important therapeutic work also may involve a patient's grappling with his or her internal world in the nonintrusive presence of the analyst. Thus, while it is an error to conceal one's reactions when openness may better serve a patient's therapeutic needs, it is an error, too, to discuss one's experience in insensitive or ill-timed ways that may disrupt patients' attempts to articulate their own experience, which sometimes can be quite fragile. Effective clinical analysts usually are able to recognize those moments in treatment when the patient needs to become constructively immersed in his or her own experience in a way that has relatively little to do, directly, with the presence of the analyst. The analyst may, in fact, through his or her very presence, make such moments possible; but still it can be intrusive to call attention to that factor in moments of a patient's self-absorption. Here I wish to emphasize the therapeutic importance of the analyst's "deep personal involvement" that so often develops in therapy (Mitchell, 1997b), which, while not necessarily articulated, can undoubtedly play a very powerful role.

Certainly it is counterproductive for analysts to introduce their own reactions in a manner that disrupts, intrudes, or makes it difficult for patients to more fully contact their own experience; rather, analysts must help patients become more fully self-aware. Analysts' intrusions are particularly problematic if they stunt a patient's growth by repeating a pattern in which the patient has been overwhelmed by a strong or dominant parental influence, and it is precisely in such instances, of course, that we are apt to see such developments. While analysts are now encouraged to talk about their own experience far more than tradition has encouraged, there undoubtedly are many occasions when they must allow analytic experiences and interactions simply to deepen or to speak for themselves.

CHAPTER 9

PSYCHOANALYSIS AND FACILITATING
PATIENTS' ADAPTIVE ACTION

So far, I have considered the mechanisms of personality change, and the analysts' participation to promote them, primarily as they operate directly within the psychoanalytic setting. Now, turning attention to a different aspect of psychoanalytic participation—the uses of analytic skills and the analyst's influence to promote patients' adaptive actions in the outer, or extraanalytic, world—I introduce an additional way of extending the reach of the two-person model. The idea of psychoanalytic activity, and of combining action-oriented techniques with analytic treatment, is not a new one.[1] In fact, it has existed and been extraordinarily controversial since the earliest days of psychoanalysis. Freud himself, speaking at the Budapest Congress in 1918, first explained that the efficacy of psychoanalysis could sometimes be enhanced by the addition of an active technique to influence behavior. Citing the example of severe agoraphobia, Freud (1919) stated, "One succeeds only when one can induce them [patients] by the influence of the analysis to . . . go into the street and to struggle with their anxiety" (p. 166). In the same published lecture Freud also spoke about the use of an active technique to deal with obsessional neuroses.

---

1. The distinction between "active" techniques and "action-oriented" techniques deserves some clarification. Activity describes intensive or extensive actions of the therapist within sessions; action-oriented techniques include those that are intended to help the patient operate more effectively in the realm of action outside of sessions.

189

Yet Freud (1912b) had earlier opposed the use of analytic activity in the form of assigning formal tasks to assist the patient. He wrote:

> It is wrong to set a patient tasks, such as collecting his memories or thinking over some particular period of his life. On the contrary, he has to learn above all—what never comes easily to anyone—that mental activities such as thinking something over or concentrating the attention solve none of the riddles of a neurosis; that can only be done by patiently obeying the psychoanalytic rule, which enjoins the exclusion of all criticism of the unconscious or of its derivatives [p. 119].

Such admonitions established the negative attitude toward analytic activity that was to endure for years to come. Theoreticians such as Ferenczi (1919, 1920, 1925) and, later, Alexander and French (1946; Alexander, 1956, 1961) encountered sharp criticism from mainstream analysts for their suggestion that analysts might potentiate analytic treatment through more active technical strategies that were directly concerned with patients' behavior. Although the innovative Ferenczi became best known for his ideas about mutual analysis, he also was the first serious pioneer with an "active" technique. Ferenczi (1920) was at pains to clarify that the intent of his approach was not at odds with Freud's "fundamental rule" of free association and other technical principles but was intended "to enable the patient, by means of certain artifices, to comply more successfully with the rule of free association and thereby to assist or hasten the exploring of the unconscious material" (p. 198). Ferenczi's clinical diaries (Dupont, 1988) describe one patient whom he told to eliminate masturbatory activity, another who was asked to stand up during a session and sing a song exactly as her sister would, and yet another who was asked to compose poetry. Delighted with the progress he attributed to these techniques, Ferenczi wrote, "It was astonishing how favorably this little interlude affected the work," and "We owed the most remarkable impulse toward betterment . . . which was rendered manifest by the help of 'activity.'" Ferenczi (1928) ultimately reached some very sensible technical conclusions about the use of active methods: that they be introduced in ways that were extremely sensitive to patients and to the psychoanalytic process, that they be applied empathically; that therapists never forbid behavior, only advise it; that new action be undertaken tentatively, and that the patient be permitted to decide the actual timing of a new activity.

Originally, Freud (1919) supported Ferenczi's experiments and, as Balint (1967) pointed out, even took credit for them. Subsequently, however, Freud and his followers renounced the approach, and Ferenczi was eventually ostracized for his radical, active ideas. In 1925, Ferenczi published a paper stressing the limitations and contraindications of active technique. Reiterating its subordination to interpretation, and describing it as a technique of last resort, he anticipated the later idea of "parameters." Following Ferenczi's unhappy experiment with active methods, the phrase "psychoanalytic activity" for many years remained an oxymoron within the psychoanalytic establishment.

Nearly a quarter century later, Alexander and French (1946) reintroduced the idea of activity to the psychoanalytic community, and again it provoked similar and more intense opposition. As we saw in chapter 5, although most of the controversy over their "flexible" approach centered on the corrective emotional experience, there were other aspects of their method that mainstream analysts found unacceptable (see Eissler, 1950). Unlike Ferenczi, whose concerns with activity were limited mostly to intrasession activity, Alexander and French were interested in the mutative role of patients' new actions and experiences outside of the psychoanalytic situation. Concentrating on the intervals between sessions, Alexander and French asserted that "the therapeutic influence of . . . actual experience [is] much greater than that of the interviews themselves which are but a 'shadow play' of real life" (p. 19). Accordingly, they suggested that the analyst "at the right moment, should encourage the patient (or even require him) to do those things which he avoided in the past, to experiment in that activity in which he had failed before" (p. 41). Such actions were thought capable of facilitating important new endings or solutions that could equally or more meaningfully occur in extrasession activities, rather than with the analyst. Like Ferenczi, Alexander and French stressed how the consequences of active techniques could be used to advance insight.

Orthodox psychoanalysts at the influential 1961 Edinburgh Symposium on "The Curative Factors in Psycho-Analysis" moved against rival psychoanalytic approaches, including Alexander's experiential one (Friedman, 1978). With exact interpretation as their battle cry, these analysts took up arms against the threatening modalities that recognized the value of relational and experiential approaches; they identified such approaches as compromises of "the best," seen as interpretive analytic work involving a transference neurosis. When the Edinburgh psychoanalytic conference adjourned, the interim course of modern American psychoanalysis had been determined. In a conservative spirit, American psychoanalysis remained deeply committed to a primarily intrapsychic psychoanalysis that minimized the therapeutic role of relational and experiential factors, extraanalytic interpersonal functioning, and the analyst's activity. In my opinion, that suppressive influence, which survives to this day, has prevented the full emergence of many participatory and helpful forms of psychoanalytic activity.

If any group in the psychological environment of the 1950s and 1960s could have raised psychoanalysts' consciousness of the advantages of practical, behaviorally oriented interventions, it would have been prominent behavior therapists, such as Wolpe, Salter, and others. It is here that we see a contemporaneous, parochial development within the field of behavior therapy that complemented and reinforced the Edinburgh psychoanalysts' position. Behavior therapy emerged during the 1950s and 60s, primarily under the auspices of academic psychologists who treated psychological problems at the superficial level of behavioral adaptation and modification. The very formation of behavior therapy has itself been understood in terms of a Kuhnian paradigm revolution that developed as a reaction against the venerated canons of psychoanalysis and vigorously sought to offer an alternative view to psychoanalysis (Eysenck, 1988; Krasner, 1988). A commitment to maintaining the purity of technique was not unique to psychoanalysts. Behavior therapists, too, resisted diluting their own doctrinaire views by the inclusion of psychoanalysts' insights and techniques that potentially could have enriched and deepened them. Because behavior therapy grew out of the tradition of experimental psychology and learning theory, high-level abstraction was eschewed and events had to be operational, measurable, and, above all, observable. As opposed to the "inner" explanations of psychoanalysis, behavior therapists sought, dichotomously, to offer "outer" explanations of the locus of causation of behavior. So vehement was the behaviorist rejection of the "mental forces" of psychoanalysis that Skinner (1974) sloughed off the mind merely as "the mentalistic problem."

Certain inherent theoretical and substantive intellectual incompatibilties thus exist that prevented combining Freudian depth psychology with a psychology of individual behavior. Indeed, even to this day, if we approach a reconciliation of these approaches emphasizing Freudian psychoanalytic insights with a psychology of behavior modification, an integration remains impossible. Analytic and behavioral paradigms are based on very different philosophical convictions, and the appeal of each undoubtedly is related to practitioners' own psychodynamics. The psychoanalytic model is basically introspective and concerned with the patient's internal world; the behavior therapy model is action oriented and directed toward external reality. Most psychoanalysts view behaviors as a surface, a source of meaningful origins in unconscious processes, enactments, conflict, psychic structures, and the past. As noted earlier, action has been seen as antithetical to insight. Even today, most analysts see behavioral interventions as too simplistic, superficial, and lacking in subtlety. Yet, when behavior therapists are accused of making people out to be too simple, they retort, psychoanalysis portrays them as too complex.

Historically, intense interdisciplinary rivalries between psychologists and psychiatrists—the former identified with academic centers and behavioral methods and the latter with medical settings and psychoanalysis—reinforced and widened the gulf between insight-oriented and action-oriented methods of therapy. Driven in part by this polarizing rivalry, psychoanalysts and behaviorists remained closed off to a cross-fertilization of ideas and thus to the possibilities of mutual invigoration and enrichment that might have resulted from considering fresh ideas originating outside of their traditional intellectual borders. An acceptance and integration of practical behavioral considerations by analysts, as well as of experiential and interpersonal ones, could long ago have enriched psychoanalytic theorizing, potentiated technique, and, overall, strengthened the psychoanalytic movement. And a recognition by behaviorists of the deeper motivational sources of behavior, especially those involved in their patients' resistances to their change methods, could have empowered their attempts to effect behavioral change. Analysts from a social work background have begun to comprise a significant force within psychoanalysis. Practitioners from that discipline, with its casework tradition, may be more inclined than analysts from other disciplines to cultivate pragmatic interests and to hone analytic skills with the practical, action-oriented methods described in these chapters.

The Cognitive "Revolution"

At around the time that Skinner (1974) referred to the "mentalistic problem" in outlining his radical form of behaviorism, psychology's cognitive revolution, articulating yet another school of psychotherapy, began to gather momentum. That development, coupled with the relational psychoanalytic evolution that also began to take root in America at the time, have been crucially important in reframing the way many analytic therapists, and especially behavior therapists, understand their work. These events have played a major role in beginning to dissolve what one might identify as an insight–action dichotomy.

Piagetian psychology considers the individual's mental processes in the context of adaptation to the external world; thus these cognitive psychological developments form a bridge between the individual's behavior and mental activity. Many behavior therapists, like analysts, began to find utility in the ability of certain Piagetian cognitive concepts to account for their developmental and clinical observations. Based primarily on commonalties of understanding but later also on similar techniques, a rapprochement gradually began to develop, first between behavior and cognitive therapies, and later, and in a more limited way, between cognitive and analytic therapies. While behavior therapists were becoming more cognitive, simultaneously, psychoanalysts were taking up Piagetian cognitive concepts that began to redefine certain earlier, energic and drive formulations.

Interest in combining the different psychotherapies had remained little more than a latent theme in the literature until, during the 1970s, the cognitive revolution served to jell a more delineated area of interest—indeed, a movement, that was to take shape during the 1980s. Wachtel (1981), for example, among the very first psychoanalysts to recognize the potential of reformulating traditional psychoanalytic concepts on the basis of Piagetian ideas, described transference as schemas in which assimilation predominates over accommodation to an inordinate degree. By 1984, with the publication of Atwood and Stolorow's *Structures of Subjectivity*, Piagetian psychoanalytic psychology had begun to take hold in psychoanalysis on a widening scale. There was talk among analysts of a psychoanalytic phenomenology, of the individual's fundamental need to maintain the organization of experience, of processes of assimilation and accommodation, with transference seen as an instance organizing activity, and of the analyst's task as helping the analysand gain insight into the ways that his or her cognitive-affective patterning activity contributed to experience. Concurrently, Beck and his associates (1979), working in cognitive therapy, also described the individual's active patterning of experience and behavior and wrote about underlying cognitive schemas as the building blocks of personality organization that shape the individual's world. Mediated by their expanding, shared interest in cognitive formulations, behavior therapists and psychoanalysts were discovering common ground. Pointed in radically different directions, remarkably, theorists in each modality independently had come upon bridges to the other. In this context, we can begin to consider how to reconcile the new role for external reality and action and an appreciation of the transactional nature of psychodynamics, and to synthesize cognitive-behavioral with analytic treatments intended to modify personality structure.

Strachey's "Mutative Interpretation" and the Analyst's Active Orientation

Although, traditionally, mutative psychoanalytic experience has been understood as occurring narrowly within the psychoanalytic situation, as we have seen, personality change proceeds along many avenues. In concentrating on the influence of intrapsychic factors, psychoanalysis has lost track of the potentials for personality change that exist in a person's extraanalytic activities and the experiences of ordinary day-to-day living. Normal life-cycle events, achieving mastery in important areas of functioning, a person's personal triumphs, defeats, and tragedies, for example, all can have profound and lasting effects on personality. Thus interactions with persons other than the analyst, while the source of the patient's difficulties, also can provide experientially rich sources of new learning and change. But the many sources of change that exist outside of the analytic relationship never have been put to therapeutic advantage systematically by psychoanalysts; rather, if not totally excluded, they have been relegated to a role of peripheral importance.

Strachey's (1934) work on "mutative interpretation" is the most frequently cited authority on why extratransference interpretations are *not* mutative. According to Strachey, interpretations of the analysand's transference reactions directed toward the analyst enable the analysand to distinguish between the reasonable, objective, and helpful analyst and the patient's archaic superego projections. Thus the patient, through introjection, replaces the earlier, bad internal object with the new, good one. The attendant relaxation of superego constraints facilitates the integration of previously warded-off material. But for this process to occur, the analyst first must be experienced by the patient, over time, as someone real, new, and different. This accomplishment, enabling the patient to accept previously repressed material involved in superego projections, explains the transforming aspects of transference interpretation.

A crucial element in mutative interpretation, according to Strachey, was that "every mutative interpretation must be emotionally immediate; the patient must experience it as something actual" (p. 352). In addition, mutative interpretations were to be governed by the "principle of minimal doses" and were to be specific, that is, detailed and concrete. Extratransference interpretations were seen as more limited because they were far less likely than transference interpretations to be given at the "point of urgency," or immediacy, since the object of the impulse to be interpreted was someone other than the immediately present analyst. Because the analysand must necessarily have a diminished sense of reality in relation to them, these interpretations were less likely to be mutative.

There is enormous danger in minimizing the importance of transference, its analysis and direct benefits. Transference and its analysis drive the psychoanalytic model, making it unique and powerful among psychotherapeutic modalities. However, that does not negate the advantages that exist in analysts' taking a broad view of new relational experience, one that encompasses extrasession actions and change, especially in the light of our growing understanding of the transactional nature of the person's mental functioning within an interpersonal field. Recent theoretical developments outline a basis for recognizing the mutative significance of extratransference phenomena. Some such theories, based on the idea of "multiple coding," for example, synthesize psychodynamic and cognitive views of mental structure and functioning. These views take account of recent insights from both psychoanalytic and cognitive psychological practice and research, and are based on data from a host of empirical findings too long to list. Without challenging the wisdom of Strachey's formulations, these theories provide a way of extending the analyst's interventions and understanding how analytic interventions involving patients' extrasession activities might also lead to structural change.[2]

To summerize Epstein's (1994) integration of the cognitive and the psychodynamic unconscious, two information-processing modes of individual psychological functioning are posited: "intuitive-experiential" and "analytic-rational," which correspond to the primary and secondary processes of psychoanalysis, respectively. The

2. See Bucci (1997) for a thoroughgoing discussion of "mutiple-coding" models of mental functioning.

intuitive-experiential system is related to affects and experience, the analytic-rational more strictly to intellectual functioning. Based on adaptational needs, most information processing is seen as occurring outside of deliberative, rational consciousness and within the experiential system, which unreflectively and intuitively organizes experience and directs behavior. The experiential system is thought to be organized as a network of adaptive and maladaptive schemas seen essentially as generalizations about life and functioning that are derived from emotionally significant past experience.

Schemas are stable structures that provide meaning to one's experience. They are associated with one's convictions and priorities, some potentially adaptive—that persistence will be rewarded, for example—and others maladaptive—that success is dangerous or that others cannot be trusted, for example. Schemas can be organized conceptually in terms of internalized relational patterns—representations of the self, others, and the interactions between them, including affects. Through the organizing activity that is associated with them, these schemas, or, better for our purposes, internalized relational patterns, determine the nature of a person's thoughts and feelings, overall experience, and actions, including overt behavior. Unlike conscious, logical ideas, these internalized relational patterns typically are preconscious and operate automatically. One can readily extrapolate how they might prompt the "familiar and familial" (Mitchell, 1988), organizing one's activity as understood in relational theoretical systems. When they are maladaptive, these relational patterns, operating as a closed system, rigidly dominate a person's response patterns. One can see how this way of formulating, emphasizing automatic efforts to establish that which is familiar in one's relational world, provides a useful way of understanding enactments.

These internalized relational patterns are based on, and are thought to be changed by, *lived experience.* Accordingly, there are two main avenues to structural change. One, closely related to psychoanalytic interpretation and insight, is to induce alterations in the patterns of the experiential system through the influence of the rational system, that is, by subjecting them to rational scrutiny and making prereflective organizing processes conscious. A second source of change is for the patient to learn *directly, from emotionally meaningful, personally significant experiences* (as through experiential learning, including aspects of transference analysis). These ways of thinking about change also account for the mutative potency of new relational experience. Moreover, understanding the change process in this way is, in certain fundamental respects, compatible with Strachey's work emphasizing how immediate, emotionally meaningful, and personally significant experience is promoted within the analytic setting.

Mutative lived experience is thus achieved through effective transference analysis, along the lines described by Strachey (1934), but also through other experiences and outside activities. Part of what Strachey was getting at, and is also achieved in extratransference interventions of the sort I am describing, is that prestructured patterns can be changed by emotionally immediate experiences that are lived through and internalized. Thus, in addition to transference analysis, there also exist naturally occurring, emotionally meaningful and personally significant extraanalytic activities and situations in the patient's life that can provide sources of change. Therapists may intervene in patients' living through of these experiences, helping them to shape new and adaptive responses and then to work through the consequences of their new actions in treatment. To illustrate, consider an underachieving man who is made anxious by the prospect of success. Analysis reveals a profound affective tie to the father involving the father's perception of the patient as inept, a perception rooted apparently in the father's own needs for dominance. The patient, having internalized the interaction with the father, has come to see himself as incapable and success as threatening. To this man, worldly success threatens the existing bond to the father and represents relinquishing the hope of ever receiving his father's affirmation. In other words, ironically, worldly success has become equated with failure in an endeavor that has profoundly motivated this man and structured the very meaning of his existence.

Were all of this to be rationally explained to the patient, it undoubtedly would fall flat, leaving him unchanged. Analysts know all too well that explanations alone have a limited capacity to promote deep change. When the analyst's interpretations are "well-timed" and attuned to intensified experiential factors, however, then the achievement of insight can advance change. (Incidentally, just as analysts seek to heighten experiential factors facilitating change through operations such as those outlined by Strachey, cognitive-behavior therapists try to take advantage of naturally occurring affective experiences through such procedures as exposure and self-monitoring, as described in the next chapter.) Thus the potential for profound change is dramatically enhanced when the patient lives directly through *personally significant* and *emotionally meaningful* experiences that provide a basis for directly repudiating, revising, or creating new internalized patterns. Whether directly through the transferential relationship with the analyst or in the ordinary process of living, under the experiential conditions of intensified emotional meaning and personal significance, structural change becomes possible.

Here is where enactments, insight, and new relational experience come into play. As was discussed in chapters 4 and 5, a patient's ability to engage others, including the analyst, in "vicious cycles" of relating has been widely documented for its role in personality disturbance. Were our hypothetical patient to overcome his transference expectations through transference interpretation and achieve an insightful experience with the analyst in which he could come to feel safe, competent, and even appreciated by the authority/analyst, he might overcome his fears of paternal abandonment or attack. With the analyst making himself available for a new object relationship in the analytic setting, the intensified affective, experiential, and historical meanings of both old and new relational experience could be reworked so that the impact of that experience is incorporated into mental structure, much as Strachey described.

But change follows many routes. Consider another scenario: Say the patient, helped by his analyst, was enabled to engineer and live through a similar new experience with another father figure, such as a boss, or directly through real achievement could discover other rewards that might offset the effects of the father–son bond. These discoveries, too, might help to create a breach in the patient's closed system by establishing additional beliefs, shifting priorities, and helping the patient become emancipated from the self-sabotaging tie to his internalized father. By promoting the formation of additional new relational patterns, modifying old ones, and prioritizing anew as the result of transferential as well as extratransferential learning experiences, the analyst, intervening to affect the patient's ordinary process of living, helps him behave differently and find new, more flexible ways of experiencing his world and his options within it.

I wish to be clear that, as analysts, we are not, of course, to be satisfied with superficial behavioral changes alone. Working to integrate behavioral changes, analysts seek to promote further psychological growth, relying on analytic concepts and processes such as working through. In order to deepen and extend the impact of superficial behavioral changes, analysts help their patients to process new behavior patterns and the associated self-experiences, feelings, and attitudes; to relate them to the old and to explore the origins of both; to compare new and old forms of interpersonal feedback; to examine relationships with childhood experience, past and present transference manifestations, and important, to understand the relation of anxieties and resistances, with parallels in the transference, associated with the formation of new, more adaptive self-and-object configurations. Moreover, as I will describe in the next chapter, analysts can take advantage of their active attempts to promote patients' constructive extraanalytic actions as a means of extending the process of transference analysis.

Until recently, much psychoanalytic theorizing, based on the one-person model of a segregated psychoanalytic situation, emphasized that insight into the transference alone is the key to change. In the approach I am offering for consideration, the analyst's involvement—first in enactments; then, through transference interpretation, progressively in new relational experience with the analyst—remains key. However, recognizing the mutative value of new experiential learning that is personally meaningful and emotionally significant—but that occurs outside of the analytic relationship—further enables analysts to consider how they might extend their influence and help patients achieve mutative outside experiences. Now, in addition to the analyst's being a source of transferential insight, the analytic relationship acts as a means of facilitating and integrating outside experiences in ways that can promote structural change.

Advantages of the Action-Oriented Approach

The legacy of the past generation of analysts is in certain respects an unfortunate one for contemporary practitioners. Past media portrayals of psychoanalysis led patients to expect that psychoanalytic insight, as if by magic, could transform them. The psychoanalytic establishment did little to correct the public perception and demystify its procedures. Thus patients came to treatment fully expecting to be able to change all at once, as the result of one or a few penetrating, dramatic discoveries. Of course, many were disappointed. Thus many analytic therapists today find themselves in a difficult position; having failed to meet the lofty expectations encouraged by earlier characterizations of the analytic process, they find themselves further challenged by a political and economic climate demanding that they be able to make the most efficient use of treatment opportunities.

Very often, therapeutic insight accrues gradually, over time and, rather than being inherently transformative, it provides a blueprint for change. The patient, recognizing what he or she is doing and has done "wrong" in the past, and why, gains freedom to take certain new and constructive actions, usually in small increments, and to gain control over and avoid other, problematic actions. Much of the work of internal change, involving what has been called the "working-through" process, can be accurately described as a "postchange" phenomenon in the sense that it promotes an integration of new self-with-other configurations and associated experiences that are encountered only after the patient has made modifications in his or her actions and ways of being. These modifications in action may occur with the analyst or with others, usually both.

It has been my experience that analytic techniques that are "behavioral" in nature in that they seek to promote experiences of favorable behavioral changes, and those which are "cognitive" that encourage new ways of organizing experience, can be implemented in ways that ultimately potentiate structural personality change. Indeed, as one comes to think about and work with these separate "nonanalytic" approaches in a way that I regard as truly integrative, a clear distinction among them often tends to fade. An effectively integrated and even seamless blending of techniques that are action oriented with those which tap traditional analytic objectives and methods can in many instances substantially enhance analysts' therapeutic efficacy.

Relational formulations recast the intrapsychic aspects of psychodynamics and extend the meaning of structure, elaborating them through behavioral and interpersonal processes. A patient's behavior is not just considered on a superficial level but is seen as integrated with the role of psychodynamics. The analytic use of action-oriented interventions incorporates an awareness that changes in internal and external patterns are interdependent and interactive and, in the context of an analytic relationship that promotes integration and working through, can proceed apace with one another. It is precisely because action-oriented interventions are attuned to the patient's actions in the field in which he or she functions, and relate the specifics and subtleties of intrapsychic life to the network of experiences and interactions that form the fabric of the person's life, that they advance the psychoanalyst's interest in modifying personality organization.

Attending to the actions of the patient outside of the consulting room avoids the negative kind of segregating of psychoanalytic treatment and arid intellectualization that characterizes the least productive forms of psychoanalytic and all forms of psychotherapy. This way of working can enable the analytic therapist to operate flexibly, helping patients achieve meaningful practical gains in outside life as they deepen their self-awareness and benefit from other aspects of treatment that are uniquely psychoanalytic, such as a mutative new relational experience with the analyst. There are other reasons for tapping the action dimension to potentiate analytic therapy. Many patients bring with them relatively few of the necessary aptitudes, skills, or even psychological curiosity, either initially or sometimes at all, to permit them to participate in an intensive, self-searching transference-countertransference exploration. Others may be preoccupied with concrete, practical, or otherwise pressing outside problems, including symptoms and forms of disturbed functioning; these factors make the personal immersion and patience required for psychoanalysis very difficult, if not impossible, for them. That is why many experienced analytic therapists already work in integrative ways—informally, that is.

While significant, these are not the only reasons for considering applying action-oriented techniques analytically to a patient's activities in the outer world. At least as important is their potential for heightening the vital *experiential* dimension of treatment and for putting to therapeutic use an emotionally meaningful and personally significant setting for change, the patient's "real life" outside, following the very same reasoning offered by Strachey and other analysts for intensifying experiential "here-and-now" work in the transference. Heightened affective experience occurring in a personally meaningful context, which is usually made possible with the analyst through transference developments, often occurs spontaneously in the challenges of the patient's outside activities, creating a favorable setting for change.

Three Forms of Psychotherapy Integration

Before going further, let us place psychotherapy integration, itself—efforts to synergistically combine diverse therapeutic modalities—in a context. My own approach, outlined in this chapter and the next, remains true to relational psychoanalysis. Applied through a two-person model of the psychoanalytic setting, it sometimes draws from the technology for behavior change that exists in cognitive-behavior therapy to *analytically* promote salutary changes. Elements of the approach have been incorporated by Wachtel in recasting, relationally, his cyclical psychodynamic approach. The theoretical form of integration that I am advancing also has been described by Messer (1992) as an example of what he calls *assimilative* integration—forms that recognize the value of diverse practices while permitting relative consistency in one's own theory and practice (here, psychoanalysis). But other forms of psychotherapy integration also have been considered. Recently, authors (Gold, 1996; Wachtel, 1997) have arrived at a tripartite classification of integrative approaches. Accordingly, three relatively distinct forms of psychotherapy integration can be identified: 1) technical eclecticism, 2) theoretical integration, and 3) the common-factors approach.

Technical eclecticism is exemplified by the approach of Lazarus (1992, 1995). Appearing at times to be little more than a hodgepodge of arbitrarily selected techniques, the eclectic approach has given the discipline of psychotherapy integration somewhat of a bad name among theoretically minded psychoanalysts and psychotherapists. Eclecticism (vs. integrationism) is a particular method that proceeds from an assessment of a patient's specific problems, defined as treatment targets, as well as the patient's resources on cognitive, affective, and interpersonal levels. The techniques of one or more modalities may then be combined on a pragmatic or "as-needed" basis that matches the patient's clinical needs with specific interventions. Eclectic practitioners are willing to recognize the independent value of, and to choose from among, established interventions without regard for theoretical origins or coherence within a superordinate theoretical framework. They are concerned, simply, with what promises to be most effective in any individual case. Accordingly, insight into a behavior may be judged most helpful at one juncture, relaxation training at another, perhaps a gestalt technique further on, a joint session with the spouse, or even a family session might seem indicated with continuing developments.

I reject the eclectic approach and endorse a second one, *theoretical integration*. Theoretical integrationists and eclectics are apt to proceed differently in their work with patients. Integrationist therapists may appear "eclectic" in the sense that they, too, are open to the possibility of drawing from diverse approaches, but they look toward a higher level of abstraction to guide and synthesize the different methods they employ. Guided by a more articulated theoretical vision, the clinical work of integrationists must reflect an internally consistent theory of personality development, functioning, and change that has broad applicability. As a result, integrationists may blend different modalities so that the constituent parts become indistinguishable, rather than simply mixing them as eclectics do. The integrationist, while perhaps no more clinically effective than the eclectic in any one case, is both grounded in and works toward a creative synthesis, an approach that will have broad clinical applicability and improve clinical work among a wide range of cases. Considering their penchant for theory, psychoanalysts are likely to prefer this approach to eclectic ways of working.

Wachtel's (1977, 1987, 1997) theorizing, a strong influence on my own thinking, offers an elegant illustration of theoretical integration. Wachtel has long been a major proponent of the view that "cyclical" psychodynamic theory offers the most advantageous way of reconciling psychodynamic and behavioral ways of understanding and treating psychological disturbances. Similar ideas are implied, if not explicit, in many other psychoanalytic formulations (e.g., Sandler, 1976a; Gill, 1982a; Atwood and Stolorow, 1984; Mitchell, 1988). More than most psychodynamic theories, the cyclical view acknowledges that situations of patient's own making play a critical role in influencing their subsequent functioning. That is because the situations that people encounter are, in large part, of their own choosing, that is, determined by their personality organization. Specifically, the patient chooses certain situations, including associates, over others; he or she perceptually organizes the nature of these situations in ways that come to shape their personal affective and cognitive impact; further, as a result of the response propensities stimulated thereby, the patient influences others to act in particular ways. Thus patients create the same situations for themselves—situations that are in part expressions of their personality organizations—over and over again. This rich array of intrapsychic, interpersonal, and contextual factors, and the complex interplay among them, determine the individual's psychological functioning. In emphasizing the cyclical quality of behavior, Wachtel (1997) thus appreciates what is *ironic* in psychological functioning, that "the ways in which our very efforts to banish certain experiences from our lives can actually contribute to bringing them about" (p. 376).

In his most recent book, Wachtel (1997) positions cyclical psychodynamic theory, which formerly was set apart from the main body of psychoanalytic theory by its association with relatively more superficial, interpersonal psychoanalytic conceptualizations, quite productively within the newer relational psychoanalytic framework. While emphasizing the depth of the cyclical psychodynamic approach anew, he also extended his earlier conceptualizations to more fully embrace systemic concerns—namely, family concerns, the implications of which he developed with his collaborator and wife, Ellen Wachtel, a family therapist. Wachtel thus moved that which was peripheral to a position of centrality—systems considerations for the individual psychotherapist and individual psychodynamics in the case of family systems therapists. He has consistently stressed the therapeutic importance of the interrelationship between the individual and the system and especially experiential factors occurring within both. Within this view, a person's internal psychological processes and behavior both are included in interventions.

A third form of psychotherapy integration is the *common-factors* approach. This approach is based on the assumption that all effective psychotherapeutic modalities share certain critical, curative features but package them differently, so to speak. Prominent psychotherapy researchers Jerome Frank, Carl Rogers, and Hans Strupp approached psychotherapy from this point of view. They have attempted to isolate the specific features existing within a variety of approaches that ultimately were therapeutic. Rogers's (1956, 1961; Rogers and Dymond, 1954) findings have been intuitively rewarding to many psychoanalysts, especially those with backgrounds in academic psychology who are familiar with humanistic forms of psychotherapy and psychotherapy research. Rogers found that, in order for a treatment relationship to result in change, the therapist had to respond with accurate empathy, unconditional positive regard and what he and his collaborators called self-congruence (related to what I have defined as authenticity). A therapist's quality of nonpossessive warmth also was an important finding.

In general, as Gold (1996) concluded, contemporary common-factors investigators have shown that relational and supportive elements based on the therapeutic relationship, and technical elements associated with new learning experiences and the opportunity to test new skills in action, are among the factors associated with all effective therapies. The convergence noted between psychoanalysis and cognitive-behavior therapy can be understood as an expression of common curative factors.

Psychoanalysis and the Current Status of Psychotherapy Integration

Although those seeking to integrate active with analytic techniques never constituted a vital force within psychoanalysis, the idea of analytic activity never completely disappeared. In the years following Alexander, scattered publications of integrative efforts continued to appear. (See Goldfried and Newman, 1992, for a review.) Relational developments and the changing clinical and economic realities of recent times have rekindled analytic therapists' interest in the ways they might use active techniques and psychotherapy integration to empower their work. Further, many young professionals approaching the field with a practical bent are nevertheless drawn to the explanatory power of psychoanalysis. More willing to challenge authority than their predecessors, these young professionals are less affected by the conservative influence that has conditioned the reactions of so many of their seniors. Thus they are more receptive to less doctrinaire and more integrative ways of thinking and working. Many of these therapists experience a greater freedom than those who came before them to practice analytic therapy in a spirit of responsible and creative empirical experimentation.

Tracing Gill's changing evaluation of the integrative ideas set forth here underscores the growing acceptance of the more active, integrative approach. While withholding a definitive opinion when analytic integration of the sort advanced here was first called to his attention, Gill (1984b) commented on the "difficulties" of psychotherapy integration. He reasoned that integration might successfully be achieved in psychodynamic psychotherapy but not necessarily in psychoanalysis, which, in his view, was distinguished by its central emphasis on the analysis of the patient's experience of the relationship, or transference analysis. Gill (1988) believed that the effect of the analyst's contribution probably could not be significantly resolved by interpretation if a certain "ill-defined" range of interaction was exceeded. Noting that that range might well differ from patient to patient, Gill observed that it remained to be empirically established. This qualification was important to Gill (1982a) since he saw it as desirable that the treatment outcome be as dependent as possible on the analysis of the transference, with the inevitably accompanying new experience, and as independent as possible of persisting transference.

Commenting directly on Wachtel's and my ideas about analyst activity and integration in his last book, Gill (1994) seemed considerably more receptive to the integrative idea. He grew to believe that help with behavior in a difficult situation might be desirable as a means of breaking an analytic impasse or an obsessional vicious cycle. He recognized that the utility of such active interventions was much more acceptable with both the recognition that interaction is inevitable and constant and attention to the analysis of such interaction. Whether the therapy remains psychoanalytic, Gill believed, depended on the nature of the deliberate interaction and whether its meaning in the transference was analyzed. Concurring substantially with the ideas I advance here, Gill concluded favorably that "once an analytic situation is established so that the two participants are agreed on the centrality of the analysis of interaction, it may be helpful to relax the strictures against interaction for a more effective therapy" (p. 57).

Psychoanalytic Realism and Helping Patients Take Action

In chapter 3 we saw that analysts historically have tended to be far more concerned with process goals (whether a patient is freely associating or resisting, for example) than with patients' reality-functioning or life goals (see Wallerstein, 1965, for a review). Thus many practitioners continue to see analytic treatment as having its greatest effect when the psychoanalytic situation is removed from the patient's day-to-day life. Note the comments of Adler (1993), who, in responding to an earlier paper of mine, encouraged analysts not to be distracted by the patient's actions in external reality. He wrote:

> In effect, the Freudian psychoanalyst's answer to the question "What do you want the patient to do?" is always predictably and monotonously the same: we want the patient to express whatever comes to mind. This most fundamental technical prescription to *let it happen* sets in motion an unpredictable process whose centrifugal tensions will reverberate through the patient's life outside the office. This injunction does not mix easily with the therapeutic ambition to *make it happen out there* [p. 586].

An analyst's commitment to understanding qua understanding is not the equivalent of a commitment to promoting change. Promoting understanding alone, as it applies exclusively to transference-countertransference processes, is compatible with segregating the psychoanalytic reality, treating it as if it were discontinuous with or separate from the rest of the patient's life. Like approaches that fail to consider the real contribution of the person of the analyst in understanding transference, analytic applications that allow the therapy to unfold without taking account of patients' progress in relation to everyday stresses and challenges, including the problems that have brought them to treatment, are flawed according to the standards of psychoanalytic realism. Remaining in touch with real, practical developments in the patient's life, especially in relation to the problem(s) that initially brought the patient to psychotherapy, heightens the relevance of the analytic process.

Historically, analysts have concentrated on transferences and resistances and left to random trial and error the patient's development of the adaptive behaviors that can play so vital a role in determining the ultimate success of an analysis. Much is gained analytically, of course, as the analysand and the analyst attempt to work through and master new situations in reality, reconciling the different consequences of both constructive and misdirected efforts. Yet leaving these adaptations to trial and error and neglecting the patient's course of action in the external world is at the very least an inefficient way of approaching analytic change, especially when one realizes that *the most important resistance that the analyst may often need to attend to is the patient's resistance to taking constructive new action.*

Consider how, for example, a patient was helped to recognize and change his own role in a troubled marital relationship, in which he felt neglected and criticized. Through treatment, the patient began to appreciate the need to become both more expressive and assertive with his wife, whose criticism he feared. We had clarified that in part his fears reflected certain characteristics of his wife, but in other ways they were based on his early interaction with an apparently borderline, severely critical mother, who at times actually assaulted him. (A sudden, loud noise, perhaps of a car backfiring, once disturbed his session. Startled, the patient shared the associations that the noise triggered. He recalled the many times when, as a small child, he would listen attentively for sounds from his mother's bedroom, anticipating that she might fly into one of her rages and find him as her target.) His initial assertive gains, through trial and error, were erratic and, as one might expect, sometimes provocative. On one occasion, he independently selected a paint color for the master bedroom and then went ahead and painted it to "surprise" his wife, without first discussing it with her. She had a keen aesthetic sense, was very invested in design, and became predictably upset with him. On another occasion, he faltered, complying with the wife's "insistence" that he not invest a small sum of money in order to put their used car in top condition, which they hoped to sell for several thousand dollars. An experienced automotive hobbyist, the patient knew a great deal about automobiles and, in fact, knew far more about this matter than his wife did. Moreover, the sale would benefit her by enabling her to replace her old car.

We explored these and other, similar interactions at some length. With regard to the selection of the bedroom paint color, taking care to recognize his fragile new assertiveness, I pointed out how "ironically" he had, in fact, acted "assertively," yet in a way that had led to criticism that might have been anticipated and avoided. We came to understand this as his contribution to perpetuating the negative interaction with his internalized critical mother. In responding to the incident related to the auto repair, however, I turned to an action-oriented technique. After exploring his anxiety about taking action despite his conviction that it was a prudent thing to do, I urged him to go ahead and have the car repaired, and then we would examine the wife's reactions. (I had the sense that he was reading too much into his wife's concerns and that she was acting out of anxiety, anger, and a lack of confidence in his judgment, understandably, based on their prior history and the recent interaction involving painting the bedroom. But I trusted that she could recognize his automotive authority. Thus I was making discriminations about her and her behavior that he was thus far unable to make.) Since he was anxious about taking action and might avoid it (procrastination was a major difficulty), I created a structure that would make it more likely that he would go ahead and, further, that would enable us to clarify the actual outcome; I encouraged him to keep a detailed diary on the interaction with his wife. Not surprisingly to me, his wife was pleased, not upset, with him for taking command in an area in which she felt less capable. Gradually, he was being helped to fine-tune his judgment and actions and to see how, through his own efforts, he was able either to perpetuate negative object relations that echoed and reinforced his early relationship with his mother or to cultivate an experience of change and his wife's appreciation.

As analysts acknowledge the desirability of including attention to patients' real-life struggles and attempts to work out the realities of everyday existence, they come to a position different from traditional views that encourage the patient's and analyst's immersion in process goals within the separate reality of the psychoanalytic situation. What is emphasized in the revised view is a psychoanalytic process that is continuous with the patient's ordinary life and that takes *progression*—not regression—as its beacon, with the analyst seeking to ensure, to the extent possible, that treatment efforts correspond with the patient's pursuit of specific life goals. There are advantages to acknowledging both the patient's *life* and *treatment* goals, and in therapeutically concentrating on both (Ticho, 1972). It is not enough merely to increase a patient's insight; what often is more important is the application of that awareness to the patient's daily life. Following Ticho, we might think of life goals as the goals patients would seek to attain if they could put their potentiality to use. They are the goals patients would aim at if their "true" capacities were freed. Here the analyst takes a position similar to that described by Loewald (1960), who, while considering such matters from a more traditional perspective including the importance of a holding environment, wrote, "The patient, being recognized by the analyst as something more than he is at present, can attempt to reach this something more" (p. 27).

Some of the understandings that are reached in an analysis carry inherent and powerful imperatives for action, and when they occur they may impel the patient directly to make significant changes toward life goals. But most treatment insights do not have that sort of effect. That is why analysts must be actively concerned with "the responsibility *of* insight" (Rangell, 1981a)—with helping patients develop and follow through on the action implications of analytic insights. Working within a classical framework, Rangell reasoned that analysis moves "to a point in treatment where positive actions become desirable if not necessary both in the analysis and in life" (p. 130). Insight followed by adaptive action results in the most effective change.

People who seem to possess what might be called a "talent" for action are among those who ordinarily make the best use of analytic therapy. They do not lean toward action as a means of avoiding insight—engaging in what analysts often call acting out—but implement it in ways that extend analytic insight. Some examples of this form of action are the person who in a timely, appropriate, and direct—but not counterphobic way, confronts the boss after realizing through the analytic work that his own submissiveness was based on a history with a domineering father, or a patient who calls again after a first date to test the patterned conclusion, questioned by the analyst, that the initial date was a bust, or the patient who seriously takes up a sport for the first time, willing to challenge a family myth that a sibling was the athletically gifted one and she was meant to be an artist.

In contrast, there are those patients who are handicapped by an inability to take constructive action. Among them are the diffusely phobic people who Rangell noted require "more realistic attention" than customarily is required in order to help them implement adaptive behavior. Other theorists (Gedo, 1998a,b, for example) also have identified patients who lack the ability to coordinate their actions with insight—not only as a manifestation of motivational factors, but on the basis of inadequate skills, or, as Rangell (1981a) put it, "intrinsically—either constitutionally or from early character development" (p. 130). These patients, in particular, benefit from psychoanalytically applied action-oriented techniques to help them address these deficiencies.

Behavioral changes resulting from therapy sometimes are dramatic. More often, as Rangell (1981a) reminds us, "the effects of analysis may manifest themselves not in a new or dramatic development, but in the more subtle or quiet 'actions' of intrapsychic life" (p. 138). These more subtle changes in action—ways of thinking or of handling one's feelings of anxiety, for example, enhanced self-esteem or improvements in the quality of affects or object relations, or even simply relief from anxiety that may or may not be acknowledged—all must be counted as successes. Yet should we not at times aim beyond these purely intrapsychic changes, provided that our actions on patients' behalf are sensitively attuned to their own life goals and limitations? And, if so, how does such a position translate into our actual clinical participation?

Shifting our thinking in this way has a very significant impact on our clinical functioning. For instance, what is learned from the analytic exploration of transference-countertransference patterns is not treated as an end in itself but is actively related to interactions with people other than the analyst, both from the past and, especially, from the present. Of course, relating a transference-countertransference pattern to other relationships must be accomplished in sensitively timed ways that do not rob transferential moments with the analyst of their immediacy, affectivity, personal conviction, and thus mutative potency. But it is not always desirable that insight remain centered on the analytic relationship, as if movement within it alone were the consummate analytic outcome. However important the analytic relationship may become—and it often becomes extraordinarily so—at some point bridges must be built between insights developed in the consulting room and their implementation in everyday life. This recognition encourages the analyst's involvement as an important, involved party in the patient's life. Concern with the patient's struggles—not the analyst's detachment from them—is valued, with interventions framed in ways that may directly help the patient take new actions that help solve life's problems.

While analysts may often have a sense that the material patients are grappling with in sessions is very important, they cannot always establish its relevance to outside problems. Of course, we cannot possibly be aware of all the aspects of change in a patient's mental functioning, not even in the analytic setting, no less when the patient is describing operating outside of it. Inevitably there will be unexpected moments when a patient's changes are called to our attention, perhaps through the reported observations of others. Still, in conducting treatment we must not be occupied with the material in a way that loses sight of the patient's practical objectives, that completely "lets it happen," as it were. Rather, the analyst attempts to complement traditional ways of listening for transference-countertransference developments, selectively explicating the relationship between the unfolding process and life goals. This view discourages analysts from simply opening and broadening the material and exploration, as through sharing one's own "musings" or "free" associations, for example, but finds value in the counterbalancing effort to elicit material that is likely to be related to patients' practical goals.

Determining which themes of the patient to follow or encourage, and which to deemphasize or even to disregard—what is and is not clinically and realistically meaningful—is not a simple matter. One cannot always know for certain whether a particular line of inquiry will turn out to be productively related to other important sets of feelings or situations, including the presenting problem. But our psychodynamic formulations ordinarily serve us well in formulating estimates of this kind. Usually, the difficulties that our patients manifest with us are continuous with those in outside life. It is a safe bet that the inability of a person to make a commitment to treatment is related, for example, to the work inhibition or other relational difficulties that brought the person to therapy, or, as another example, that a patient's conflicts about discussing matters of mutual attraction are related to intimacy problems with which he or she is grappling. These connections often can be made manifest in highly productive ways.

If the therapist develops a sense, over time, that the sessions are unproductive or unrelated to the very real issues that brought the patient to treatment, then he or she can introduce and examine this possibility with the patient. Doing so has the effect of keeping the treatment on course with the patient's life goals while advancing the exploration. Emphasizing psychoanalytic realism in this way is not seen as suggesting that the analyst create a hurried, pressured, or insensitive analytic atmosphere. On the contrary, pressure is inimical to the sort of holding environment and underlying empathy that are essential to facilitating patients' psychological growth. I recently felt frustrated as I listened to a talented, highly accomplished patient discuss giving up a new and potentially rewarding career opportunity without trying very hard to find ways of applying her abilities to its challenges. As I grappled with my feelings, I finally decided to explicitly address the *disparity* between our apparently different reactions to her situation. In so doing I chose to question with her whether my reaction was based on her actual life goals or on my own goals for her. We clarified this disparity, which extended an ongoing discussion of her own conflicted ambitions, but now in its relation to her "pushy" mother and the patient's veiled wishes to thwart her, bringing to light a relational pattern that had remained obscure.

We see from the example how a relational understanding of personality organization lends itself to utilizing interventions geared toward enhancing the patient's functioning in everyday life. If, as in the one-person model of the psychoanalytic situation, the patient's mind is regarded as isolated, that is, as somehow cut off from the interpersonal field, then the analyst's interventions must be applied in ways that exclude or at least minimize externals in order to concentrate on internal structures and processes. The intervention in the example—my highlighting the patient's and my own different views by sharing a personal reaction in order to question, ultimately, the patient's conduct in the work setting, in the context of transference analysis—would be inappropriate. This is also an example of how thinking about structure relationally invites the analyst to conceptualize and intervene in terms of both internal relational patterns *and* external object relationships.

Conclusion: The Active Analyst and One-Person and and Two-Person Psychoanalytic Models

Both the redefined role of external reality that is inherent in the two-person model and the model's focus on action are among the developments that make it possible for analysts to give attention to behavior change (chapter 3). Certainly it is not enough that an action-oriented method be employed simply because it is known to be helpful to many people, as in technical eclecticism. Rather, an active method is applied because it does not violate but advances the basic *psychoanalytic* processes that organize the approach. In other words, awareness of the various underlying psychoanalytic theoretical assumptions may suggest or contraindicate the use of certain active techniques.

The analyst's activity thus finds new viability in relational psychoanalysis and a two-person model. The attempt to compartmentalize the patient into "inner" and "outer," to dichotomize treatment into insight-oriented and action-oriented modes, and the customary distinctions between psychoanalysis and psychoanalytic psychotherapy, all break down in the light of the implications embraced by such theorizing. The relational system of understanding takes a view of psychic structure that is fundamentally different from the classical model. In it, internal structures are seen as continuously interacting with the patient's relational field and his or her actions, overt behavior, and interpersonal dealings within it. With personality structure, motives, behavior, the resulting self–other configurations in the external world, and feedback seen as interacting elements in self-regulatory and field-regulatory mechanisms, behavior may at times become an important intervention focus in fostering enduring personality change.

CHAPTER 10

USING ACTION-ORIENTED
TECHNIQUES ANALYTICALLY

*D*uring the fourth year, the major focus of Carrie's twice-a-week treatment had become her anger and the splitting mechanisms she often used to defend against it. She typically experienced her own anger innocently as the result of her victimization by others. Psychodynamically, this split appeared to be associated with her own disavowed aggression and a protective attitude toward others, related to a fear that her anger would destroy her relationships. We had explored this dynamic in our relationship, an exploration that had been limited because very little anger had been expressed or, as far as I could tell, even felt toward me. At this point in treatment, I was being preserved as a good object, as she had always dealt with her father.

Carrie, a 28-year-old Asian-American woman, handled her first pregnancy, and the birth and early months of her daughter's life, well. But when her daughter became a toddler, Carrie became increasingly frustrated with her daughter's tendency to "test" her. If the child "misbehaved" in one or another age-appropriate way, such as having a toilet accident, Carrie might experience that as a deliberate act of defiance against her. A concern with how the quality of her mothering would appear to others aggravated her mounting frustration. Mother and daughter both had become "bad" in her estimation. At times, this concern resulted in uncontrolled anger, and she described minor instances of "shoving" and "roughing up" the child. In one isolated instance, the patient pushed her daughter, who fell and was bruised. Afterward, the patient was deeply remorseful, experiencing this event as dramatic evidence of her unacceptable anger and inadequate self-control.

Gradually, Carrie was helped to recognize some superficial, repetitive elements from her own childhood experience. She grasped in a general way that she was acting as her own mother had; her mother had a temper and also had been obsessively concerned with the reflection of her daughter's (the patient's) behavior as it reflected on her mothering skills. Problematic indeed was the patient's intractable identification with this aggressive aspect of her mother, which, in the context of her predominant experience as a victim, often surfaced as if it were an unfamiliar part of herself over which she had little if any control.

From her past history of episodic angry outbursts, it was understandable that, despite her moderate gains in self-regulation and self-esteem, Carrie continued to be frightened over an inability to contain her aggression toward her daughter. In an anxious, obsessive way, shame and self-control became perseverative themes throughout our sessions. Frightened and self-condemning, she became fixated on her capacity for anger and its expression but did not seem able to move with this concern or to deepen her understanding of it. I felt stymied. Familiar with a cognitive-behavioral anger management method, I grappled with the decision over whether or not to introduce the structured approach into the treatment in order to break the obsessive vicious cycle, since the patient had worked psychoanalytically in a generally beneficial way.[1]

This therapeutic choice point (Messer, 1986) illustrates several complex issues associated with the use of action-oriented techniques in analytic therapy. I wondered how it would affect the treatment to respond to the patient actively, by assisting her with action-oriented techniques to cope more effectively with anger toward her daughter. How would it affect the pathogenic maternal identification? Might the psychodynamic and transferential manifestations of that identifi-

1. I have become much more comfortable using integrative methods, especially in "seamless" ways, which I describe later in this chapter. I use this example, drawn from my early experience with these methods, because I believe it addresses many of the concerns of readers. It is common to experience discomfort, although it diminishes with successful clinical implementation, in breaking with tradition to introduce such techniques to patients. As Leo Stone (1961) observed, the theoretical conception of the psychoanalytic situation "has great influence and power, occasioning self-consciousness or even guilt when its outlines are transgressed" (p. 18).

cation, of shame, anger, and the patient's subtle appeal for help with self-control, be addressed more productively, overall, through the inquiry alone, rather than at the additional level of action? How would such an intervention affect the analysis of the transference? Might it disrupt the patient's subsequent participation in the inquiry? And from the behavioral perspective, would it really work? What about the impact of transference on the learning of coping techniques?

The question of *when* action-oriented techniques might be employed most beneficially is not a simple one for analytic therapists to answer. When introduced and worked with appropriately, interventions modifying action can contribute to structural change. Depending on many intrapsychic and interactional variables operating within the treatment, however, action-oriented interventions undoubtedly can be more helpful at certain times than at others. Conceivably, too, they might have a detrimental impact, as when the analyst employs active techniques *instead of* working analytically, that is, colluding with the patient's resistance to the examination of issues that are more beneficially addressed through an analytic inquiry. Thus, in the instance with Carrie I considered the possibility that I might have become "pulled into" the transference by employing action-oriented techniques related to a counterproductive enactment associated with another important issue of hers, that she not be treated as though she were "different," that is, damaged. Such considerations, related ultimately to clinical judgment, are particularly compelling in relation to the introduction of active, especially action-oriented techniques, by the analytic therapist and require thoughtful consideration.

I did not feel "under fire," so to speak, to do something. Since I did not experience undue interactional pressure, I did not consider projective identification as a potential complicating factor. I sensed that the treatment had become bogged down and that I had exhausted interpretive possibilities with Carrie. When I tried to understand the potential meaning that the action-oriented intervention might have for Carrie in terms of possible internalized object relationships and associated enactments, no contradictory relational configuration occurred to me. On the contrary, the provision of practical assistance seemed actively responsive to her in precisely the way her parents had failed. I, unlike her parents, was responding to what seemed to me her legitimate needs—in this instance, to her life goal of being a good parent. I was aware, nevertheless, that down the line we probably would discover other meanings my understanding and participation might have, both for me and for her. Accordingly, I decided to offer Carrie cognitive-behavioral anger management techniques (similar to those implemented by Novaco, 1975, Meichenbaum, 1977, and Deffenbacher and Stark, 1992).

I wish to be clear that the action-oriented technique was not inspired primarily by the goal of providing a new relational experience in the sense outlined by the developmental-arrest theorists (Winnicott, 1960; Kohut, 1984) or by Alexander and French (1946). I believe that one definitely could employ action-oriented techniques within those frameworks, but that is not my interest. Conceptualized with an object relations emphasis, a primary goal of the treatment was the exploration and modification of the patient's internalized and external relational patterns. Since the analytic interaction provides an introjective basis for advancing structural change through new relational experience, I wished to be as certain as possible that the active intervention would not replicate the parental behavior that had contributed to the patient's difficulties but instead would frame an adaptive introject that might facilitate, and not impair, the development of adaptive structure. To provide the patient with insight, the interaction around the technique had to be analyzed.

In conceptualizing the provision of this help principally in terms of object relations, I considered further diminishing Carrie's problematic identification with her disturbed mother. Helping Carrie develop a constructive way of dealing with the child when she was angry could advance her differentiation from disturbed aspects of the internalized mother. The interaction surrounding the active intervention itself would provide a potential opportunity for an adaptive internalization, as well as an identification with the therapist. Fostering more competent psychological skills for handling anger also would contribute to a positive revision of certain self-representations, narrowing the gap with her ideal self and thus diminishing feelings of shame and enhancing self-esteem. I further anticipated that, by helping to shape more adaptive parental behavior and a new, more positive alignment with her child, important new material could be mobilized for the analysis. Anger management techniques also reduced the possibility of physical harm or psychological damage to the child, although the risk of the former, while frightening to the patient, seemed negligible to me.

I first explained the rationale for the action-oriented technique and summarized the formal procedures, which Carrie found agreeable. As I introduced them, I modified the intensive procedures, condensing and spreading out over several months, meeting twice weekly, what a cognitive-behavior therapist might accomplish in a dozen or so sessions, in order to blend them with the analytic process. Thus any potential disruptiveness was minimized, and an opportunity was provided to explore Carrie's reactions to me in this more active capacity, as well as to the techniques themselves. I taught her relaxation skills and diaphragmatic breathing (Barlow and Cerny, 1988) to help her moderate her physiological reactions when angry. Next, I asked her to maintain a detailed diary describing situations with her daughter that provoked her. Subsequently, these entries were discussed in our sessions, with word-for-word attention to her record of associations to the child's behavior, including images and sensations. (These conscious data are the "automatic thoughts" of cognitive therapists.)

As Carrie and I went over her diary, she was helped to gain distance from, and to evaluate, her anger-provoking thoughts and the evocative situations themselves. I pointed out, and she realized, the exaggerated sense of certainty experienced with her automatic thoughts—as if she could read the child's mind and malicious intentions, as part of a tendency to personalize the child's motives. (For example, "She's just doing that to make me angry again!") We also developed a practical strategy, helping her to avoid angry confrontations by emphasizing practical goals. Thus, in coping with provocative situations, she would first take a moment to spontaneously bring about a self-calming state of relaxation; then, using a coping statement, she would further compose and focus herself, asking, "What is it I *really* want to accomplish here?"

Next we developed a hierarchy, progressing from the least to the most provocative situations she had encountered during several weeks of diary keeping. We would develop a deeply relaxed state and Carrie then "rehearsed," through visualization and the use of her relaxation skills and coping statement, calmly and effectively managing her daughter's behavior and her angry reactions to them. We examined the situations, developed specific strategies for handling them, and evaluated their potential success. Proceeding up the hierarchy, we gradually focused on implementing the skills that were successfully mastered through "cognitive rehearsal" in everyday interactions with the child. Although I initially taught her the techniques and then loosely "supervised" her work with them by discussing diary entries and evaluating results with her, Carrie conducted most of the work, including the practice and implementation, independently between sessions.

Importantly, we used the action-oriented techniques to advance the analytic inquiry. One useful way was to look at Carrie's written material to elaborate the construction of her inner relational world. She was able, spontaneously, to recognize that many of the angry thoughts recorded in her diary "echoed the voice" (her words) of her own mother, now internalized. Thus she was helped to appreciate more fully and better understand that identification. For instance, she saw her tendency to view the child as defiant and to overreact to the child's normal testing behavior in ways that her mother had frequently overreacted to her own developmentally normal actions. These insights were reinforced by discussions of ongoing interactions with her mother, and Carrie's mother's interactions with her granddaughter. All this helped her to grasp the sources of her own behavior and to gain better control over it.

As we scrutinized Carrie's actions in relation to the child's actual behavior, a process of projective identification with the child was clarified. That is, examination of certain of her attempts to "discipline" the child revealed how her verbal and nonverbal behavior, ostensibly motivated to bring about compliance, actually prompted the child to mischievously "go too far" rather than to obey. In this way Carrie was helped to realize how she was covertly encouraging the child to misbehave and "taunt" her, causing the child thereby to provoke Carrie's anger. She gained further control over her behavior with that awareness. This pattern also was gradually understood as corresponding to her childhood experience of *mutual* provocation with her mother, thus helping her to own her own anger in a nonjudgmental way. I understood this enactment in terms of a dissociated, provocative maternal introject that had been largely obscured by the patient's self-representation as victim.

Over time, Carrie's growing awareness of her part in these aggressive exchanges, understood in terms of a similar enactment with her own mother, helped make it possible for her to take greater responsibility for her own contribution to confrontations earlier felt to be instigated entirely by others. Less frequently did anger seem to come over her as though not her own. I reasoned that, historically, Carrie may have secretly identified with her mother's indirectly provocative behavior in order to convert the passive experience of abuse to an active one, thereby achieving a sense of control. Now the interaction pattern of eliciting the "naughty" child's behavior preserved the object tie to the abusive mother, while also mitigating guilt.

Let us consider more directly the *analytic* impact of the action-oriented intervention. Carrie reacted intensely to my active response to her. A very powerful transferential meaning that the intervention had for her was discovered to be associated with the wish, previously warded off, to activate her ineffectual father, who had failed to intervene and stop her mother's abusive behavior. Comparing my behavior to her father's, she reached the anguish, profound disappointment, and rage associated with his passivity, especially in relation to his failure to put an end to her mother's abuse of her. Previously, that disappointment had been grasped only intellectually. It later seemed that it had been necessary for her to repress such feelings in order to maintain the father, as she had maintained me, as a good object. Shielding us from anger and disappointment provided a further basis for her more stable, acceptable, and less toxic, victim identification, associated with a relatively more positive attachment, compared with the internalized angry mother. Anger toward me never became a significant element in the treatment; but following the action-oriented intervention, for the first time, her relationship with her father, and her deeply conflicted feelings toward him, became meaningfully accessible, both to her and to the inquiry.

As a result of these combined interventions, Carrie became able to handle her anger more effectively and comfortably than before. I also observed unexpected gains: she became more fully able to experience and spontaneously express her appreciation and affection toward her child and to respond to her more decisively. Formerly equating maternal participation with destructiveness, she had withheld herself; especially when she and her daughter were in the presence of her husband, she deferred excessively to him, while remaining emotionally distant from the child. As anticipated, improved self-regulation and the enhanced quality of Carrie's parenting combined with other analytic gains to produce strengthened feelings of self-esteem. The analytic work had enhanced the action of the active technique and, in turn, had been enhanced by it.

Specific Technical Considerations

Therapeutic "Choice Points"

Therapeutic choice points (Messer, 1986) mark those moments when a therapist weighs the relative benefits of action-oriented and insight-oriented techniques. Choice points apply to the use of action-oriented techniques in formal or modified forms. They can be framed usefully in terms of whether, for a particular patient and at a particular time, the goals of treatment are best furthered by the continuing exploration alone or by the addition of some action-promoting technique and the exploration that results from it. While an action-oriented approach may be therapeutic for a patient at one point, at another time the same approach might not be in the patient's interests.

A decision to introduce action-oriented techniques into analytic therapy must be based on thoughtful consideration of each patient's overall therapeutic needs, including, especially, the state of the transference-countertransference relationship. In this way, therapists can minimize the risk that, through activity, they may participate in counterproductive enactments—their, and the patient's unconscious, collusive structuring of the interaction that interferes with articulating relational patterns when that can be most useful to the patient. As a check, when the possibility of introducing action-oriented techniques occurs to a therapist, he or she should always first evaluate that possibility as a potential countertransference signal. The impulse to offer an action-oriented technique may have complex and potentially countertherapeutic sources and meanings—among them, projective identifications and the unconscious role relationships the patient may be seeking to establish that generally are more usefully explored and understood rather than enacted.

In thinking about choice points, analytic therapists must avoid thinking dichotomously—that they are working *either* analytically *or* behaviorally. It is not that a technique that points toward action will necessarily close off analytic potentials or block insight; more likely it will create a different (and sometimes richer) avenue toward achieving it. Simply because I have responded actively to a patient's wish for my help with becoming more assertive does not necessarily mean that I will not get to deal with his resistances to being more fully assertive with me and with others, or with conflicts about my unresponsiveness, for example. Whether one frustrates or responds to the patient's needs, there always will be consequences that offer material to be dealt with analytically, provided that the exploration of interactions remains primary and that the patient feels safe to talk openly about his or her experience with the analyst.

The introduction of an action-oriented technique might wisely be held in abeyance until the therapist feels confident that the technique is responsive to the patient's valid therapeutic needs. Over time, one is able to more effectively evaluate indications and contraindications in relation to the shifting clinical and psychodynamic context in which the technique is to be introduced, including the transference-countertransference configurations. One might wonder, for exam-

ple, why do I have the idea of relaxation techniques with this particular patient (and not with another anxious patient) in the first place?
Why does it come up at this particular time? What is the symbolic and
historical meaning of this interaction, and how might my actions fit
into the patient's internalized relational world? Could my activity
here be a response to the patient's passive longings, or an enactment
to avoid the patient's anger at me following a personal failure that
he or she felt reflected poorly on the therapy, for example? Might
my inclination to act here be a countertransferential attempt to take
control or to dominate the patient that originates from my own feeling of threat? How does this action correspond to our agreed-upon
intentions and to the patient's life goals? These are only a few of the
many complex considerations that come into play when one is considering introducing action-oriented techniques into the interactive
matrix. It is only in retrospect that the pair can appreciate some of
the many transferential and countertransferential meanings that
such an intervention may have but that never can be fully understood.

The Analyst's Stance

What distinguishes a stance that facilitates the analytic therapist's use
of action-oriented techniques from a more conventional one?
Analysts who give attention to their patients' actions need not depart
very much from more familiar ways of attending to their patients'
communications. They must, of course, be more sensitive to their
patients' realistic surround, to the personalities and actions of those
who populate it, to the patients' conduct within it, and to the reverberating consequences of individual actions. Under certain conditions, from that balanced stance, analysts may choose to intervene
actively to influence behaviors to help patients achieve important life
goals, as with Carrie. This is done in analytic ways, that is, in a manner considering psychodynamics, resistances, transference, and countertransference, and that seek to promote psychological growth
through awareness and new experience. One must be careful to avoid
counterproductive forms of analytic enactment. But all of this is familiar to experienced analytic therapists.

  As in all analytic approaches, attentive, empathic listening prevails,
enabling the therapist to grasp, in order to clarify, the patient's experience, both with the analyst and with others, that is, as understood
in and through the analyst's subjective reality. There are many times

when the analyst may even immerse himself or herself in the internal experience of the patient. At times, however, he or she also may enter the extrasession reality of the analysand, both introspectively and extrospectively, that is, both feeling his or her way into the patient's experience of interactions and also observing them "from outside" (Wolf, 1988). Here the analyst is concerned not only with the patient's psychic reality but also with practical reality and how the patient interacts with others in the relational world and how they respond; here attention is directed away from narrow applications of empathy and toward an understanding of relationships with others, their settings, and the actions and interactions they involve.

All psychoanalysts attend to patients' overt behaviors; but, from a traditional point of view, patients' behaviors, like other individual expressions, are understood symbolically, primarily as a source of information about the patient's internal psychodynamic processes. What is not necessarily appreciated from the monadic perspective is the specificity of context and its relevance to mental transactions—how the particulars of the relational world elicit particular intrapsychic responses and how the patient, through his or her actions, shapes his or her relational world, including interpersonal feedback patterns that are of psychodynamic consequence. In this extension of the two-person model, one might think of the external relational world as an integral part of the analytic field.

When seeking to influence behavior in positive ways—in teaching a structured technique, for example—the analyst is not just concerned with the patient's behavior with the analyst as a source of psychodynamic material, although it always retains that meaning. The analytic therapist applying action-oriented techniques is concerned with more than an exploration of the meanings and motivations underlying the patient's transferential behavior. He or she also attends to enactments outside of sessions, to the patient's life goals and progress toward them, and to practical, adaptive potentials that might be developed through facilitated behavior changes that the analyst can directly help the patient work toward and integrate within sessions.

When the analyst turns to action-oriented techniques, the active collaboration takes a somewhat different direction, but only partially and temporarily does it reorder the priorities of understanding and behavior change. The analyst's attempts to understand never fully cease, even while he or she is teaching improved skills of assertiveness or relaxation, for example. The goal of the interaction at a particular moment may be to potentiate adaptive behavior or to modify an enactment in the patient's outside life, but in a way that can advance important psychoanalytic goals: the analysis of transference and structural change.

Action-Oriented Techniques, Transference Analysis, and "Working Through"

Action-oriented techniques are introduced with several aims in mind. On the most superficial level, they are intended to promote adaptive behavior. When I say superficial, I do not mean to belittle the importance of this level of impact. It may be highly consequential, as we saw with Carrie, whose improved mothering skills benefited her family life and her feelings about herself. But we saw in that example, too, that the analyst employs these techniques in ways that advance psychological growth by modifying personality organization. Thus there is nothing superficial about the action of the techniques themselves when they are used in these ways. In addition to their embodying constructive interactions that themselves can become internalized, these interventions achieve deeper aims as the patient and analyst deal analytically with the techniques' impact on various levels of the patient's relational matrix (internal as well as external), especially by "working through" new forms of action and feedback.

Superficial changes brought about through the use of action-oriented resources can be integrated analytically, especially in the working-through process, to promote structural change and help the patient move out of closed-system ways of relating. Analysts must clarify, especially, the transferential meanings of learning the technique specifically within the therapy relationship. Ironically, this is a point made by Strachey (1934) (whose work I described in chapter 9) in reasoning why transference interpretations alone are mutative. He explained that extratransference interpretations act as "feeders" for the transference situation and so pave the way for mutative transference interpretations. The introduction of action-oriented techniques is usually uniquely evocative for patients, and the analyst's attention to, and skillful work with, that (transferential) reaction is crucially important for achieving the fullest possible success with these interventions. Like their practical impact, the potential transferential meanings of action-oriented interventions always must be carefully considered beforehand. The transferential meaning an action-oriented technique has for the patient, related to the relational configurations that are formed through the technique's introduction, which may be explored analytically, can be usefully understood, over time, in terms of the patient's relational patterns.

A superficial level of meaning is defined by the intent formed by the analyst's and patient's mutually agreed-upon therapeutic objectives—say, to help the patient manage anger. That goal, based on the analyst's and the patient's best thinking and constructive collaboration, can be understood as an expression of the potentially positive new relationship with the analyst, consistent with therapeutic objectives. The technique is introduced with the patient's explicit agreement that it is responsive to his or her needs. But the intervention will nevertheless be experienced in transferential terms that deviate from that baseline and that are analyzable in relation to that baseline as a reference point. As with any interaction, the countertransference meaning of the intervention involves potentially unconscious elements for the analyst, as well as for the patient, that may come to light only later as the participants engage in the inquiry that follows.

It can be seen, then, that the introduction of action-oriented techniques invokes many psychological processes in the patient that are similar to the patient's responses to more conventional analytic interventions (Wachtel, 1993a). When an analyst interprets or is silent, the patient experiences this action in a manner that corresponds to his or her significant organizing activity and relational patterns. Thus one patient might appreciate the analyst's silence as thoughtful, while another might experience the same behavior anxiously or angrily as an abandonment. Overall, it is little different with action-oriented techniques. The therapist's manifest intentions are stated, but there always remains ambiguity in the experience and actions of others (the therapist). Thus a patient who is taught relaxation, for example, may likewise experience the analyst across a wide range of transferential possibilities—as responsive, manipulative, protective, abandoning, intrusive, or in a variety of ways determined by his or her psychodynamics. These responses, of course, may be analyzed.

Certainly there can be significant problems with an analytic stance that uniformly, consistently, aggressively, or in ill-timed ways exerts influence toward action, in other words, does so nonempathically or *at the price of valuable reflection.* That is where the danger of the analyst's enacting the role of the dominating, intrusive, or ambitious parent might come in, for example. Without a vigilance that seeks to clarify the interaction and the patient's experience of it, any activity of the therapist, including that geared toward having an impact on the patient's actions in the external world, may become nonanalytic and counterproductive. Thus, in using formal action-oriented techniques one can try to teach them gradually, in stages, spaced over many sessions, or otherwise introduce them in ways that enable the pair to remain in touch with, and to analyze, the patient's experience of them.

Action-Oriented Techniques as New Relational Experience: A Failed Application

In working with Carrie, I tried to anticipate the meanings that the active intervention might take on within her internalized relational world. Roughly, I turned out to be correct, correct enough, at least. As I hoped, she experienced my behavior as an act of attentiveness and strong support rather than as proof that she was damaged. But I could not anticipate how intense her reaction would be. My surprise resulted, in part, from my sense of caution in approaching action-oriented techniques; I was more concerned at that time with avoiding detrimental activity (through a counterproductive enactment, or what one-person-model analysts call countertransference enactment) than sensitive to the positive new relational experience (a therapeutic enactment) that our interaction might represent. I would say that Carrie experienced a very important and mutative new relational experience with me; the action-oriented methods combined in a strong and favorable way with the analytic procedures we employed, allowing us to advance her psychological growth.

However, there also may be times when, on the basis of similar reasoning, a therapist might decide not to employ these techniques with a patient. For instance, one patient with a tendency to sexualize others' attentions and to relate in seductive ways aimed at manipulating others' responses, insisted that I teach her methods for relaxation. I felt that, if I were to agree to her demands, I would be allowing myself to be used in a negative, inauthentic way that would repeat problematic aspects of her past and would represent acting *rather than* analyzing. Nor did I wish to respond actively while *simultaneously* analyzing my participation, as I might in another instance. My judgment at the time was that introducing an action-oriented technique would represent giving ground to a manipulation and would violate relational analytic goals of achieving mutual authenticity and intimacy, thus serving her resistance rather than growth. Rather, we analyzed her demands, including my reactions to them, and eventually came to see how the relaxation procedure she desired represented an expression of seductive wishes toward me. (Incidentally, at a later date in the treatment, after aspects around manipulation had been largely righted between us, the patient was able to use certain related methods to advantage.)

Consider an example of how an action-oriented intervention went wrong because the therapist, who lacked adequate training in psychodynamics, did not consider the meanings of the transference-countertransference patterns in relation to the patient's internalized relational world. The patient, a young woman who had been sexually abused by her father in childhood, was supported by her therapist in her wish to confront her father and entire family with this traumatic piece of their history. The therapist became deeply absorbed in helping the patient prepare for the confrontation, so deeply absorbed, in fact, that he lost his analytic bearings. By actively helping the patient "rehearse" for the confrontation, he acted as a coach, which at times can be quite constructive, but only if one remains aware of the many potential levels of symbolic meaning one's actions and the intervention might have for the patient. After this patient precipitously bolted from treatment, the case came to my attention, and the therapist and I attempted to reconstruct what had happened.

We considered several possible reasons for the failure of the technique. First of all, the action-oriented technique may have been ill-conceived from the start. What did the act of confronting her family mean to the patient? It may have been experienced by the patient as an identificatory act, expressing in a retaliatory way the patient's own capacity to abuse. If so, without the patient's getting a grip on that meaning of the experience, the therapist's premature, enthusiastic sponsorship of her taking action would be extremely threatening. What did the transference-countertransference configuration symbolize to the patient? What did it mean to her to confront the entire family, including her mother, who had played a passive role, and a sister who, as far as she knew, had not been abused by the father?

After some exploration, the therapist and I concluded that the act of rehearsing with the patient had not been adequately thought through and probably represented an enactment, a mutually preconscious form of participation that was eventually experienced as profoundly threatening to the patient's internalized bond to her mother. The therapist, working so hard to help and be the good mother, was, without adequate awareness of the implications, acting in precisely the way the patient's mother had failed to act, that is, actively acknowledging and addressing the problem. That basic configuration, which in my interaction with Carrie had developed into a salutary form of new relational experience, here proved disastrous for two possible reasons that we could reconstruct. First, the alliance with the therapist/advocate threatened the patient's loyalties to her failed mother—both the internalized and actual relationship. (The mother would be among those "attacked" in the family confrontation.) Second, an analytic context had not been established in which the pair could explore, consider, understand, and thereby integrate the various meanings of the act of confrontation and its rehearsal, especially the meaning for the patient of the therapist's participation in it. In other words, the therapist did not consider or explore how these external actions might fit into the patient's internal relational world, that is, he did not employ them analytically.

Beyond the practical, adaptive changes that are aimed at, the therapist's introduction of action-oriented interventions ideally involves therapeutic interactions that themselves are adaptive and that represent new relational experience. When the therapist teaches formal relaxation, as when he or she speaks calming words in soothing tones to a patient who is recalling intensely distressing events, it may advance the establishment of a self-calming interaction as the basis of an internalized relational pattern. When the therapist avoids participating in counterproductive enactments and engages constructively when using active techniques, the interactions around the active techniques can offer positive relational experiences, or therapeutic enactments, that may be inherently healing, especially when they are new or contrast with the patient's expectations. Consider a further example of a therapist who calmly and attentively helped a patient to learn skills for overcoming anxiety attacks. The therapist's behavior stood in sharp contrast to that of the patient's anxious, overconcerned mother and his inattentive, scornful father. Since we can never be certain beforehand of a patient's experience of our actions, it is important to analyze the way the patient organizes the meanings of these interventions so as to cultivate their positive meanings.

Introducing Action-Oriented Techniques "Neutrally"

Although aspects of the analyst's "neutral" attitude are extremely important, it becomes clear that, as neutrality is applied to a two-person model, and especially to action-oriented techniques, the traditional concept reaches a conceptual breaking point. If the concept is employed, as in the one-person model, as part of a package requiring that the analyst, in order to facilitate treatment, should conceal his or her personal characteristics so as to remain anonymous, should abstain from gratifying the patient, or should avoid influencing while remaining immune to the patient's influence, then the concept has little or no utility (or even possibility). When analysts align themselves actively with fostering patients' adaptations clearly they are not acting neutrally according to Anna Freud's (1936) equidistance definition. Yet within *all* psychoanalytic approaches, including monadic and dyadic models, essential elements of the analytic process ordinarily included under the rubric of neutrality come into play, and that is also the case in applying action-oriented interventions. These elements include analysts' monitoring and moderating their own experience and participation, avoiding the undue imposition of personal values or their own issues, and trying to guide themselves according to patients' true capacities and life goals, rather than the analyst's own desires. Within a two-person view that sees influence as mutual and asymmetrical and that values the analyst's fuller activity and participation so as to advance an analytic process, the major contribution of analytic neutrality is that it keeps at the forefront of the analyst's critical awareness the need for a balance between constructive participation, on one hand, and self-monitoring, on the other. That undertaking includes the analyst's efforts to remain as aware as possible of his or her actions, how they relate to the patient's, and the impact of the analyst's personality and actions on the patient.

How can one integrate formal action-oriented techniques "neutrally?" One way that a respect is shown for the patient's autonomy, abilities, and life goals is through the empathic manner in which action-oriented techniques are introduced. Here the therapist minimizes the taking of initiative from the patient. After careful reflection on the psychodynamics, transference-countertransference configurations, and reality considerations of the patient, the technique under consideration is first described to the patient as a potential resource. The therapist might say something like, "There's a behavioral technique that you might find helpful. Let me describe it to you and we can see whether you're interested in learning more about it." Without further pressure from the therapist, the patient is then helped to decide whether or not he or she wishes to learn and subsequently employ the method. Often, even when these techniques are rejected by the patient, the possibility of action techniques alone stimulates important associative material and highlights resistances, the analysis of which may advance the therapy.

Once mastered, the patient's application of action-oriented techniques remains largely a matter for the patient to manage. This attitude applies alike to the patient's initial agreement to undertake these techniques and to the subsequent decision to apply them, which recognizes the patient's autonomy. Although, as in exploring all resistances, the therapist continues to show an interest in the fate of these techniques, trying to understand why the patient might have failed to use them in a situation in which they might have been helpful, nevertheless the therapist avoids becoming too invested in behavior change or whether or not the patient draws on the techniques. Instead, the patient's use, misuse, or failure to use the techniques provides additional clinical and therapeutic material that may be used to illuminate the dynamics and the transference.

Discovering a Resource in Cognitive-Behavior Therapy

Interventions pointed toward action can take many forms, some quite subtle and others more formal and structured. Subtle interventions that facilitate new action are pervasive in analytic technique and may involve suggestion. For instance, all analysts can appreciate the suggestive implications of a question like, "What do you imagine might happen if you were to say something about that to her?", which is laden with suggestive elements. In another example, Mitchell (1993) described exploring with a patient why a particular, obvious course of action had not occurred to him.

To consider the more formal sorts of action-oriented methods that analysts might apply in their work, let us turn to cognitive-behavior therapy where we find a number of structured techniques that analysts might draw from to enhance their work. Let us consider the modality of cognitive-behavior therapy itself before examining some specific techniques that might be used analytically. Strictly cognitive interventions might be grouped on two levels: those which seek superficially to modify a person's conscious thought processes and ideation, and those which seek to modify underlying cognitive structures. An example of the former is teaching a patient adaptive coping statements or deliberate "self-talk" for self-calming to replace counterproductive, anxiety-provoking internal dialogue. (Carrie used a coping statement, "What is it I *really* want to accomplish here?", to manage anger.)

Cognitive "restructuring" is the basic cognitive technique for modifying underlying schemas. The term is derived from the therapies proposed by Beck (Beck et al., 1979), Ellis (1973), and Meichenbaum (1977). It involves a variety of therapeutic approaches whose major mode of action is modifying the patient's thinking and the premises, assumptions, and attitudes underlying those cognitions. The goal, following a rationalist model, is to help the patient identify specific misconceptions, distortions, and maladaptive attributions and to test their validity and reasonableness (Meichenbaum, 1977). Promoting an "empirical" or "scientific" attitude through a guided examination of the available evidence, cognitive therapists help patients test the validity of their automatic thoughts as conclusions. According to Beck and his associates (1979), "The essence of reality testing is to enable the person to correct his distortions. An analysis of meaning and attitudes exposes the unreasonableness and self-defeating nature of the attitudes" (p. 155).

There are difficulties integrating a rationalist cognitive model of this kind with the relational, or relational-constructivist, stance (Frank, 1993a). Specifically, analytic techniques typically seek to expand and elaborate the subjective expressions of the patient and to understand their basis in the patient's constructions, whereas rationalist cognitive techniques involve a persuasive attempt to directly influence the patient's beliefs and thought processes through reason. It is as though the therapist has an appreciation of reality that always is "realer" than the patient's. Recent psychoanalytic formulations acknowledging perspectival realism cannot easily be reconciled with a stance resulting in a therapist's efforts to "correct distorted cognitions." That is not to say that relational analysts cannot help patients "reality-test"; but reality testing becomes a dialectical comparison between a patient's and a therapist's constructed realities, rather than a therapist's rationality and a patient's irrationality. The constructivist influence that has recently developed in cognitive therapy (Guidano and Liotti, 1986; Guidano, 1991; Mahoney, 1991, for example) helps to overcome this limitation by offering a greater compatibility with the relational psychoanalytic approach. More like the analytic view, constructivist cognitive approaches also do not concentrate narrowly on modifying target behaviors or symptoms.

Wachtel (1997) has taken the position that rationalist forms of cognitive therapy such as the approaches of Ellis and Beck have contributed only modestly to the evolution of psychotherapy integration. I agree that that is the case when we assess the treatment benefits occurring at the deepest structural levels. Cognitive formulations, compared with psychodynamic ones, tend to be too narrow in their grasp of the complexity of personality functioning, and these interventions, too intellectual. It has been my experience, however, that, even when they are taken at the surface level, the most superficial cognitive strategies, such as coping statements to promote new behaviors, sometimes can be used with analytic ones in ways that help to promote deep change (as we saw with Carrie).

In cognitive-behavior therapy, as distinct from strict cognitive therapy, cognitive restructuring and other structured methods are integrated with behavioral techniques. Following the assumption that behavioral alterations can lead to cognitive change and vice versa, this technical integration emphasizes the therapeutically useful interplay between behavior change and insight. The major arena of change is the lessons learned as the patient applies to real life the exercises developed in the therapy, rather than direct interactions with the therapist, as in the analytic model.

Typically, *planned homework assignments* in the form of "behavioral experiments" are collaboratively developed. These activities are intended to help patients recognize, test, and ultimately revise dysfunctional interpretations or expectations associated with underlying schemas, to cope more effectively, and to develop new behavior patterns in their outside lives. For example, a patient who holds the maladaptive belief that he will be rejected if he is assertive may be asked by the therapist to apply assertive skills he has learned in sessions in specific situations and then to carefully monitor the responses to it; the hope is that he will learn that his assumptions and fears are erroneous and will go on to refine these skills. As part of an active psychoanalytic approach the analyst might also encourage the patient to undertake carefully timed and developed "assignments" that organically and empathically develop from the analytic work and then analyze and work through their consequences.

Self-monitoring techniques are frequently employed by cognitive-behavior therapists to clarify clinical phenomena and to chart patients' progress.[2] A patient might agree to maintain an ongoing, written record of the occurrence or nonoccurrence of a predefined

---

2. The reader interested in learning more about self-monitoring and other techniques reported in this section may wish to refer to Barlow and Cerny (1988).

behavior or symptom: for example, when it occurred, where, with whom, and what he or she was thinking and feeling at the time. Although analytic therapists may at first feel awkward asking patients to perform tasks such as keeping diaries, they can be used analytically, as in the example of Carrie. A further example of the value of this technique is found in integrative work with a patient who had anger outbursts dangerously disruptive to his professional responsibilities. He was highly intelligent, but because of anxiety-based cognitive difficulties with focusing and memory, the dynamics of his anger were difficult to clarify using analytic methods of transference-countertransference analysis alone. And characterizations of his relationships with others were obscured by his specific deficits. Thus it was very difficult for both of us to gain insight into the sources of the patient's anger episodes. However, a detailed diary helped to clarify the contextual and experiential aspects of the patient's anger in situations outside of treatment. The diary, which included not only his observations but also *verbatim* thoughts, demonstrated explicitly how the patient was perceiving defensive, "bullying" aspects of himself in others and thus personalizing otherwise innocuous situations that he read as threatening to his sense of importance. Moreover, the process of diary-keeping, while creating distance, also strengthened this patient's capacity for self-observation and, thus, self-control in these anger-filled, threatening situations.

Through diary-keeping, another resistive, adolescent young woman who episodically mutilated her arms and wrists with a razor, and for whom it was difficult to articulate her experience, was able to identify that such episodes always followed conflict with, and resulting rage toward, her mother. Similarly, an otherwise high-functioning man in his sixties experienced psychotic-like outbursts of rage during which he railed aloud at imagined, "unfair" authorities. He viewed these episodes as "crazy," yet could not control them. Usually, the rages occurred in solitary moments, while shaving in front of a mirror, for example, or at other times when immersed in fantasy, but he occasionally would slip into these episodes within earshot of others, with such outbursts resulting in a deep sense of humiliation. So dissociated was his behavior that even with extreme effort he was unable to recall the rages in sufficient detail to examine their antecedents or contents. Self-monitoring through diary keeping helped to counter dissociative trends and to facilitate sharpened recall so the rages could be more fully explored and understood in sessions. Moreover, attempts to monitor these outbursts through diary-keeping provided a way of becoming aware of the rages early in their development, thereby helping to bring them under the patient's conscious control. In this instance, as in the earlier example, monitoring, alone, had direct therapeutic benefits.

Keeping a diary between sessions can benefit certain patients by helping them gather material for their sessions and can help others by promoting a continuity between the work of sessions and their lives outside, even encouraging them to apply the insights of sessions. Overall, diary keeping can help certain analytic patients become more aware of their inner lives and feelings and can sensitize them to the reactions of others. Many patients suffering from hysterical defensive styles experience psychogenic cognitive impairments of memory, concentration, and global or diffuse thinking, for example (Shapiro, 1965). Others, relying on extensive dissociation, or who suffer with attention deficits, also lack self-reflective ability. In an analytic context, some of these patients might be helped by formal self-monitoring techniques such as diaries to help focus themselves and to "get in touch" with their inner lives. These techniques can sensitize patients to cognitive and affective experiences, facilitating the process of problem-clarification and self-awareness.

Another adult patient could be treated for just one year by a student therapist. He was fixated in the paranoid-schizoid mode of experiencing and was profoundly attached to his mother, with whom he lived, virtually without boundaries. His therapy was thought to be promoting, iatrogenically, an exclusive attachment to the therapist, similar to that with the mother; apart from sessions, the patient stopped going out of the house altogether and spent much of his time writing fiction. The therapist resourcefully employed the patient's interest in writing and a diary to encourage the patient to venture into the world. The "dialogue" he thereby maintained with himself about his experiences fostered his exposure (see below) to frightening new experiences and thus the process of individuation. In this instance, the therapist chose not to discuss the diary entries with the patient but instead encouraged him to retain them as a part of his "private" life. Often the diary format alone promotes insight by permitting the patient to gain distance from his thoughts and ways of organizing experience, and to recognize that the reality of the moment is not absolute, immutable, or unalterable but, rather, is something that is constructed. In enhancing skills of self-observation, formal self-monitoring techniques also promote a sense of personal agency.

A therapist's assigning self-monitoring can be experienced, within the transference, in a variety of ways. One patient's subsequent noncompliance with a collaboratively developed homework assignment was clearly her defiant way of proving that the therapist could not gain control over her. Another's conscientiously prepared and typewritten diary was my initial, first-hand introduction to her perfectionism, related to her need always to be the best—in this instance, my best patient. When I first began to experiment with self-monitoring, I asked a passive patient to undertake a diary-keeping task to help him overcome procrastination, which was a major issue. He was to record the thoughts and feelings that came up as he approached an avoided task. I should have known better than to experience surprise when he kept putting off completing the assignment. When we explored his procrastination, which came directly into our relationship as a result of the action-oriented technique, I learned of his anxiety that I would see how dull he was and then would become critical and rejecting—a fear that had inhibited him throughout his life.

Ever since Wolpe's (1958) development of an abbreviated application of clinical *relaxation training* for systematic desensitization, this technique has had an enormous impact on the field of cognitive-behavior therapy. Although there are many distinct clinical relaxation procedures, progressive relaxation training, discovered by Edmund Jacobson (1929), probably has the broadest clinical utility. Relaxation practice can be effective in treating a wide range of problems, including sleep disturbances, headache, hypertension, neuromuscular tension, some forms of anxiety, and poor anger control (Lichstein, 1988). Because these self-calming techniques usually can be learned in a matter of weeks and have such broad applicability, they have become a sort of aspirin in the hands of many cognitive-behavior therapists. Combined with other methods, such as controlled breathing, relaxation protocols have been expanded for the successful treatment of panic disorder (Barlow and Cerny, 1988).

Exposure therapy is another widely used behavioral technique. According to Marks (1981), who described the application of this procedure to phobias, "the phobic is persuaded to enter and stay in his or her phobic situation until he or she feels better, and to do this repeatedly until it becomes so customary that it holds no more terrors" (p. 45). Exposure can be imaginal or actual, as we saw in visualized and real rehearsals with Carrie. All forms of exposure often are combined with other cognitive and behavioral techniques, such as *response prevention* to treat compulsive rituals. Here the assumption is that, if a conditioned response is withheld, its strength will diminish. In compulsive hand washing, for example, the compulsive act of washing is prevented and the person is forced to deal with and master the anxiety that drives it (such as contamination anxiety). In treating obsessive-compulsive disorder, the technique of response prevention requires that the therapist act as an enforcer of sorts; the technique therefore is not readily compatible with an empathic analytic stance. However, I have described how exposure with response prevention was used analytically to help a patient overcome a behavior pattern of striking out in anger, to master her feelings of anxiety, and to gain control of her behavior associated with rejection (Frank, 1990).

Systematic desensitization is another combined application of exposure therapy. Here active exposure to the problem is gradual, providing the patient with an opportunity to accomplish mastery at lower levels of challenge before taking on higher levels of threat. (I used a hierarchical approach of this kind with Carrie.) Exposure techniques like "implosion" and "flooding" are extreme; they are unlikely to conform to the empathic requirements of the psychoanalytic setting.

Analytic Therapy, Psychological and Behavioral Skills

Typically, analysts address motivational issues—not coping skills. Yet recent attention to the interaction between motivational factors and skills, largely neglected by analysts in the past, suggests that analytic treatment often can be enhanced when accompanied by interventions that supplement patients' behavioral as well as psychological capabilities. Many analysts (for example, Basch, 1988; Gedo, 1988a,b; Lichtenberg, 1989; Lichtenberg et al., 1992) have recognized the importance of the patient's fundamental motivational need for exploration, competence, and mastery and have shown how those needs contribute to the development of self-esteem. Levenson (1983) also noted that deficient semiotic skills play a major role in personality disturbances and can be improved through analytic therapy.

Gedo (1988a,b) has suggested that maladaptive behavior produced by the repetition of response patterns developed in early childhood can be distinguished from similar behaviors that result from the failure of a person, for whatever reason, to acquire essential psychological skills; such failure Gedo called "apraxia." Although motivational factors and skills, with their reverberating effects, may be quite difficult to separate from one another clinically, Gedo, meaningfully, has nevertheless identified the important contributing role of *skills deficits* in impaired psychological functioning. His work suggests that, once a holding environment is established, analysts often need to address not only underlying motivational factors but also competencies and skills. Among the deficits of certain patients, Gedo described an inability to conduct attentive, expressive conversation, to identify one's own feelings, to trust one's own perceptions, and to effectively plan a course of action. Actual skills deficits may result from particular internalized relational patterns as well as help shape them.

If the analyst is sensitive to marginal deficits, and especially if the patient has a talent for action, such skills can be conveyed readily and informally. All it may take is something like an analyst's pointing out a patient's apparent lack of enthusiasm in expressing an idea that he or she feels strongly about to a group of colleagues, for example. With patients suffering from apraxia, however, an analysis may well bog down as the result of pronounced skills deficiencies, in which case no amount of interpretation and psychoanalytic insight can have a significant effect. Here open-ended exploration offers the patient far less traction than a specific focus on deficits and how to cope with them, sometimes through homework and active techniques, such as role playing, integrated with the analytic process.

Many skills deficits that impede an analysis can be taught in structured ways (see, e.g., Goldfried, Decenteceo, and Weinberg, 1974; Meichenbaum, 1977). These skills and behaviors include simple actions like initiating conversations and making requests and more complex ones like negotiating, managing employees, and public speaking. Even leadership is a performing art, and much of it can be taught, especially to talented students. Assertiveness (Galassi and Galassi, 1978; Jacubowski and Lange, 1978; Masters et al., 1987), sound problem-solving skills (Meichenbaum, 1977), and psychological skills such as self-calming (Lichstein, 1988) also can be taught. In addition, teachable skills can alleviate psychological symptoms, such as panic disorder (Barlow and Cerny, 1988) and anger management difficulties (Novaco, 1975; Deffenbacher and Stark, 1992).

Modifying Formal Behavioral-Cognitive Techniques for Analytic Therapy

As an analyst in training I was reproached by a supervisor for allowing a patient to make use of his journal in treatment. The supervisor explained to me that keeping and reporting on a journal was too intellectual and distracted the patient from transference-analytic work. Yet it has become clear to me that the technique of diary-keeping and also behavioral experiments often lend themselves quite readily to, and can empower, analytic ways of working, especially when one is working with patients with limited capacities for self-reflection and for applying the insights of sessions to outside life. While prescriptive applications clearly are doomed to fail, and clinical judgment must always play a significant role in the therapist's functioning, certain of these action-oriented techniques, properly administered, can be more readily integrated than others. On the other hand, certain techniques, such as relaxation training, must be applied more sparingly, depending on clinical considerations. And applying exposure therapy with response prevention, which often requires a therapist's narrow symptomatic focus and enforcement rather than empathy, often creates significant difficulty in working analytically.

Sound clinical work always requires that the therapist tailor the process to the individual patient. In so doing, the therapist draws on a repertoire of skills in sensitively shaped and timed ways that match the clinical requirements of specific moments. Rather than applying action-oriented techniques in their fully structured, and often programmatic, forms, therefore, analytic therapists often can modify these techniques to suit particular situations. As in the example of Carrie, these techniques may be abbreviated, condensed, spread out over many sessions, or otherwise adapted to harmonize with the analytic process and particular patients' needs, without losing their effectiveness.

Certain key concepts from cognitive-behavior therapy (rather than specific techniques) also can be selectively incorporated into analytic strategies. For instance, the analytic therapist who recognizes the advantages of the cognitive-behavior therapist's exposure therapy might, like a behaviorally oriented colleague, encourage patients, at the right time, to initiate certain specific actions; but, although analysts might wish to promote favorable practical developments, they also would encourage such behavior with the anticipation of developing rich material for analytic sessions. In the same vein, taking a page from the cognitive-behavior therapist's treatment manual for obsessive-compulsive disorder, which involves response prevention, the analytic therapist might actively discourage obsessional patients from dissipating anxiety through compulsive actions, even develop strategies for doing so, and instead encourage them to experience, examine, and master that anxiety with the analyst. As another example, in working with phobically anxious patients, thinking in terms of anxiety hierarchies, or what cognitive-behavior therapists call graded exposure, leads analysts to encourage patients to seek out those outside experiences that maximize the chances of patients' meeting with success while minimizing the chances of a setback through failure. Once less challenging situations have been mastered, then the therapist might build on those more limited successes and gradually help the patient master more stressful conditions.

"Seamless" Integration

By "seamless" integration, I refer to interventions in which the boundaries between insight-oriented and action-oriented techniques become indistinguishable. Here, the threads of the integrative intervention become seamlessly woven together in "a mode of working that is *at once* psychoanalytic and active, that aims to explore and understand *and* to help the patient give shape to his yearnings in ways that render them more realizable" (Wachtel, 1993a, p. 600). Seamless forms of integration, which analytically oriented therapists seem able to apply far more comfortably than formal methods, recognize that the progressive edge of structural change is not necessarily found in the activities of the psychoanalytic situation alone, but in new and constructive actions that may occur outside as well as within the analyst's office. With an awareness of the integral role that behavior change can play in structural change, the analytic therapist can find many occasions for introducing such integrative techniques.

Consider the example of an intervention I used in treating a patient I will call John. John's experience with his father was quite dramatic. As an only child, he had been very close to his father during his early years. He idolized his father and felt his strong, positive participation in his daily development, especially in athletics like playing ball and cycling. When John reached early adolescence, he began to come into his own and to distinguish himself at school socially, athletically, and academically. At that time, a series of events occurred, and, quite precipitously, the parents divorced; the father left the home. Angry and devastated, John felt that he had been abandoned by his coach, ally, companion, and inspiration. The quality of the father and son relationship never again would be the same, and over the years, especially with the father's remarriage, the two drifted apart. At that time, John and I now realized, he fell into a depression; he came to see himself no longer as a "star," as he recalled his standing in seventh grade, but as a high school "cutup" and "clown." He managed to rebound and do fairly well in college, although clearly he did not perform up to potential. Now, just out of college, he sought therapy for the first time because he felt unable to "get into" his job.

During the course of therapy, John was passed over for an assignment, one that he was uniquely qualified for and that through our work together he had come to permit himself to want very much. In addition to dealing with his feelings about this disappointment, we very carefully reviewed what had happened and what he might have done to bring it about. We discovered how the seeds of the rejection probably lay in his interactions with his direct supervisor. John felt extremely conflicted toward the supervisor; he admired him a great deal, but while drawn to him he also found himself feeling extremely intimidated by him. We discovered that, paradoxically, in his anxiety John had been shielding his special qualifications for this particular assignment from the supervisor. Forming what I would call a seamlessly integrated intervention—one that would promote exploration and insight and also encourage action in ways that might enable him more adequately to fulfill his life goals, I said to him, "It sounds as though you may have been afraid to show him your capability in the way you've been daring to show it to others lately, out of the fear that if you really are good—too good, a star—you probably will lose this father's new-found support." I am describing a specific intervention here, but it is worth noting that the theme it captures was a central one, both in the transference and outside, in John's treatment.

Let us examine several elements of this intervention. First of all, it encouraged John's adaptive action, specifically, expressing his capabilities in an appropriate way. The intervention also recognized and reinforced the behavioral gains John recently had made ("the way you've been daring to show others lately") and framed them in a way that could absorb the setback and encourage his continued new action. The intervention also called John's attention to the role of anxiety and his fear of repeated disappointment ("You may have been afraid . . . ") in this maladaptive pattern. Crucially, the intervention linked the current, self-protective interaction with the supervisor with the pivotal internalized relationship with the father and the historic role of the father's abandonment, which John imagined his success had brought on. The anxiety is the key element that John picked up on and that we then worked with in the session.

In my experience, analytic therapists who integrate action-oriented methods generally progress from discrete toward seamlessly integrative ways of working. At first analysts may find the idea of their initiatives difficult to balance with analytic orientations. Homework assignments, for example, do not always blend easily with an analytic manner of working that emphasizes patients' initiatives. But after they apply action-oriented techniques in formal ways and become convinced of the efficacy of mediated behavior change, analytic therapists are apt to see the value of an emphasis on action in working analytically. Extending the implications of a two-person model, therapists can actively potentiate the action dimension in personality change, thereby heightening the experiential elements of their analytic methods, often through very real, practical gains in their patients' daily lives, while simultaneously enhancing the analytic relationship and transference analysis and deepening the results of treatment.

CHAPTER 11

FOCUSED INTEGRATIVE PSYCHOTHERAPY

*W*hen polled directly, a great many analytic therapists state that long-term treatment is the modality of choice for most patients. Yet how do these clinicians reconcile their position with the surprising finding of large studies like the National Medical Expenditures Survey (Olfson and Pincus, 1994), with its sample of 38,000 individuals, that the vast majority of Americans (84%) do not continue beyond the 20th session of psychotherapy? It behooves analytic therapists, especially in the current social, political, and economic climate, to give attention to short-term forms of treatment. I realize that many analysts have turned summarily from this challenge, protesting against the very destructive aspects of shortened therapies, especially as they are imposed by HMOs and managed care organizations. Other practitioners, however, find interest in these applications, as do I, for several reasons unrelated to managed-care practice. A major one is to avoid repeating the errors of the past; mainstream analysts of the 1960s, for example, rejected Alexander's contributions out of hand, including those of value. The principles of personality change and clinical efficacy are to be learned from short-term as well as long-term methods, from cognitive-behavior therapy as from psychoanalysis, and from other modalities as well, with which this book is not directly concerned. What is crucial is that analysts not approach brief therapy models with the idea of displacing longer term work but to enrich and empower it, as well as to extend therapists' clinical efficacy in instances when only short-term treatment possibilities exist. Focused integrative psychotherapy synthesizes traditional analytic insights with those of time-limited and cognitive-behavior therapies.[1]

Background

There is nothing new about the idea of shortening psychotherapy.[2] Concerns with the length of treatment developed with Freud (1919), who as early as 1918, following World War I, astutely anticipated short-term developments when he said:

> It is very probable, too, that the large-scale application of our therapy will compel us to alloy the pure gold of analysis freely with the copper of direct suggestion. . . . But, whatever form this psychotherapy for the people may take, whatever the elements out of which it is compounded, its most effective and most important ingredients will assuredly remain those borrowed from strict and untendentious psycho-analysis [p. 168].

We have seen that Ferenczi, and later Alexander and French, provoked intense resistance and controversy when they attempted to accelerate treatment by activating the analyst. We saw, too, that, historically, a segregation has long existed between analytic and cognitive-behavior therapies (chapter 9). A similar separation has been maintained between advocates of long-term analytic treatment and short-term psychodynamic treatment approaches, and as in the past, it is not only psychoanalysts who are responsible for this separation. The bold claims of many proponents of brief therapy have done little to promote rapprochement.

Malan (1980), for example, in his zeal for the short-term approach, likened its significance to that of Freud's discovery of the unconscious, and, in 1976, saw Davanloo's work as "destined to . . . revolutionize both the practice and the scientific status of dynamic psychotherapy within the next 10 years" (p. 20).

Whether or not Malan's enthusiastic prophecy was realized is questionable. In any event, such claims leave us with a question: If brief therapy can accomplish so much in so short a time, then how does

---

1. Since elements of cognitive-behavior therapy were discussed in chapter 10, I do not discuss them further in this chapter.
2. Many efforts to shorten analytic therapy involve forms of psychotherapy integration. For a historical review see Goldfried and Newman (1992).

one make the case for long-term therapy? One answer was provided by Davanloo (1978) when he noted that only about one-quarter in his research of screened patients (130 of 575) were found appropriate for this modality. Nonetheless, responsible analytic observers such as Wolberg (1980) have noted that in the majority of instances, patients seeking psychotherapy can achieve satisfactory results working short-term and, from a perspective emphasizing cost effectiveness, that all patients might be viewed as potential candidates for short-term therapy before longer term methods are undertaken. The data supporting Wolberg's observation, including considerable empirical evidence for the effectiveness of short-term approaches, are nevertheless mixed. Messer and Warren (1995), summarizing an array of studies, concluded, in the most general terms, that, while the percentage of persons helped tends to increase with the duration of therapy and long-term therapy offers greater breadth of change, time-limited therapy is helpful to a substantial proportion of patients—as helpful and lasting as time-unlimited therapy in many of its effects. The time clearly has come for analytic therapists to thoughtfully and seriously explore ways in which the insights and methods of different modalities, including brief psychodynamic therapy, might be combined to empower and accelerate their work.

Brief Psychodynamic Therapy

Brief psychodynamic therapy represents a tradition in its own right. Among the most prominent contributors to this approach are Balint (Balint, Ornstein, and Balint, 1972), Malan (Malan and Osimo, 1992), Sifneos (1992), Davanloo (1978, 1980), Wolberg (1980), Mann (1992), Strupp and Binder (1984), and Luborsky (1984).[3] The distinction between one-person and two-person models of treatment, so meaningful in understanding the differences among psychoanalytic approaches, applies to short-term treatment paradigms as well. Malan, Davanloo, and Sifneos offer methodologies developed within a one-person model; they emphasize conflicts between intrapsychic processes, such as drive derivatives and ego defenses. Two-person model approaches to brief therapy like those of Luborsky and Strupp and

---

3. Because I cannot review all the brief therapy approaches comprehensively here, I have provided one or two recent references for each. In addition to primary sources, the interested reader may wish to examine the more extensive review by Messer and Warren (1995).

Binder, grew out of relational theories and emphasize interpersonal conflicts such as those between interpersonal wishes and feared outcomes. Two-person model interventions, extending the field of action of the therapy beyond the consulting room in a manner compatible with that proposed in this book, are concerned with recurrent patterns of maladaptive behavior and, specifically, how they are maintained in the interactions of the individual. A third group of theorists (Mann, for example) espouse a hybrid model. As with long-term treatment, the differences between one-person and the two-person models are meaningful.

Patient Selection

Many authors have specified a range of selection criteria to identify patients who are likely to respond well to their approaches. Essentially, these are patients who are able to engage in short-term treatment rapidly and constructively and then terminate therapy expeditiously. In selecting patients, some theorists emphasize specific psychiatric syndromes and psychodynamic diagnoses; others stress personal characteristics, especially patients' motivation for therapy. Overall, diagnostic factors seem less adequate as predictors of outcome than how well, empirically, a person responds to treatment. Thus a prospective patient's response to a preliminary trial of therapy is highly valued by virtually all contemporary practitioners of brief therapy.

Some therapists select only high-functioning persons. Sifneos (1992), for example, selected patients possessing notable ego strength and ruled out those with severe pathology for his "short-term anxiety-provoking psychotherapy." For STAPP, people must be strongly and realistically motivated in order to do well. They must have a good history of object relations and be intelligent, psychologically minded, insightful, introspective, and curious about themselves. Another favorable prognostic sign, related to the talent for action, is a patient's willingness to experiment with adaptive behaviors. In a trial of therapy, patients who respond actively, who are able to identify and work effectively within a single focus, who have a constructive response to trial interpretations, and who seem flexible, with a capacity to experience, tolerate, and express feelings, also are seen as having favorable prognoses. Clearly, these are the same people who would do well in full-scale psychoanalysis and, probably, in any form of psychotherapy.

Other brief therapists are less selective and are willing to treat a broader range of patients. Malan (Malan and Osimo, 1992), for example, although willing to treat people who were not necessarily highly integrated, excluded those with "complex" or "deep-seated" pathology that might have been associated with a potential for psychotic, depressive, or suicidal breakdowns. Malan also ruled out patients with gross acting out, substance abuse problems, or unsupportive environments. For Malan, a trial of therapy must provide the therapist with a clear grasp of the patient's psychodynamics and reveal the patient's favorable response to interpretation, especially in the focal area. Wolberg (1980) described three distinct "classes" of short-term therapy patients, each with a particular configuration of symptomatic, behavioral, and characterological features corresponding to different treatment needs and methods. Together with patients' motivation, Strupp and Binder (1984), in their "time-limited dynamic therapy," like Luborsky (1984), stressed as selection factors a patient's ability to frame the problem in terms of interpersonal relationships and to form a mature, trusting relationship, or alliance, with the therapist.

The Dynamic Focus

Following the seminal work of Thomas French (1958, 1970), most brief analytic therapists define and limit their therapeutic objectives through the delineation of a dynamic focus. In working through focal problems, patients gain mastery over a significant problem area in their lives. Interpreted in various ways, the concept of a focus remains central in virtually all contemporary systems, since most therapists assume they must narrow the scope of the work in order to assure the most efficient use of time. The dynamic focus usually involves a formulation about a circumscribed, ongoing adaptive problem and its relation to early experience and to a historical, underlying conflict. It is responsive to the questions: What is a dynamic understanding, or working model, of the patient's problem in functioning that has brought this patient to treatment? How does that understanding illuminate the most relevant, efficient treatment?

The dynamic focus may take many forms. Based on practitioners' own theoretical orientations and the patients with whom they work, theorists define different problem areas in terms of specific underlying conflicts and therapeutic strategies. For Sifneos (1992), for example, the focus is to involve a triangular, or oedipal, conflict. But for Davanloo (1978, 1980) the focus also might be preoedipal; in fact, Davanloo is willing to address more than one focus in a single treatment. In Balint et al.'s (1972) "focal psychotherapy" there were "focal *aims*," which, developed from a psychodynamic formulation, served as a beacon to the therapist in guiding a reparative therapeutic interaction that strongly emphasized the patient's new relational experience with the therapist. For Mann (1992), the focus stresses empathy and addresses the patient's "chronic and current pain," related to a negative self-image. He also stresses the impact of termination. For Strupp and Binder (1984), the focus is a salient cyclical psychodynamic pattern. It is framed as a working model, a focal narrative, rather than an absolute truth. Similarly, Luborsky (1984) describes a tripartite "core conflictual relationship theme" as the focus; it involves a person's wish, need, or intention (e.g., to be accepted), a response from the other (e.g., rejection), and a response of the self (e.g., anger). This theme captures the central pattern, script, or schema that each individual follows in conducting relationships.

Although many brief therapists insist on defining a clear focus at the time of the initial evaluation, others identify the focus gradually through an interpretive theme that is thought to crystalize over several sessions. Strupp and Binder (1984), like Wolberg (1980), emphasize that refining the focus is the actual work of the therapy. For these authors, the focus operates as a guiding heuristic that gains meaning and credibility as the work progresses; when the focus no longer has explanatory power and fails to act as a source of useful strategy, another, more plausible focus may be substituted.

The Contract

Most brief therapists establish a "contract" with patients early in treatment. Typically, this agreement makes explicit that treatment will be brief and will be limited to the defined focus. There are many differences in the specific arrangements that particular practitioners establish. Mann (1992), for example, in whose view the termination process plays a central therapeutic role, always specifies, in the initial interview, the exact number of sessions (12) and a definitive date of termination. In this way, interruptions, such as planned vacations and holidays, are specifically anticipated. Mann initially defines a "central issue" with the patient, with the understanding that it can be modified as treatment proceeds. Sifneos (1992) first states that the treatment will last "several months" (actually, 12 to 20 sessions). Like Davanloo (1978, 1980) (for whom treatment lasts 5 to 40 sessions), he does not prescribe a precise duration or termination date in advance, but during the initial evaluation he does clearly inform the patient of the brevity and narrow focus of treatment. Like many cognitive-behavior therapists, Wolberg (1980) was clear with patients at the outset that therapy required their active effort, including homework, in order to translate insights into action. Wolberg also stressed that the patient must continue with deliberate therapeutic work after treatment formally ended. While practitioners like Malan and Osimo (1992) and Wolberg permit and even encourage subsequent meetings after termination, others, like Mann (1992) and Sifneos (1992), make clear, initially, that there must be no further contact after the final session.

Technique

Generally speaking, brief-therapy strategies, especially those following a one-person model, promote rapid insight into the area of focal distress and thus help patients get in touch with "true" feelings. Therapists also provide reparative interpersonal experiences and facilitate improved adaptations, especially those following a two-person model. Although the duration of such treatments ranges from 5 to 40 sessions, most authors seem to favor 10 to 20. Technique is active, with virtually all brief therapies implemented once, sometimes twice, a week, with therapist and patient seated face to face. The therapist guides the patient by selectively keeping the work on the focus. While technique is, in this sense, directive, giving advice usually is eschewed.

Another common form of directiveness is encouragement of a patient's adaptive behaviors. Wolberg (1980), for example, encouraged deliberate behavior change and capitalized on cognitive and behavioral elements of the change process by explicitly teaching a "more constructive life philosophy." Mann (1992) and Wolberg (1980) advise the use of suggestion; a confident demeanor is intended to promote patients' hope and encourage their expectations that the therapeutic pair can achieve a great deal together in a short time.

As in traditional psychoanalysis, the material of the therapy includes the patient's associations, memories, fantasies, dreams, and the like, with the process understood through such traditional conceptualizations as transference, resistance, and interpretation. This material contributes to the therapist's psychodynamic understanding of the patient's psychological functioning, sometimes at profound levels; but in formulating interventions, most brief therapists emphasize the present, pointing their comments toward relatively superficial, derivative levels related to the focus. In contrast, Malan (Malan and Osimo,

1992) and Sifneos (1992), operating in a one-person model, suggest that deep and correct interpretations of forbidden content sometimes can be offered early on in treatment.

Transference interpretations, highly valued in most brief dynamic therapy systems, are employed both to safeguard the working alliance, so crucial if working in a confrontive manner, and to provide insight. Some therapists advise using transference interpretations early; others use them only when they judge transference to have become a resistance. Interventions may be employed to elaborate the connections among the present, the transference, and past experience (Malan and Osimo's, 1992, "triangle of person"), relating them to defenses, anxiety, and underlying impulses ("triangle of conflict"). For Sifneos (1992) and Davanloo (1978, 1980), there is a relentless, confrontive chipping away at the patient's defenses in order to reveal underlying anxiety and conflict. Here the atmosphere is often provocative, tense, and pressured. Others, like Balint et al. (1972), Mann (1992), Strupp and Binder (1984), and Wolberg (1980), while perhaps applying a degree of therapeutic pressure to move things along, through exhortation and confrontation, for example, also emphasize the need for a supportive, warm, and empathic therapeutic atmosphere. Numerous strategies help to prevent the formation of a crystalized attitude toward the therapist ("transference neurosis") that might undermine the therapeutic alliance. Among them are rapid reframing of transference reactions in terms of developmental events and outside relationships, disconfirming the patient's transferential view of the therapist, offering support, and encouraging neutral self-examination. Strupp and Binder (1984) ackowledged the "principle of least possible confrontation."

Therapeutic Action

Basing their understanding on the one-person model, Davanloo (1978, 1980), Malan and Osimo (1992), and Sifneos (1992) attribute the therapeutic action and structural change to correct interpretations and patients' resulting insights into focal conflicts. Davanloo (1978, 1980) also notes the importance of "releasing hidden feelings" as part of the interpretive process. In my opinion, however, new interpersonal experience, even when unspecified, also plays a major role. For instance, Davanloo has described how patients, under the pressure of persistent confrontation of their defenses, often become enraged at the therapist. The therapist, not responding in kind but remaining composed in the face of the patient's attack, provides the patient with an opportunity for a new experience of safety and mastery—not only in relation to threatening aggressive impulses, but with another, nonretaliatory person, the therapist.

Interpersonal curative factors are stressed in the approaches of Balint et al. (1972), Strupp and Binder (1984), and Luborsky (1984), all of which promote new mastery within the safety of the treatment relationship. These theorists have extended the field of therapeutic action beyond that occurring directly with the therapist and have emphasized interpersonal factors that *maintain* maladaptive patterns, such as self-perpetuating interaction patterns. Mann also stresses the curative importance of positive, empathic relational experience, rather than interpretation. In the most recently developed of these approaches, Luborsky (1984), and Strupp and Binder (1984) emphasize the role of insight and new experience as dual mechanisms that participate in the therapeutic action. These authors have formulated insightful modification of maladaptive interpersonal patterns as a major goal of treatment.

Termination

Some short-term therapists, most notably Mann, have addressed the significance of termination process extremely effectively. They have shown how that process, related to issues of separation-individuation, becomes a meaningful focus having therapeutic power in its own right. In addition to the selection of relatively well-integrated patients who are capable of terminating expeditiously, several other technical factors combine to contain regression and thus to permit a fairly abrupt ending to treatment. They include the brevity of treatment, high levels of therapist activity, and early transference interpretation. If the patient has loss as a focus, or if there are multiple issues ("foci") or clinical complexities, then, within certain approaches, termination may require special management. Mann (1992) believes, and most psychoanalysts would agree, that a successful termination process involving constructive new relational patterns provides patients with a unique growth opportunity to develop healthy, new introjects. As noted, many brief therapists insist that there be no further contact following termination. Others, however, such as Wolberg (1980), caution that following such rigid rules can be countertherapeutic; these authors recommend follow-up sessions, as needed. Strupp and Binder (1984) also recognize that treatment sometimes must be extended.

Implications for Analytic Therapy

We might ask, what can analytic therapists accustomed to working long-term learn from the short-term dynamic therapies? Most traditional analysts have enormous respect for the value of time as a factor in the analytic process. For these analysts, who generally tend to expand the focus rather than narrowing it, brief approaches represent an inherently limited and inevitably superficial way of working. Each of these groups (brief and long-term, analytically oriented therapists) thus makes certain assumptions that are very different from the other's. Traditional analysts usually reject the circumscribed focus and high levels of therapist activity that are advanced by brief therapists. There is evidence, nonetheless, that psychoanalytic psychotherapy, a method that has been distinguished in the past as less intensive, more interactive, and often shorter term than formal psychoanalysis, may sometimes produce results that are comparable to psychoanalysis in both nature and stability (Wallerstein, 1986). This evidence supports the potential value of, in some cases, accelerating and narrowing a treatment with relatively modest goals, compared with more open-ended treatment.

Let us first review the positions of two preeminent psychoanalysts, Roy Schafer and Merton Gill, on short-term applications of psychoanalysis. Schafer's (1973) position on "brief psychoanalytic psychotherapy" remains the same today as it was when he first articulated it. He spoke of a treatment lasting one year. Overall, Schafer seemed to regard brief therapy as a preliminary process through which many patients might be introduced to a superior, longer term, and more thoroughgoing analytic experience. Schafer, rather than promoting the rapid achievement of deep insight into a narrow focus, the usual strategy of brief therapists, emphasizes the benefits of insight into the scope, multiplicity, and complexity of the patient's problems. He writes that, as the unhurried, nondirective, analytic exploration proceeds, gradually drawing out and delineating unarticulated phenomena—including conflict, defense, resistance, and especially transference—patients ideally become aware of the central role of conflict in their existence and develop a greater appreciation of their own role in apparent passivity. Even without elaborate interpretation, Schafer observes, a process of self-discovery occurs with the benign analyst, and a new, organized way of framing one's problems develops, leading to relief of the patient's suffering. As the patient realizes that he or she has been active in his or her own suffering, a sense of hopelessness and fragmentation diminishes. The patient also may reclaim disavowed affects and begin to grasp that he or she may become active in other, more constructive ways that can alter present, future, and even the past through active reformulations of experience.

Schafer asserts, contrary to many brief psychodynamic psychotherapists, that there can be only a limited attempt in this approach to begin to articulate transference and resistance in relation to difficulties in other relationships. Significantly, in Schafer's view, the termination—though fraught with potential emotional difficulties for patient and therapist alike, including their grappling with the disappointments that are inherent in the limitations of any analytic treatment—provides an excellent opportunity to begin to understand the patient's responses to separation in relation to the dynamic conflicts that treatment has addressed.

Gill (1984a), in a paper significant in that it both revised the author's earlier, influential views of the distinction between psychoanalysis and psychotherapy and also reexamined the psychoanalytic situation in the light of one-person and two-person psychological distinctions, took an explicit position with regard to brief analytic therapy. He gave the example of a nine-month, once-a-week treatment (36 sessions). Gill's essential methodology for a time-limited approach, similar to that for time-unlimited approaches, was the analysis of transference (the patient's experience of the relationship) as far as it could be carried. If the analysis of the transference-countertransference interaction in the here-and-now can be considered a focus, then Gill's approach is focused, and, in that respect, is closer to brief psychodynamic approaches than most analytic positions, including Schafer's. He also stressed the value of early interpretations of disguised expressions of the transference in the here-and-now, as opposed to historical exploration and genetic interpretation. Reasoning in the manner of some brief therapists, Gill stressed that transference interpretations that apply to relationships outside the analysis have far less mutative value than those directly involving the analyst. Again like brief therapists, he pointed out that this technique avoids the artificial development of a regressive transference neurosis, which he saw as iatrogenically induced. Rather than the rapid, confrontive approach of many brief therapists, however, he advanced a gradual procedure, carefully attuned to the patient's resistances and proceeding from more superficial to deeper levels of material.

In an ideal world, a "complete" psychoanalysis would be given as much time as it requires. But we do not live in an ideal world, and thus most analysts are not strangers to working within a relatively short-term framework, a term dictated by the academic year, for example. Although Schafer and Gill had different emphases, both believed that analysts should operate in the same way, basically, whether working long-term or short-term. It is my belief that there are many instances of short-term treatment, especially those concerned with actual symptoms, when a shift in the time frame dictates a shift in approach. Let us consider ways in which analytic therapists might advantageously integrate elements from brief therapy in modifying their approaches for work with patients that they know, beforehand, will be short-term. In so doing, some practitioners, who maintain one-person model commitments may appreciate approaches such as Malan's, with its emphasis on working actively with content, accurate interpretation, and insight. Others, especially those endorsing relational points of view, may favor the insights of Balint, Luborsky, and Strupp and Binder, stressing new relational experience. And still others may find Wolberg's approach, with its stress on practical action, including cognitive and behavioral methods, most congenial. The point is that one need not subscribe to any particular form of brief psychodynamic therapy in order to put the broad insights of that modality to therapeutic advantage in analytic therapy.

In beginning treatment with patients, for example, it is advantageous, in general, that the intended duration of treatment, or that the time frame is open-ended, be made clear. A therapist's willingness to remain open to the possibility of extending therapy, rather than limiting the number of sessions, has critical clinical implications and must be considered in relation to each individual case. The specter of termination always looms over, and inevitably shapes, the process of psychotherapy. Therapists must always be clear in their own thinking about the termination process, its meaning and therapeutic role, and how it is best negotiated with individual patients (Frank, 1998). These are factors that become highlighted by short-term therapy.

Working long-term, some psychoanalysts make little concentrated effort to develop an organized understanding of patients' psychodynamics; rather, they trust that refinement of their understanding will come about spontaneously, gradually, and incrementally. These analysts thus adopt a relatively inactive role, even in history taking, for example, assuming that relevant material will unfold over the course of treatment. This reactive, abstinent psychoanalytic stance often is carried over to less ambitious, shorter-term treatments that typically involve scaled-down goals and diminished session frequency, inappropriately in my view. The extent to which a therapist follows the patient's lead, permitting the emerging material to define the direction of the treatment and to provide refinements of the therapist's psychodynamic formulation, as opposed to the extent to which one takes the initiative, drawing actively from formulations to guide the exploration, is a complex technical matter. The therapist's organized understanding of the dynamic focus, providing a tentative conception of the work that needs to be done, forms a dynamic tension with a more open-ended, exploratory approach that is mediated by a recognition of the complexity and ambiguity of personality and of therapeutic processes. The latter orientation is reinforced by the therapist's recognition that the patient is the final expert on himself. In time-limited approaches, following foci that are not salient runs the risk of inefficiency and of diluting therapeutic efficiency; but if a long-term therapist promotes work in a focus too stringently, he or she runs the opposing risk of cutting off potentially rewarding areas of exploration.

The less active approach derived from standard technique, emphasizing that the therapist consistently must follow the lead of the patient's associative drift, is disadvantageous to many once- (and even twice-) a-week patients who are seen relatively short-term. In the light of the findings of time-limited psychotherapy and the growing appreciation of interpersonal mechanisms in the therapeutic action, an interactive approach and the use of a focus appear to be more productive, short-term, than an abstinent one. An analytic focus may be defined in any of the following ways, alone or in combination: a symptom (such as anxiety or depression), a central conflict or developmental arrest, a disturbance of the self-image, a salient interpretive theme, a troubled relationship, or a cyclical psychodynamic pattern (Strupp and Binder, 1984). Working short-term, the therapist often must conceptualize a hierarchy of focal areas of dysfunction in order to answer the question, how can I intervene most meaningfully, having the most significant therapeutic impact in the shortest (or anticipated) period of time? Given short-term capabilities, ambitious goals give way to achievable ones. Short-term approaches require that therapists participate more actively, including completing a thorough evaluation and history at the beginning of treatment and regularly reviewing process notes in order to effectively guide the progress of treatment. Rather than simply opening up the associative process, as through sharing their own associations, for example, therapists also act to confine patients' material to themes judged most relevant to agreed on therapeutic objectives.

As in long-term analysis, new relational experience has been stressed in certain brief psychodynamic therapy approaches, initially by Balint et al. (1972), who spoke of the treatment in terms of the patient's attempts at repetition and the therapist's efforts to have certain aspects of the unresolved past problem "come out right this time, with the therapist as the replica of important figures in . . . [the patient's] early life" (p. 133). Luborsky (1984) and Strupp and Binder (1984) also emphasize the new relationship that is made possible by the therapist's trying to forge insightful new relational experiences with the patient rather than by repeating problematic enactments. Insight remains important in the latter views, but perhaps less so than in the one-person model; and interpretation, rather than attempting to bring unconscious contents into consciousness, is thought to facilitate patients' new kinds of experience of self with others. While there has been a tendency to regard the direct promotion of behavior change as an objectionable practice in traditional analytic technique, some brief therapists, like Sifneos (1992) and Wolberg (1980), have noted the value of encouraging patients to initiate adaptive action. I have made a similar recommendation for long-term work in this book.

The "foreverness" of open-ended treatment, while promoting an atmosphere enabling a patient to feel safe to express and work out certain deeply complicated issues, also can function in deleterious ways. Long-term therapy can indulge patients' as well as therapists' avoidance of termination, which is, for therapists, often reinforced by emotional as well as financial concerns. Yet the specter of termination is an important consideration in any analytic treatment; it organizes much of a patient's material as the pair struggles with the paradoxes inherent in the analytic relationship and other relationships, such as the patient's becoming deeply involved and yet facing the relationship's very real limitations, especially in time. Time-limited therapies highlight therapeutic potentials that are associated with the termination process itself, especially when an absolute termination date is set in advance. Handled well by the therapist, an imposed termination can be related productively to many of the psychodynamic issues that treatment has addressed along the way. Approached skillfully, focused termination work consolidates analytic therapy, deepening and extending it. Unfortunately, because of the many complicated countertransference concerns that can develop around ending, many long-term treatments end in ways that are less than salutary. Therapists may either "hold on" to patients too long, or, reacting against that impulse, stimulate feelings of rejection in patients. Short-term therapists remind analysts of the importance that patients end their treatment with enhanced feelings of self-esteem related to the therapeutic work they have accomplished.

Practitioners may find that a participatory analytic orientation creates many constructive possibilities that a more reactive stance does not, especially in short-term work. Nevertheless, it is difficult for some analysts accustomed to working longer term to shift to short-term applications. It is not simply what is asked of therapists *technically* that accounts for this difficulty. In long-term therapy, a mutually gratifying bond of intimacy often develops between patient and therapist. That bond includes what I have identified as the affectional aspect of the nonobjectionable positive countertransference (chapter 8). Because short-term treatment requires the therapist to engage and then to let go very quickly, he or she forgoes much of this form of affective gratification. Such affective reactions of the therapist, while natural and capable of being applied constructively in long-term work, as well as becoming detrimental, are more likely to give rise to intensified countertransference problems in the hurried therapeutic atmosphere that is characteristic of short-term therapy.

Focused Integrative Psychotherapy

Several of these themes—working in a focus, promoting adaptive action, and achieving new relational experiences outside as well as within the psychoanalytic relationship, plus using cognitive-behavioral strategies—all are drawn together in a short-term approach I have used and call focused integrative psychotherapy. Focused integrative psychotherapy can have particular advantages when one is working under significant time constraints and especially when actual symptoms, maladaptive forms of interpersonal behavior, and characterological features combine to play a role in a patient's difficulties. One way of formulating a focus combines internalized object relations and problematic interpersonal patterns. A working model can be developed that relates maladaptive behaviors and symptoms to rigid, internalized symbolizations of the self and others, including expectations of them, and their interactions.

Clinical Example

David, 25 years old, came to see me with the presenting complaint of "a little trouble with public speaking." Initially, he struck me as being quite arrogant. The idea of coming for therapy seemed beneath his dignity and required that he admit and face being afraid, specifically, of public speaking. Taking tranquilizers, which he had attempted at his internist's recommendation, also was unacceptable to him. Because of his limited budget (and, no doubt, his negative feelings toward therapy), David had budgeted a fixed sum for therapy, an amount that would allow us to work together no longer than six months. Ordinarily, I might have referred him to a practitioner with a lower fee, but because his goals were primarily limited to a symptom, and probably would be responsive to an integrative approach, I thought reasonable results could be achieved within 20 sessions.

To realize his ambitions within the industry in which he worked, David would have to remain highly visible and frequently give formal presentations, which caused him intense anxiety. As we discussed his problem with public speaking, I recognized and pointed out to him that, in addition to his very distressing and limiting public-speaking symptom, he had other inhibited forms of self-expression—feeling self-conscious, for example, even when chatting with a small group of associates. He also became exceedingly uncomfortable and halting in his initial presentation while discussing himself with me. Thus we came to see David's difficulties not in terms of his public-speaking symptom alone, which reached the proportions of a phobia—although that problem remained in the forefront of our work together—but also in terms of his expressing himself confidently in a variety of circumstances. Behind his cocky façade, his fear, on a conscious level, was that he would not be intelligent enough. Feelings of self-disparagement, experienced in terms of his manhood, followed his avoiding situations calling for self-expression and caused him additional distress.

Analogous to his conflicts over public speaking, in his vocational dealings with others he maintained a private, grandiose sense of his capabilities, yet felt the need to conceal himself as a result of conflicting fears of humiliation over being discovered as a fraud. These fears had been exacerbated by certain earlier experiences, including some in his career. In a job he held while in college, motivated to earn extravagant praise and yet to avoid feared criticism from authority figures, he had engaged in an inappropriately grandiose but secretive scheme that, when discovered, resulted in his dismissal. He also felt a deep resentment toward senior colleagues who had authority over him, which at times surfaced as a rebellious, belligerent attitude. Further, although his career had begun reasonably well and it seemed quite possible that he might fulfill his aspirations, he was deeply conflicted about success and, believing himself to be inept, dared not believe too strongly the evidence of his own capabilities.

I learned that, while growing up, David had been harshly and unpredictably disparaged by his father, often in the presence of his mother and "baby" sister (four years younger). The father was an extremely powerful man, a CEO with a large firm, who dominated and abused others, including his wife and son. On occasion, the father would castigate and even beat David publicly over minor transgressions, causing his son to experience a profound sense of humiliation. David first coped with his father's verbal and physical abuse by trying to please and avoid provoking him, a strategy he learned was impossible; he also developed a façade, trying to impress others, including family members, with his boldness, while feeling himself as actually shaky and inadequate. He also was extremely close to his mother, with whom he identified. She was a delicate woman who acted submissively toward her domineering husband. She prized her only son, emphasizing his manliness and similarity to her own idolized father, who had died when she was a young girl. At times when the father was harsh with her, David wanted to rise to his mother's defense but was afraid to do so. He also felt diminished by his perception that his sister, exceptionally bright, was more capable at school. That which David entertained in fantasy, he expressed only indirectly—a wish to become the family champion and win the admiration of his mother and sister. To do so was terribly threatening, of course, and would incur the risk of going toe to toe with his dreaded father. Being more challenging and expressive also jeopardized his hope that at some time his father might show affection and admiration for David's capabilities.

These issues, all represented in his internalized relational matrix, had become problematic for David, and crystallized in his fears of public speaking. The internalized relational configuration with the father, mediated by that with the mother (and sister), provided a way of understanding David's personality organization. We understood his public-speaking difficulty in terms of conflicting ties to a sadistic, disparaging father (fearing disparagement by authority figures), on one hand, and to an adoring, worshipful mother who expected a great deal, on the other (and thus his seeking extravagant praise).

His father's attacks, physical as well as psychological, had taken a great toll on David, and he was deeply conflicted over actualizing his own capacities, especially in a competitive setting. Basically, he had learned that the safest way to avoid assault, to preserve feelings of connection to the father, and to maintain his self esteem was to operate with inhibition and compliance. Yet that represented a conflicted path in that it did not allow him to realize the hopes his mother had instilled in him. In addition to the public-speaking phobia, these opposing allegiances, reflected in the patient's conflicted self-concept, were played out in vocational and other interpersonal patterns that ultimately confirmed his negative expectations.

Public speaking was tantalizing to David. It represented the conflictual opportunity to seize the role of hero but also the possibility of humiliating attack. Understandably, he would quake with anxiety when speaking publicly, for there was no way he could hide and yet speak effectively to a receptive group of his colleagues, many senior to him. Doing well at public speaking represented an expression of David's suppressed wish to stand up to his demeaning father and become a leader, which stimulated his terror of attack and humiliation in that setting, either as its agent or its object. Doing poorly at public speaking would, preconsciusly, allow him to remain safe—safer, at least, than standing up to and threatening the father, which is what public shows of competence symbolized—and yet it also represented a humiliating defeat. Autonomous achievement was thus exceedingly conflictual, having become confused with gratifying mother and overthrowing father, that is, with an oedipal triangle.

It was this overall configuration—the anxiety symptom, or phobia; the maladaptive interpersonal pattern (which, not surprisingly, became manifested in the transference); and the associated self-esteem issues, all interrelated—that defined the therapeutic focus. As in so many instances, understanding David's specific symptom within the context of his character pathology had considerable value. Accordingly, symptomatic patterns are seen as extensions of character pathology; symptoms are actualizations of unconscious conflicts that are expressed more diffusely throughout a person's personality structure and relationships. Thus symptomatic relief reverberates throughout a person's personality, with the result that many patients who come to therapy seeking symptomatic relief, and who are successfully treated for their symptoms with the aid of integrative action-oriented techniques on a short-term basis, subsequently decide to address further the characterological issues that have been brought to their attention during the earlier, more focused intervention.

This way of understanding David's core psychodynamics not only provided historical and structural ways of understanding his difficulties but also defined the course of treatment. As one element, it suggested the possible benefits of an insightful new experience with a therapist/father, one who could be resilient, supportive, and non-critical in a relationship that enabled David to discover and work through the dangers he experienced in relation to self-expression. Predictably, the focus became apparent in the transference; David dealt with me initially in a glossy manner that, when examined, was understood as a way of protecting himself from the possibility of my disparaging observations of him. When this development was addressed, he was able to reveal his concerns over being discovered as inept as a psychotherapy patient. He spontaneously recalled memories of hiding from his father, who often became attacking and punitive, most painfully at those times when he needed and sought his father's assistance. Insight into this pattern, together with the achievement of a relationship with me that might provide reparation for it, could help him understand and overcome his fears.

David progressively revealed himself to me, gradually expressing many different aspects of himself—tenderness and felt vulnerabilities that he dared never before to express toward other males, as well as more familiar patterns involving challenging behaviors. There were many confrontational moments, as well as revelations of felt weakness, which became the stimulus for respectful exploration but not retaliation. David's anxieties and resistances to revealing these aspects of himself were understood in terms of the dynamics and anxieties of the father–son relationship. Had he revealed these feelings within the family setting, clearly he would have been actively humiliated.

The psychodynamic formulation of the focus also suggested specific ways of working with David through action-oriented techniques to help him overcome his phobia. Thus, with my willingness to form with him an encouraging but realistic new relationship unlike that with either parent, the treatment progressed on a second level, an exposure strategy to help him overcome the circumscribed anxiety symptom. I encouraged David to take on incrementally more challenging presentations and to observe his own experience and impact on others carefully, and we would discuss his reactions in detail. In certain sessions, at his suggestion, we went over presentations that had been videotaped (for training purposes) by his firm and observed in reassuring but realistic ways that his expectations for his performance had been unreasonably high. We noted, more superficially, that despite his internal experience his felt distress was hardly visible to others. Together we attempted to understand the sources of his discomfort and to develop specific strategies for handling them. We recognized his need to swagger during presentations and to stifle potentially valuable discussions that stimulated fears of not knowing answers he (incorrectly) believed he should know, and we identified his inclination to anticipate questions defensively, as if other males in the audience, as a rule, wanted to show him up, as he thought his father might. The ways that he experienced presentations were examined and understood in the light of the dangers of the paternal relationship and the ways he had learned to protect himself within it. We noted the irony so common in psychological functioning, that self-protective efforts—swaggering and defensive superficiality, for instance, and haughty responses to the views expressed from the audience—invited the very antagonism he sought to protect himself against. David's reactions to the exposure methods were further used to facilitate transference analysis, but only as seemed relevant to, and in ways hoped to advance, insight into the dynamic focus.

Through my analytic role, and especially the psychoeducational one David had urged me to take on, and that I had accepted, I was operating as a critical authority. Thus David and I were participating together in a relationship rich in its potential to become either a counterproductive enactment or an authentically new relational experience. At times he would experience me as critical when it was not my intention to be, and we would grapple with that disparity. Sometimes he reported that he had begun to feel more successful at public speaking. At other times, he experienced reversals and attempted to use them, defensively, to show that I, not he, was a failure. All this material was actively related to focal concerns with retaliation for self-expression and was elaborated within the framework of the paternal relationship.

The intensity of his fears of assault and his need for self-protection were highlighted dramatically at one point when I introduced the idea of formal progressive relaxation training. That proposal, apparently a dramatic reminder of his traumatic physical beatings at the hands of the father, caused him to feel extremely anxious and elicited threatening, conscious associations to actual, physical assault. If he were to let down his guard, he feared, I might actually assault him, as his father had. In the moment it was experienced, that transference reaction seemed very real to him, although almost immediately afterward he reality tested and rejected it. (Time did not permit us to adequately understand and work through that reaction, which was undoubtedly rich in its meanings and powerful in its impact on David's overall adaptation. Remember, David was to be seen once-a-week for 20 sessions. Perhaps a more intensive analytic regimen would have permitted further work with the dissociative implications of this significant material.)

Experiences with others also were therapeutically important. We related the conflicts that came up between us to those with other males in his firm, with whom David, expressing alternative poles of the conflict with his father, tended to relate either compliantly or belligerently. Thus the interpersonal treatment goal—to promote David's ability to risk being more effectively expressive and to free that behavior from conflicts over aggression and fears of retaliation—corresponded to goals conceptualized at the levels of symptom and character.

There was reason to assume that David came to internalize a view of the benevolent therapist/father as constructive, resilient, and tolerant, with attendant changes in his sense of self in relation to the father and thus in his expectations of others. With an array of feelings, including delight, disappointment, and anxiety, David gradually was beginning to recognize more clearly and to appreciate that people did not retaliate when he presented himself with a greater strength, which had felt to him somehow like a weakness at first. In other words, he came to feel safer following a course different from that which perpetuated old, submissive patterns; and he learned, to a limited and yet meaningful degree, that he no longer needed to appease or live up to internalized and projected parents. That is, he needed less to prove himself and thus felt less embattled each time he presented himself, especially to other males. Mastering setbacks that in the past he would have avoided, he became more willing to present himself authentically to others and even tested his relationship with his father. Thus, changes at the level of action became integrated with the multiple levels of affect, cognition, perception, and symbolization. Life in general and public speaking in particular lost some of their danger.

David and I agreed to end our work on schedule and rather unceremoniously. I would have been delighted to extend the therapy had that been his decision. Certainly we were both aware of the remaining issues, and had spent time discussing them. But he was grateful for what we had been able to accomplish in 20 sessions, which seemed to have made a significant difference in his life, overall, including symptomatic progress. There were some mutual feelings of disappointment as we ended, common for therapists, especially those accustomed to working longer term. David's disappointment seemed related to our falling short of a fuller "cure." My own was related to the inability to address certain issues further, particularly an undercurrent of resentment that I sensed that had not become adequately resolved and that, as a transference resistance, might have prevented greater therapeutic success. I also wished our work had provided him with an even more solid sense of his own worth.

Nor were we able to work intensively with the termination process. But we could only accomplish so much in 20 sessions, and this approach is not intended to develop all the rich therapeutic potentials of working with termination per se. When practical goals are weighted heavily among treatment objectives, profound considerations related to time and the impact of ending the relationship cannot be addressed conscientiously, compared with models such as Mann's, for example. Two factors mitigate the inability of this model to address termination issues intensively. One relates to applying the approach only with appropriate patients—those who can tolerate ending abruptly, for example, and who bring a combined symptomatic-characterological-interpersonal focus, so that short-term symptomatic relief has great significance. Another is a recognition of the possibility of continuing treatment at some time in the future. In closing, I wish to point out that this way of working is intended in no way as a substitute for long-term work; it can, however, represent an effective, integrative modality with a place within an analytic therapist's broad repertoire of techniques.

AFTERWORD

A book published in the final year of the millennium, and at the centennial of psychoanalysis, invites a look, both ahead and back, in order to place its ideas in a historical perspective. Surprisingly, it was only as I neared the completion of this book and was preparing to present some of the material to a group of colleagues at the National Institute for the Psychotherapies, that I realized how directly these ideas extend those addressed in my earlier, edited volume, *The Human Dimension in Psychoanalytic Practice*. On an impulse, I took the earlier volume off the shelf and thumbed through my Introduction. There I found that I had framed the challenge to the contributors in terms of "the positive role of the analyst's personal involvement" and discussed "the real relationship . . . characterized by an affectional bond of mutual trust and respect, and where the analyst is willing to fully experience and to be experienced, on an authentically human level."

Decades have passed and yet these very phrases might be found among those I have written here. Perhaps the French claim is true: "Plus ça change, plus cêst la même chose"—The more things change, the more they remain the same. But the zeitgeist and recent theoretical developments have provided a climate and language of ideas that enable one to amplify and advance seminal ideas such as those contained in the earlier book, an effort I shared with others. I have attempted to present these ideas here in more thoroughly articulated and clinically applicable ways.

Historically, this is a moment of heterodoxy unlike any before it in psychoanalysis. The many ways in which psychoanalysis is both understood and approached technically give testimony to an appreciation of the complexity of the therapeutic action in psychoanalysis. I think it probable that we never will thoroughly understand that process. However, the reader must have become aware that, in my view, relational theory holds enormous value. It offers a broad synthesis of many useful ways of thinking about what we actually do as analysts, what really is helpful to patients. Further, it confirms, while providing ways of organizing, much of what I have gathered from my own experience in the consulting room. Like the complementary, individual voices in a choir, relational analytic ideas form a larger synthesis, usually resulting in interesting harmonies and only occasionally in dissonance. It is capable of embracing, synthesizing, and generating developments such as those presented here.

Psychoanalysis has been and is being approached from many angles, but relatively little theorizing emphasizes the action dimension in analysis or, most certainly, incorporates action-oriented interventions. I have placed the action dimension of personality change, once excluded altogether by monadic conceptualizations of psychoanalysis, at center stage. Tracing the role of action—both analysts' and patients', within and outside of treatment sessions—in the process of personality change, I pursued its implications on the basis of the two-person model of the psychoanalytic process. In so doing, I have taken this book where analysts in the past were forbidden to go; I have attempted to turn to advantage what once was thought detrimental—analysts allowing themselves to become involved in patients' lives, as defined here, and, further, knowingly influencing patients' behavior.

I have suggested that analysts' reluctance to extend their influence beyond the confines of the analyst's office and outside of the analytic relationship stems from an anachronistic conception of the psychoanalytic process that is inappropriate when considered in the light of a two-person model and its very different ways of conceptualizing action and reality. I reasoned that by understanding and harnessing the action dimension more effectively, we often can accomplish a great deal more psychoanalytically than when we work in more traditional ways. Thus, although this work withstands analytic scrutiny according to most current standards, not long ago ideas of this kind would have been judged a heresy. Even today, I am certain, many readers will disagree with the direction taken here.

In emphasizing action, interaction, and integration it has not been my intention to minimize or exclude the significance of other important relational processes, but to advance an understanding of them. I attempted to place these ideas within the broad framework of an evolving psychoanalytic realism that considers the analyst as a real person, the analytic relationship as real, having much in common with other important relationships of the patient, and that redirects analysts' attention to patients' practical, day-to-day functioning and presenting problems, in addition to psychoanalytic process goals. In my opinion, such realism serves many patients' interests more effectively than forms of theorizing and practice that emphasize fantasy and metaphorical meanings in ways that create a psychoanalytic reality that is removed from the individual's ordinary life.

Extending the field of analytic interventions and change beyond the consulting room, accomplished here by integrating behavioral-cognitive methods, is seen as a very important development. Increasing numbers of analysts, especially younger colleagues, are finding fewer and fewer opportunities to practice psychoanalysis as we have known it, intensively. They, more than established practitioners, have had to demonstrate their clinical efficacy in differently creative, flexible, and often short-term forms of practice. I have tried to write responsively to the concerns of both groups—those who might wish to apply these insights in more customary and intensive psychoanalytic ways, and those who might wish to expand their clinical flexibility in ways that combine analytic with other insights and methods.

Santayana (1905–1906) wrote that a conception not reducible to the small change of daily experience is like a currency not exchangeable for articles of consumption; it is not a symbol but a fraud. These words challenging the value of abstract ideas that lack practical significance are severe. Yet as I consider the past of psychoanalysis, I am troubled by the observation that, for too long, too many American psychoanalysts remained far removed from clinical reality—from people, their ordinary problems, and their struggles to overcome them. This deficiency is reflected in a past literature in which analysts too often seemed to cherish people less than their own precious concepts, stilted theories, and, especially, vaunted techniques, often idealized at a cost to patients. I find it remarkable that past analytic treatments have not always been evaluated by the actual results they have accomplished in patients' real lives, but by how "well" they were conducted.

I have described a psychoanalytic approach that helps people deal with their psychological suffering on practical as well as profound levels. I have drawn from the technology of cognitive-behavior therapy to strengthen an area in which, in my opinion, psychoanalysis has remained relatively weak—the practical, helping patients directly improve their day-to-day functioning and alleviate their distress. But if analysis has been deficient in this regard, what it has done best among all the psychotherapeutic modalities is heal the individual through a relationship, at profound levels. I have challenged the idea that analysts' paying attention to practical concerns necessarily results in sacrificing the more profound changes analytic patients are able to achieve. Thus I have attempted to synthesize both these levels.

We have seen that progress during the first century of psychoanalysis was substantially slowed by interdisciplinary rivalries, professional politics, and the fragmentation that ensued. As psychoanalysis enters its second century, I hope we will go forward in a spirit of greater openness, integration, and consolidation of our accumulated clinical wisdom. With this book, I have offered a step in that direction.

REFERENCES

Abend, S. (1982). Some observations on reality testing as a clinical concept. *Psychoanal. Quart.*, 51:218–238.

Adler, E. (1993). Commentary on Frank's "Action, Insight, and Working Through" from the perspective of Freudian analysis. *Psychoanal. Dial.*, 4:579–588.

Alexander, F. (1956). *Psychoanalysis and Psychotherapy: Developments in Theory, Technique, and Training.* New York: Norton.

——— (1961). *The Scope of Psychoanalysis.* New York: Basic Books.

——— & French, T. M. (1946). *Psychoanalytic Therapy: Principles and Application.* New York: Ronald Press.

Anderson, R. & Cissna, K. N., eds. (1997). *The Martin Buber–Carl Rogers Dialogue: A New Transcript with Commentary.* Albany: State University of New York Press.

Appelbaum, G. (1999). Considering the complexity of analytic love: A relational perspective. Presented as part of the National Institute for the Psychotherapies Professional Association Focus Series, New York, April.

Arlow, J. (1984). The psychoanalytic process in regard to the development of transference and interpretation. In: *Psychoanalysis: The Vital Issues, Vol. 2,* ed. G. H. Pollock & J. E. Gedo. New York: International Universities Press, pp. 21–44.

——— (1985). The concept of psychic reality and related problems. *J. Amer. Psychoanal. Assn.*, 33:521–535.

——— & Brenner, C. (1988). The future of psychoanalysis. *Psychoanal. Quart.*, 57:1–14.

——— (1990). The psychoanalytic process. *Psychoanal. Quart.*, 59:678–692.

Aron, L. (1990). One-person and two-person psychologies and the method of psychoanalysis. *Psychoanal. Psychol.*, 7:435–475.

——— (1992). Interpretation as expression of the analyst's subjectivity. *Psychoanal. Dial.*, 2:475–507.

——— (1996). *A Meeting of Minds: Mutuality in Psychoanalysis.* Hillsdale, NJ: The Analytic Press.

——— (1997). Self-disclosure and the interactive matrix. *Psychoanal. Dial.*, 7:315–318.

——— & Bushra, A. (1998). Mutual regression and altered states. *J. Amer. Psychoanal. Assn.*, 46:389–412.

——— & Harris, A., eds. (1993). *The Legacy of Sándor Ferenczi.* Hillsdale, NJ: The Analytic Press.

Atkins, N. (1970). Action, acting out and the symptomatic act. *J. Amer. Psychoanal. Assn.*, 18:631–643.

Atwood, G. E. & Stolorow, R. D. (1984). *Structures of Subjectivity: Explorations in Psychoanalytic Phenomenology.* Hillsdale, NJ: The Analytic Press.

——— ——— & Trop, J. L. (1989). Impasses in psychoanalytic therapy: A royal road. *Contemp. Psychoanal.*, 25:554–573.

Bacal, H. (1985). Optimal responsiveness and the therapeutic process. In: *Progress in Self Psychology, Vol. 1*, ed. A. Goldberg. New York: Guilford Press, pp. 202–227.

——— (1990). Does an object-relations theory exist in self psychology? *Psychoanal. Inq.*, 10:197–220.

——— & Newman, K. (1990). *Theories of Object Relations.* New York: Columbia University Press.

Bacciagaluppi, M. (1989). Erich Fromm's views on psychoanalytic "technique." *Contemp. Psychoanal.*, 25:226–243.

Bader, M. J. (1995). Authenticity and the psychology of choice in the analyst. *Psychoanal. Quart.*, 64:282–304.

Balint, M. (1950). Changing therapeutic aims and techniques in psychoanalysis. *Internat. J. Psycho-Anal.*, 31:117–124.

——— (1967). Sándor Ferenczi's technical experiments. In: *Psychoanalytic Techniques: A Handbook for the Practicing Psychoanalyst*, ed. B. B. Wolman. New York: Basic Books.

——— Ornstein, P. H. & Balint, E. (1972). *Focal Psychotherapy: An Example of Applied Psychoanalysis.* London: Tavistock.

Barlow, D. H. & Cerny, J. A. (1988). *Psychological Treatment of Panic.* New York: Guilford Press.

Basch, M. F. (1988). *Understanding Psychotherapy: The Science Behind the Art.* New York: Basic Books.

Beck, A., Rush, A. J., Shaw, B. F. & Emery, G. (1979). *Cognitive Therapy of Depression.* New York: Guilford Press.

Beebe, B. & Lachmann, F. (1992). The contribution of mother-infant mutual influence to the origin of self- and object representations. In: *Relational Perspectives in Psychoanalysis*, ed. N. J. Skolnick & S. C. Warshaw. Hillsdale, NJ: The Analytic Press, pp. 83–117.

Benjamin, J. (1990). An outline of intersubjectivity: The development of recognition. *Psychoanal. Psychol.*, 7 (Suppl.):33–46.

Bion, W. R. (1959). Attacks on linking. *Internat. J. Psycho-Anal.*, 40:308–315.

Bird, B. (1972). Notes on transference: Universal phenomena and hardest part of analysis. *J. Amer. Psychoanal. Assn.*, 20:267–301.

Boesky, D. (1982). Acting out: A reconsideration of the concept. *Internat. J. Psycho-Anal.*, 63:39–55.

——— (1990). The psychoanalytic process and its components. *Psychoanal. Quart.*, 59:550–584.

Bollas, C. (1983). Expressive uses of the countertransference. *Contemp. Psychoanal.*, 19:1–34.

——— (1987). *The Shadow of the Object.* London: Free Associations.

——— (1989). *Forces of Destiny.* London: Free Associations.

——— (1992). *Being a Character.* New York: Hill & Wang.

Bromberg, P. (1986). Discussion of "The wishy-washy personality" by A. Goldberg. *Contemp. Psychoanal.*, 22:374–387.

——— (1994) "Speak! That I may see you": Some reflections on dissociation, reality, and psychoanalytic listening. *Psychoanal. Dial.*, 4:517–548.

Buber, M. (1957). Mutuality and therapy. In: *The Martin Buber–Carl Rogers Dialogue: A New Transcript with Commentary*, ed. R. Anderson & K. N. Cissna. Albany: State University of New York Press, 1997.

Bucci, W. (1997). *Psychoanalysis and Cognitive Science: A Multiple Coding Theory.* New York: Guilford Press.

Burke, W. (1992). Countertransference disclosure and the asymmetry/mutuality dilemma. *Psychoanal. Dial.*, 2:241–271.

Chrzanowski, G. (1980). Collaborative inquiry, affirmation, and neutrality in the psychoanalytic situation. *Contemp. Psychoanal.*, 16:348–366.

Chused, J. F. (1991). The evocative power of enactments. *J. Amer. Psychoanal. Assn.*, 39:615–639.

——— & Raphling, D. L. (1992). The analyst's mistakes. *J. Amer. Psychoanal. Assn.*, 40:89–116.

Crastnopol, M. (1997). Anonymity, desire, and authenticity in the analytic relationship. *Psychoanal. Dial.*, 7:327–336.

Davanloo, H. (1978). Evaluation, criteria for selection of patients for short-term dynamic psychotherapy: A metapsychological approach. In: *Basic Principles and Techniques in Short-Term Dynamic Psychotherapy.* New York: Spectrum Publications, pp. 9–34.

——— (1980). *Short-Term Dynamic Psychotherapy.* New York: Aronson.

Davies, J. M. (1994). Love in the afternoon: A relational reconsideration of desire and dread in the countertransference. *Psychoanal. Dial.*, 4:153–170.

——— (1998). Between the disclosure and foreclosure of erotic transference-countertransference: Can psychoanalysis find a place for adult sexuality? *Psychoanal. Dial.*, 8:747–766.

Deffenbacher, J. L. & Stark, R. S. (1992). Relaxation and cognitive-relaxation treatments of general anger. *J. Counsel. Psychol.*, 39:158–167.

Dewald, P. (1976). Transference regression and real experience in the psychoanalytic process. *Psychoanal. Quart.*, 45:213–231.

——— (1990). Conceptualizations of the psychoanalytic process. *Psychoanal. Quart.*, 59:693–711.

Dupont, J., ed. (1988). *The Clinical Diary of Sándor Ferenczi.* Cambridge, MA: Harvard University Press.

Ehrenberg, D. B. (1982). Psychoanalytic engagement: The transaction as primary data. *Contemp. Psychoanal.*, 18:535–555.

——— (1984). Psychoanalytic engagement, II. *Contemp. Psychoanal.*, 20:560–583.

——— (1992). *The Intimate Edge.* New York: Norton.

Eissler, K. (1950). The Chicago Institute of Psychoanalysis and the sixth period of the development of psychoanalytic technique. *J. Gen. Psychol.*, 42:103–157.

——— (1953). The effect of the structure of the ego on psychoanalytic technique. *J. Amer. Psychoanal. Assn.*, 20:104–143.

Elkin, I., Shea, M. T., Watkins, J. T., Imber, S. D., Sotsky, S. M., Collins, J. F., Glass, D. R., Pilkonis, P. A., Leber, W. A., Docherty, J. P., Feister, S. J. & Parloff, M. B. (1989). National Institute of Mental Health treatment of depression collaborative research program: General effectiveness of treatments. *Arch. Gen. Psychiat.*, 46:971–982.

Ellis, A. (1973). *Humanistic Psychotherapy: The Rational-Emotive Approach.* New York: McGraw-Hill.

Epstein, L. (1995). Self-disclosure and analytic space. *Contemp. Psychoanal.*, 31:229–236.

——— & Feiner, A., eds. (1979). *Countertransference.* New York: Aronson.

Epstein, S. (1994). Integration of the cognitive and the psychodynamic unconscious. *Amer. Psychologist*, 49:709–724.

Eysenck, H. J. (1988). Psychotherapy to behavior therapy: A paradigm shift. In: *Paradigms in Behavior Therapy: Present and Promise*, ed. D. B. Fishman & F. Rotgers. New York: Springer, pp. 45–76.

Fairbairn, W. R. D. (1952). *An Object Relations Theory of the Personality.* New York: Basic Books.

——— 1958). On the nature and aims of psychoanalytical treatment. *Internat. J. Psycho-Anal.*, 39:374–385.

Farber, L. H. (1967). Martin Buber and psychotherapy. In: *The Philosophy of Martin Buber*, ed. P. A. Schilpp & M. Friedman. LaSalle, IL: Open Court, pp. 577–602.

Ferenczi, S. (1919). Technical difficulties in the analysis of a case of hysteria. In: *Further Contributions to the Theory and Technique of Psycho-Analysis*, ed. J. Rickman. London: Hogarth Press, 1950, pp. 189–197.

——— (1920). The further development of an active therapy in psycho-analysis. In: *Further Contributions to the Theory and Technique of Psycho-Analysis*, ed. J. Rickman. London: Hogarth Press, 1950, pp. 198–217.

——— (1925). Contraindications to the "active" psycho-analytical technique. In: *Further Contributions to the Theory and Technique of Psycho-Analysis*, ed. J. Rickman. London: Hogarth Press, 1950, pp. 217–230.

——— (1928). The elasticity of psycho-analytic technique. In: *Final Contributions to the Problems and Methods of Psychoanalysis*, ed. M. Balint. London: Hogarth Press, 1955, pp. 87–101.

——— (1931). Child analysis in the analysis of adults. In: *Final Contributions to the Problems and Methods of Psychoanalysis*, ed. M. Balint. London: Hogarth Press, 1955, pp. 126–142.

——— (1933). Confusion of tongues between the adult and the child. In: *Final Contributions to the Problems and Methods of Psychoanalysis*, ed. M. Balint. London: Hogarth Press, 1955, pp. 136–167.

Fosshage, J. (1990). The analyst's response. *Psychoanal. Inq.*, 4:601–622.

——— (1992). Self psychology: The self and its vicissitudes within a relational matrix. In: *Relational Perspectives in Psychoanalysis*, ed. N. J. Skolnick & S. C.

Warshaw. Hillsdale, NJ: The Analytic Press, pp. 21–42.

—— (1994). Toward reconceptualizing transference: Theoretical and clinical considerations. *Internat. J. Psycho-Anal.*, 75:265–280.

—— (1995). Countertransference as the analyst's experience of the analysand: Influence of listening perspectives. *Psychoanal. Psychol.*, 12:375–391.

Fourcher, L. A. (1992). Interpreting the relative and absolute unconscious. *Psychoanal. Dial.*, 3:317–329.

Frank, K. A., ed. (1977). *The Human Dimension in Psychoanalytic Practice.* New York: Grune & Stratton.

—— (1990). Action techniques in psychoanalysis. *Contemp. Psychoanal.*, 26:732–756.

—— (1992). Combining action techniques with psychoanalytic therapy. *Internat. Rev. Psycho-Anal.*, 19:57–79.

—— (1993). Action, insight, and working through: Outlines of an integrative approach. *Psychoanal. Dial.*, 3:535–577.

—— (1997a). Focused integrative psychotherapy. In: *The Impact of Managed Care on the Practice of Psychotherapy: Innovation, Implementation, and Controversy*, ed. R. A. Alperin & D. G. Phillips. New York: Brunner/Mazel, pp. 79–104.

—— (1997b). The role of the analyst's inadvertent self-revelations. *Psychoanal. Dial.*, 7:281–314.

—— (1998). Ending an analytic relationship. In: *Clinical Controversies*, ed. P. Carnochan. *The Psychologist Psychoanalyst*, Winter 1997–1998, pp. 20–25.

Franklin, G. (1990). The multiple meanings of neutrality. *J. Amer. Psychoanal. Assn.*, 38:195–220.

French, T. M. (1958). *The Integration of Behavior.* Chicago: University of Chicago Press.

—— (1970). The cognitive structure of behavior. In: *Psychoanalytic Interpretations: The Collected Papers of Thomas M. French.* Chicago: Quadrangle Books, pp. 296–323.

Freud, A. (1936). *The Ego and the Mechanisms of Defense. Writings, 2.* New York: International Universities Press.

Freud, S. (1910). The future prospects of psychoanalytic therapy. *Standard Edition*, 11:141–151. London: Hogarth Press, 1957.

—— (1912a). The dynamics of transference. *Standard Edition*, 12:97–108. London: Hogarth Press, 1958.

—— (1912b). Recommendations to physicians practising psycho-analysis. *Standard Edition*, 12:111–120. London: Hogarth Press, 1958.

—— (1913). On beginning the treatment. *Standard Edition*, 12:121–144. London: Hogarth Press, 1958.

—— (1914). Remembering, repeating and working-through (Further recommendations on the technique of psycho-analysis II). *Standard Edition*, 12:145–156. London: Hogarth Press, 1958.

—— (1915). Observations on transference love (Further recommendations on the treatment of psychoanalysis, III). *Standard Edition*, 12:157–171. London: Hogarth Press, 1958.

—— (1917). Introductory lectures on psychoanalysis: Part III. General theory of the neuroses. *Standard Edition*, 16:412–430. London: Hogarth Press, 1963.

—— (1919). Lines of advance in psycho-analytic therapy. *Standard Edition*,

17:157–168. London: Hogarth Press, 1955.

———— (1920). Beyond the pleasure principle. *Standard Edition*, 18:7–64. London: Hogarth Press, 1955.

———— (1923). The ego and the id. *Standard Edition*, 19:13–66. London: Hogarth Press, 1961.

———— (1931). Female sexuality. *Standard Edition*, 21:225–246. London: Hogarth Press, 1961.

———— (1937). Analysis terminable and interminable. *Standard Edition*, 23:209–254. London: Hogarth Press, 1964.

Friedman, L. (1978). Trends in the psychoanalytic theory of treatment. *Psychoanal. Quart.*, 47:524–567.

Friedman, M. (1994). *The Healing Dialogue in Psychotherapy.* Northvale, NJ: Aronson.

Fromm-Reichmann, F. (1950). *Principles of Intensive Psychotherapy.* Chicago: University of Chicago Press.

Gabbard, G. O. (1994). Commentary on papers by Tansey, Hirsch, and Davies. *Psychoanal. Dial.*, 4:203–213.

———— (1996). The analyst's contribution to the erotic transference. *Contemp. Psychoanal.*, 32:249–273.

———— (1998). Commentary on paper by Jody Messler Davies. *Psychoanal. Dial.*, 8:781–790.

Galassi, M. & Galassi, J. (1978). Assertion: A critical review. *Psychother.: Theory, Res. & Pract.*, 15:16–29.

Gedo, J. (1988a). Character, dyadic enactments, and the need for symbiosis. *Psychoanal. Inq.*, 8:459–471.

———— (1988b). *The Mind in Disorder.* Hillsdale, NJ: The Analytic Press.

Ghent, E. (1989). Credo: The dialectics of one-person and two-person psychologies. *Contemp. Psychoanal.*, 2:169–211.

Gill, M. M. (1954). Psychoanalysis and exploratory psychotherapy. *J. Amer. Psychoanal. Assn.*, 2:771–797.

———— (1982a). *Analysis of Transference, Vol. I: Theory and Technique.* New York: International Universities Press.

———— (1982b). The analysis of the transference. In: *Curative Factors in Dynamic Psychotherapy*, ed. S. Slipp. New York: McGraw-Hill, pp. 104–126.

———— (1983). The interpersonal paradigm and the degree of the therapist's involvement. *Contemp. Psychoanal.*, 19:200–237.

———— (1984a). Psychoanalysis and psychotherapy: A revision. *Internat. Rev. Psycho-Anal.*, 11:161–179.

———— (1984b). Psychoanalytic, psychodynamic, cognitive behavior, and behavior therapies compared. In: *Psychoanalytic Therapy and Behavior Therapy: Is Integration Possible?* ed. H. Arkowitz & S. B. Messer. New York: Plenum Press, pp. 179–187.

———— (1988). Converting psychotherapy into psychoanalysis. *Contemp. Psychoanal.*, 24:262–274.

———— (1994). *Psychoanalysis in Transition: A Personal View.* Hillsdale, NJ: The Analytic Press.

Gold, J. R. (1996). *Key Concepts in Psychotherapy Integration.* New York: Plenum

Press.

Goldberg, A. (1988). *A Fresh Look at Psychoanalysis: The View from Self Psychology.* Hillsdale, NJ: The Analytic Press.

Goldfried, M. R. & Newman, C. F. (1992). A history of psychotherapy integration. In: *Handbook of Psychotherapy Integration,* ed. J. C. Norcross & M. R. Goldfried. New York: Basic Books, pp. 46–93.

————— Decenteneo, E. & Weinberg, L. (1974). Systematic rational restructuring as a self-control technique. *Behav. Ther.,* 5:247–254.

Gray, P. (1994). *The Ego and the Analysis of Defense.* Northvale, NJ: Aronson.

Green, A. (1975). The analyst, symbolization and absence in the analytic setting (on changes in analytic practice and analytic experience): In memory of D. W. Winnicott. *Internat. J. Psycho-Anal.,* 56:1–22.

Greenacre, P. (1954). The role of transference: Practical considerations in relation to psychoanalytic therapy. *J. Amer. Psychoanal. Assn,* 2:671–684.

Greenberg, J. R. (1986). Theoretical models and the analyst's neutrality. *Contemp. Psychoanal.,* 22:87–106.

————— (1991). Countertransference and reality. *Psychoanal. Dial.,* 1:52–73.

————— (1992). *Psychoanalytic Interaction.* Paper presented at the spring conference of the National Institute for the Psychotherapies, New York, April.

————— (1995a). Psychoanalytic technique and the interactive matrix. *Psychoanal. Quart.,* 64:1–22.

————— (1995b). Self-disclosure: Is it psychoanalytic? *Contemp. Psychoanal.,* 31:193–205.

————— & Mitchell, S. A. (1983). *Object Relations in Psychoanalytic Theory.* Cambridge, MA: Harvard University Press.

Greenson, R. R. (1965). The working alliance and the transference neurosis. *Psychoanal. Quart.,* 34:155–181.

————— (1967). *The Technique and Practice of Psychoanalysis, Vol. 1.* New York: International Universities Press.

————— (1971). The "real" relationship between the patient and the psychoanalyst. In: *The Unconscious Today: Essays in Honor of Max Shur,* ed. M. Kanzer. New York: International Universities Press, pp. 213–232.

Guidano, V. F. (1991). *The Self in Process: Toward a Post-Rational Cognitive Therapy.* New York: Guilford Press.

————— & Liotti, G. (1986). *Cognitive Processes and Emotional Disorders: A Structural Approach to Psychotherapy.* New York: Guilford Press.

Guntrip, H. (1968) *Schizoid Phenomena, Object Relations, and the Self.* New York: International Universities Press.

————— (1971). *Psychoanalytic Theory, Therapy, and the Self.* New York: Basic Books.

————— (1975). My experience of analysis with Fairbairn and Winnicott (how complete a result does psychoanalytic therapy achieve?). In: *The Human Dimension in Psychoanalytic Practice,* ed. K. A. Frank. New York: Grune & Stratton, 1977, pp. 49–68.

Heimann, P. (1950). On countertransference. *Internat. J. Psycho-Anal.,* 31:81–84.

Hirsch, I. (1987). Varying modes of analytic participation. *J. Amer. Acad. Psychoanal.,* 15:205–222.

————— (1994). Countertransference love and theoretical model. *Psychoanal. Dial.,*

4:171–192.

——— (1998). The concept of enactment and theoretical convergence. *Psychoanal. Quart.*, 67:78–101.

Hoffer, A. (1993). Freud's relevance to contemporary psychoanalytic technique: Commentary on André Haynal's "Ferenczi and the origins of psychoanalytic technique." In: *The Legacy of Sándor Ferenczi*, ed. L. Aron & A. Harris. Hillsdale, NJ: The Analytic Press, pp. 75–80.

Hoffman, I. Z. (1983). The patient as interpreter of the analyst's experience. *Contemp. Psychoanal.*, 19:389–422.

——— (1991). Discussion: Toward a social-constructivist view of the psychoanalytic situation. *Psychoanal. Dial.*, 1:74–105.

——— (1992a). Expressive participation and psychoanalytic discipline. *Contemp. Psychoanal.*, 28:1–15.

——— (1992b). Some practical implications of a social-constructivist view of the psychoanalytic situation. *Psychoanal. Dial.*, 2:287–304.

——— (1996). The intimate and ironic authority of the psychoanalyst's presence. *Psychoanal. Quart.*, 65:102–136.

——— (1998). *Ritual and Spontaneity in the Psychoanalytic Process: A Dialectical-Constructivist View*. Hillsdale, NJ: The Analytic Press.

Interbitzen, L. B. & Levy, S. T. (1994). On grist for the mill: External reality as defense. *J. Amer. Psychoanal. Assn.*, 42:763–788.

——— (1998). Repetition compulsion revisited: Implications for technique. *Psychoanal. Quart.*, 67:32–53.

Jacobs, T. (1986). On countertransference enactments. *J. Amer. Psychoanal. Assn.*, 34:289–308.

Jacobson, E. (1929). *Progressive Relaxation*. Chicago: University of Chicago Press.

Jacubowski, P. & Lange, A. J. (1978). *The Assertive Option: Your Rights and Responsibilities*. Champaign, IL: Research Press.

Kanzer, M. & Blum, H. (1967). Classical psychoanalysis since 1939. In: *Psychoanalytic Techniques: A Handbook for the Practicing Psychoanalyst*, ed. B. B. Wolman. New York: Basic Books, pp. 93–146.

Kernberg, O. (1976). *Object Relations Theory and Clinical Psychoanalysis*. New York: Aronson.

Klein, M. (1946). Notes on some schizoid mechanisms. *Internat. J. Psycho-Anal.*, 33:433–438.

Knoblauch, S. (1996) The play and interplay of passionate experience: Multiple organizations of desire. *Gender & Psychoanal.*, 1:323–345.

Kohut, H. (1971). *The Analysis of the Self*. New York: International Universities Press.

——— (1977). *The Restoration of the Self*. Chicago: University of Chicago Press.

——— (1984). *How Does Analysis Cure?* ed. A. Goldberg & P. Stepansky. Chicago: University of Chicago Press.

Krasner, L. (1988). Paradigm lost: On a historical/sociological/economic perspective. In: *Paradigms in Behavior Therapy: Present and Promise*, ed. D. B. Fishman, F. Rotgers, et al. New York: Springer, pp. 23–44.

Kubie, L. S. (1939). A critical analysis of the concept of a repetition compulsion. *Internat. J. Psycho-Anal.*, 20:390–402.

Lachmann, F. & Beebe, B. (1992). Representational and selfobject transferences:

A developmental perspective. In: *New Therapeutic Visions: Progress in Self Psychology, Vol. 8*, ed. A. Goldberg. Hillsdale, NJ: The Analytic Press, pp. 3–15.

——— (1995). Self psychology, later the same day. *Psychoanal. Dial.*, 5:415–419.

Langs, R. J., ed. (1981). Truth therapy/lie therapy. In: *Classics in Psychoanalytic Technique*. New York: Aronson, pp. 495–515.

——— (1982). Countertransference and the process of cure. In: *Curative Factors in Dynamic Psychotherapy*, ed. S. Slipp. New York: McGraw-Hill, pp. 127–152.

Laplanche, J. & Pontalis, J. B. (1973). *The Language of Psychoanalysis*. New York: Norton.

Lazarus, A. A. (1992). Multimodal therapy: Technical eclecticism with minimal integration. In: *Handbook of Psychotherapy Integration*, ed. J. C. Norcross & M. R. Goldfried. New York: Basic Books, pp. 231–263.

——— (1995). Different types of eclecticism and integration: Let's be aware of the dangers. *J. Psychother. Integration*, 5:27–39.

Levenson, E. A. (1972). *The Fallacy of Understanding*. New York: Basic Books.

——— (1981). Facts or fantasies: The nature of psychoanalytic data. *Contemp. Psychoanal.*, 17:486–500.

——— (1983). *The Ambiguity of Change*. New York: Basic Books.

——— & Feiner, A. H., eds. (1991). *The Purloined Self: Interpersonal Perspectives in Psychoanalysis*. New York: Contemporary Psychoanalytic Books.

Levy, S. T. & Interbitzen, L. B. (1990). The analytic surface and the theory of technique. *J. Amer. Psychoanal. Assn.*, 38:371–391.

——— (1992). Neutrality, interpretation, and therapeutic intent. *J. Amer. Psychoanal. Assn.*, 40:989–1011.

Lichstein, K. L. (1988). *Clinical Relaxation Strategies*. New York: Wiley.

Lichtenberg, J. D. (1989). *Psychoanalysis and Motivation*. Hillsdale, NJ: The Analytic Press.

——— Lachmann, F. & Fosshage, J. L. (1992). *Self and Motivational Systems: Toward a Theory of Psychoanalytic Technique*. Hillsdale, NJ: The Analytic Press.

Lindon, J. A. (1994). Gratification and provision in psychoanalysis: Should we get rid of "the rule of abstinence"? *Psychoanal. Dial.*, 4:549–582.

Lipton, S. D. (1977). The advantages of Freud's technique as shown in the analysis of the Rat Man. *Internat. J. Psycho-Anal.*, 58:255–273.

——— (1983). A critique of the so-called standard psychoanalytic technique. *Contemp. Psychoanal.*, 19:35–52.

Little, M. (1951). Countertransference and the patient's response to it. *Internat. J. Psycho-Anal.*, 32:32–40.

——— (1957). "R"—The analyst's total response to his patient's needs. *Internat. J. Psycho-Anal.*, 38:240–254.

Loewald, H. W. (1960). On the therapeutic action of psychoanalysis. *Internat. J. Psycho-Anal.*, 41:16–33.

Luborsky, L. (1984). *Principles of Psychoanalytic Psychotherapy: A Manual for Supportive-Expressive Treatment*. New York: Basic Books.

Mahoney, M. J. (1991). *Human Change Processes: The Scientific Foundation of Psychotherapy*. New York: Basic Books.

Malan, D. (1980). The most important development in psychotherapy since the discovery of the unconscious. In: *Short-Term Dynamic Psychotherapy, Vol. 1*, ed.

H. Davanloo. New York: Aronson, pp. 13–23.

———— & Osimo, F. (1992). *Psychodynamics, Training, and Outcome in Brief Psychotherapy.* Oxford, U.K.: Butterworth-Heinemann.

Mann, J. (1992). Time-limited psychotherapy. In: *Handbook for Short-Term Dynamic Psychotherapy*, ed. P. Crits-Christoph & J. P. Barber. New York: Basic Books, pp. 17–44.

Marks, I. M. (1981). *Cure and Care of Neurosis.* New York: Wiley.

Maroda, K. (1991). *The Power of Countertransference.* New York: Wiley.

Masters, J. C., Burish, T. G., Hollon, S. D. & Rimm, D. C. (1987). *Behavior Therapy: Techniques and Empirical Findings*, 3rd ed. San Diego: Harcourt Brace Jovanovich.

McLaughlin, J. T. (1981). Transference, psychic reality, and countertransference. *Psychoanal. Quart.*, 50:639–664.

———— (1991). Clinical and theoretical aspects of enactment. *J. Amer. Psychoanal. Assn.*, 35:557–582.

Meichenbaum, D. (1977). *Cognitive-Behavior Modification.* New York: Plenum Press.

Menaker, E. (1990). Transference, countertransference, and therapeutic efficacy in relation to self-disclosure by the analyst. In: *Self-Disclosure in the Therapeutic Relationship*, ed. G. Stricker & M. Fisher. New York: Plenum Press, pp. 103–116.

Messer, S. B. (1986). Behavioral and psychoanalytic perspectives at therapeutic choice points. *Amer. Psychol.*, 41:1261–1272.

———— (1992). A critical examination of belief structures in integrative and eclectic psychotherapy. In: *Handbook of Psychotherapy Integration*, ed. J. Norcross, M. R. Goldfried et al., New York: Basic Books, pp. 130–165.

———— & Warren, C. S. (1995). *Models of Brief Psychodynamic Therapy: A Comparative Approach.* New York: Guilford Press.

Mitchell, S. A. (1988). *Relational Concepts in Psychoanalysis: An Integration.* Cambridge, MA: Harvard University Press.

———— (1992). True selves, false selves, and the ambiguity of authenticity. In: *Relational Perspectives in Psychoanalysis*, ed. N. J. Skolnick & S. C. Warshaw. Hillsdale, NJ: The Analytic Press, pp. 1–20.

———— (1993). *Hope and Dread in Psychoanalysis.* Cambridge, MA; Harvard University Press.

———— (1997a). *Influence and Autonomy in Psychoanalysis.* Hillsdale, NJ: The Analytic Press.

———— (1997b). Two quibbles: Commentary on Kenneth A. Frank's paper. *Psychoanal. Dial.*, 7:319–322.

———— (1998). Fairbairn's object-seeking: Between paradigms. In: *Fairbairn, Then and Now*, ed. N. J. Skolnick & D. E. Scharff. Hillsdale, NJ: The Analytic Press, pp. 115–135.

Modell, A. H. (1984). *Psychoanalysis in a New Context.* New York: International Universities Press.

———— (1991). The therapeutic relationship as a paradoxical experience. *Psychoanal. Dial.*, 1:13–28.

Moore, B. E. & Fine, B. D., eds. (1990). *Psychoanalytic Terms and Concepts.* New

Haven, CT: American Psychoanalytic Association and Yale University Press.

Nagel, T. (1986). *The View From Nowhere.* New York: Oxford University Press.

———— (1995). *Other Minds: Critical Essays.* Oxford: Oxford University Press.

Novaco, R. W. (1975). *Anger Control.* Lexington, MA: Lexington.

Ogden, T. H. (1982). *Projective Identification and Psychotherapeutic Technique.* New York: Aronson.

———— (1994). *Subjects of Analysis.* Northvale, NJ: Aronson.

Olfson, M. & Pincus, H. A. (1994). Outpatient psychotherapy in the United States. II. Patterns of utilization. *Amer. J. Psychiatr.*, 151:1289–1294.

Orange, D. M. (1995). *Emotional Understanding.* New York: Guilford Press.

———— Atwood, G. & Stolorow, R. (1997). *Working Intersubjectively: Contextualism in Psychoanalytic Practice.* Hillsdale, NJ: The Analytic Press.

Oremland, J. (1991). *Interpretation and Interaction: Psychoanalysis or Psychotherapy?* Hillsdale, NJ: The Analytic Press.

Panel (1992). Enactments in psychoanalysis. J. T. McLaughlin, Chair. M. Johan, Reporter. *J. Amer. Psychoanal. Assn.*, 40:827–841.

Pine, F. (1985). *Developmental Theory and Clinical Process.* New Haven, CT: Yale University Press.

———— (1993). A contribution to the analysis of the psychoanalytic process. *Psychoanal. Quart.*, 62:185–205.

Pizer, S. (1992). The negotiation of paradox in the analytic process. *Psychoanal. Dial.*, 2:215–240.

———— (1998). *Building Bridges: The Negotiation of Paradox in Psychoanalysis.* Hillsdale, NJ: The Analytic Press.

Poland, W. S. (1986). The analyst's words. *Psychoanal. Quart.*, 55:244–272.

Psychoanalytic Inquiry (1990). The "corrective emotional experience" revisited. 10:285–458.

Racker, H. (1968). *Transference and Countertransference.* New York: International Universities Press.

Rangell, L. (1981a). From insight to change. *J. Amer. Psychoanal. Assn.*, 29:119–141.

———— (1981b). Psychoanalysis and dynamic psychotherapy: Similarities and differences twenty-five years later. *Psychoanal. Quart.*, 50:665–693.

———— (1990). *The Human Core: The Intrapsychic Base of Behavior.* New York: International Universities Press.

Reich, A. (1951). On countertransference. *Internat. J. Psycho-Anal.*, 32:25–31.

———— (1960). Further remarks on countertransference. *Internat. J. Psycho-Anal.*, 41:389–395.

Renik, O. (1993a). Analytic interaction: Conceptualizing technique in light of the analyst's irreducible subjectivity. *Psychoanal. Quart.*, 62:553–571.

———— (1993b). Countertransference enactment and the psychoanalytic process. In: *Psychic Structure and Psychic Change: Essays in Honor of Robert S. Wallerstein, M.D.*, ed. M. J. Horowitz, O. F. Kernberg & E. M. Weinshel. Madison, CT: International Universities Press, pp. 135–158.

———— (1995). The ideal of the anonymous analyst and the problem of self-disclosure. *Psychoanal. Quart.*, 64:466–495.

———— (1996). The perils of neutrality. *Psychoanal. Quart.*, 65:495–517.

———— (1998). Getting real in analysis. *Psychoanal. Quart.*, 67:566–593.

Rickman, J. (1951). Number and the human sciences. In: *Selected Contributions to Psycho-Analysis*, ed. W. C. M. Scott. New York: Basic Books, 1957, pp. 218–223.

Rogers, C. (1956). Client-centered therapy: A current view. In: *Progress in Psychotherapy*, ed. F. Fromm-Reichmann & J. L. Moreno. New York: Grune & Stratton, pp. 199–209.

———— (1961). *On Becoming a Person: A Therapist's View of Psychotherapy*. Cambridge, MA: Riverside Press.

———— & Dymond, R. F., eds. (1954). *Psychotherapy and Personality Change*. Chicago: University of Chicago Press.

Rubens, R. L. (1996). The unique origins of Fairbairn's ideas. Review of *From Instinct to Self: Selected Papers of W. R. D. Fairbairn, Vols. I & II*, ed. D. Scharff & E. F. Birtles. *Psychoanal. Dial.*, 1:413–435.

Rycroft, C. (1968). *A Critical Dictionary of Psychoanalysis*. New York: Basic Books.

Sampson, H. (1992). The role of "real" experience in psychopathology and treatment. *Psychoanal. Dial.*, 2:509–528.

Sandler, J. (1976a). Countertransference and role-responsiveness. *Internat. Rev. Psycho-Anal.*, 3:33–42.

———— (1976b). Dreams, unconscious fantasies, and "identity of perception." *Internat. Rev. Psycho-Anal.*, 3:33–42.

———— (1981). Unconscious wishes and human relationships. *Contemp. Psychoanal.*, 17:180–196.

———— Dare, C. & Holder, A. (1973). *The Patient and the Analyst: The Basis of the Psychoanalytic Process*. New York: International Universities Press.

———— & Sandler, A. (1984). The past unconscious, the present unconscious, and the interpretation of the transference. *Psychoanal. Inq.*, 4:367–400.

———— (1993). Psychoanalytic technique and theory of psychic change. In: *Psychic Structure and Psychic Change: Essays In Honor of Robert S. Wallerstein, M.D.*, ed. M. J. Horowitz, O. F. Kernberg & E. M. Weinshel. Madison, CT: International Universities Press, pp. 57–75.

Santayana, G. (1905–1906). *The Life of Reason*. New York: C. Scribner's Sons.

Schafer, R. (1973). The termination of brief psychoanalytic psychotherapy. In: *Retelling a Life: Narration and Dialogue in Psychoanalysis*. New York: Basic Books, 1992, pp. 292–304.

———— (1976). *A New Language for Psychoanalysis*. New Haven, CT: Yale University Press.

———— (1983). *The Analytic Attitude*. New York: Basic Books.

———— (1993). Two discussions of "theory in vivo" by Dennis Duncan: I. *Internat. J. Psycho-Anal.*, 74:1163–1167.

Schur, M. (1966). *The Id and the Regulatory Principles of Mental Functioning*. New York: International Universities Press.

Searles, H. F. (1975). The patient as therapist to his analyst. In: *Countertransference and Related Subjects*. New York: International Universities Press, 1979, pp. 380–459.

———— (1979). *Countertransference and Related Subjects*. New York: International Universities Press.

—— (1986). *My Work With Borderline Patients.* Northvale, NJ: Aronson.

Shapiro, D. (1965). *Neurotic Styles.* New York: Basic Books.

Shulman, D. G. (1995). The analyst's equilibrium: Countertransferential management and the action of psychoanalysis. Presented at the spring meeting of American Psychological Association Division of Psychoanalysis (39), Santa Monica, CA, April.

Sifneos, P. E. (1992). *Short-Term Anxiety-Provoking Psychotherapy.* New York: Basic Books.

Silberstein, L. J. (1989). *Martin Buber's Social and Religious Thought.* New York: New York University Press.

Singer, E. (1977). The fiction of analytic anonymity. In: *The Human Dimension in Psychoanalytic Practice,* ed. K. A. Frank. New York: Grune & Stratton, pp. 181–192.

Skinner, B. F. (1974). About Behaviorism. New York: Knopf.

Slavin, J. H., Rahmani, M. & Pollock, L. (1998). Reality and danger in psychoanalytic treatment. *Psychoanal. Quart.,* 67:191–217.

Smith, B. L. (1990). The origins of interpretation in the countertransference. *Psychoanal. Psychol.,* 7:89–104.

Spillius, E. B. (1988). *Melanie Klein Today: Development in Theory and Practice, Vol. 1, Mainly Theory; Vol. 2, Mainly Practice.* London: Routledge.

Stein, M. H. (1966). Self-observation, reality, and the superego. In: *Psychoanalysis: A General Psychology: Essays in Honor of Heinz Hartmann,* ed. R. M. Loewenstein, L. M. Newman, M. Schur & A. J. Solnit. New York: International Universities Press, pp. 275–294.

Stern, D. N. (1985). *The Interpersonal World of the Infant: A View from Psychoanalysis and Developmental Psychology.* New York: Basic Books.

Stern, D. B. (1989). The analyst's unformulated experience of the patient. *Contemp. Psychoanal.,* 25:1–33.

—— (1997). *Unformulated Experience: From Dissociation to Imagination in Psychoanalysis.* Hillsdale, NJ: The Analytic Press.

Stolorow, R. D. (1992). Subjectivity and self psychology. In: *The Intersubjective Perspective,* ed. R. Stolorow, G. Atwood & B. Brandchaft. Northvale, NJ: Aronson, 1994, pp. 43–55.

—— & Atwood, G. E. (1992). *Contexts of Being: The Intersubjective Foundations of Psychological Life.* Hillsdale, NJ: The Analytic Press.

—— (1997). Deconstructing the myth of the neutral analyst: An alternative from intersubjective systems theory. *Psychoanal. Quart.,* 66:431–449.

—— Brandchaft, B. & Atwood, G. E. (1987). *Psychoanalytic Treatment: An Intersubjective Approach.* Hillsdale, NJ: The Analytic Press.

—— & Lachmann, F. (1984/1985). Transference: The future of an illusion. *The Annual of Psychoanalysis,* 12–13:19–37. New York: International Universities Press.

—— Orange, D. M. & Atwood, G. (1998). Projective identification begone! Commentary on paper by Susan H. Sands. *Psychoanal. Dial.,* 8:719–725.

Stone, L. (1954). The widening scope of indications for psychoanalysis. *J. Amer. Psychoanal. Assn.,* 2:567–594.

———— (1961). *The Psychoanalytic Situation.* New York: International Universities Press.

———— (1981). Notes on the noninterpretive elements in the psychoanalytic situation and process. *J. Amer. Psychoanal. Assn.*, 29:89–118.

Strachey, J. (1934). The nature of the therapeutic action of psycho-analysis. In: *The Evolution of Psychoanalytic Technique*, ed. M. S. Bergmann & F. R. Hartman. New York: Basic Books, 1976, pp. 331–360.

Strupp, H. H. & Binder, J. L. (1984). *Psychotherapy in a New Key: A Guide to Time-Limited Dynamic Psychotherapy.* New York: Basic Books.

Sullivan, H. S. (1953). *The Interpersonal Theory of Psychiatry.* New York: Norton.

Tansey, M. J. & Burke, W. F. (1989). *Understanding Countertransference: From Projective Identification to Empathy.* Hillsdale, NJ: The Analytic Press.

Tarachow, S. (1963). *An Introduction to Psychotherapy.* New York: International Universities Press.

Tauber, E. S. (1954). Exploring the therapeutic use of countertransference data. *Psychiatry*, 17:331–336.

Ticho, E. (1972). Termination of psychoanalysis: Treatment goals, life goals. *Psychoanal. Quart.*, 41:315–332

Tolpin, M. (1983). Corrective emotional experience: A self-psychological reevaluation. In: *The Future of Psychoanalysis*, ed. A. Goldberg. New York: International Universities Press, pp. 368–380.

Tower, L. (1956). Countertransference. *J. Amer. Psychoanal. Assn.*, 4:224–255.

Tyson, P. (1986). Countertransference evolution in theory and practice. *J. Amer. Psychoanal. Assn.*, 34:251–274.

Viderman, S. (1979). The analytic space: Meaning and problems. *Psychoanal. Quart.*, 48:257–291.

Wachtel, P. L. (1977). *Psychoanalysis and Behavior Therapy: Toward an Integration.* New York: Basic Books.

———— (1981). Transference, schema and assimilation: The relevance of Piaget to the psychoanalytic theory of transference. In: *Action and Insight.* New York: Guilford Press, 1987, pp. 26–44.

———— (1983). You can't go far in neutral: On the limits of therapeutic neutrality. In: *Action and Insight.* New York: Guilford Press, 1987, pp. 176–184.

———— (1987). *Action and Insight.* New York: Guilford Press.

———— (1993a). Active intervention, psychic structure, and the analysis of transference: Commentary on Frank's "Action, Insight, and Working Through." *Psychoanal. Dial.*, 3:589–603.

———— (1993b). *Therapeutic Communication: Principles and Effective Practice.* New York: Guilford Press.

———— (1997). *Psychoanalysis, Behavior Therapy, and the Relational World.* Washington, DC: American Psychological Association.

Wallerstein, R. S. (1965). The goals of psychoanalysis: A survey of analytic viewpoints. *J. Amer. Psychoanal. Assn.*, 13:748–779.

———— (1986). *Forty-Two Lives in Treatment: A Study of Psychoanalysis and Psychotherapy.* New York: Guilford Press.

———— (1990). The corrective emotional experience: Is reconsideration due? Psychoanal. Inq., 10:288–324.

Webster's Ninth New Collegiate Dictionary (1988). Springfield, MA: Merriam-Webster.

Weiss, J. (1988). Testing hypotheses about unconscious mental functioning. *Internat. J. Psycho-Anal.*, 69:87–95.

———— (1990). The centrality of adaptation. *Contemp. Psychoanal.*, 26:660–676.

———— (1993). *How Psychotherapy Works: Process and Technique.* New York: Guilford Press.

———— & Sampson, H. (1986) *The Psychoanalytic Process: Theory, Clinical Observation.* New York: Guilford Press.

Winnicott, D. W. (1949). Hate in the countertransference. *Internat. J. Psycho-Anal.*, 30:69–75.

———— (1951). Transitional objects and transitional phenomena. In: *Through Pediatrics to Psycho-Analysis.* New York: Basic Books, 1975, pp. 229–242.

———— (1958). *Collected Papers: Through Pediatrics to Psycho-Analysis.* New York: Basic Books.

———— (1960). *The Maturational Processes and the Facilitating Environment.* London: Hogarth Press.

———— (1971). *Playing and Reality.* London: Tavistock.

Wolberg, L. R. (1980). *Handbook of Short-Term Psychotherapy.* New York: Theime-Stratton.

Wolf, E. (1988). *Treating the Self: Elements of Clinical Self Psychology.* New York: Guilford Press.

Wolpe, J. (1958). *Psychotherapy by Reciprocal Inhibition.* Stanford, CA: Stanford University Press.

Wolstein, B. (1959). *Countertransference.* New York: Grune & Stratton.

———— (1981). The psychic realism of psychoanalytic inquiry. *Contemp. Psychoanal.*, 17:399–412.

Zetzel, E. R. (1956). Current concepts of transference. *Internat. J. Psycho-Anal.*, 37:369–376.

INDEX

Abend, S., 39
abstinence, 20, 49, 77
  as retraumatizing, 71, 107
accommodation, 44
  done secretly. *See* rectification
  mutual, 92–94, 100
acting out, 28, 47, 210
  action equated with, 29
  action *vs.*, 30
action. *See also* patient(s), taking
    constructive/adaptive action
  and corrective emotional
    experience, 73
  dangers, 164
  defined, 26–27, 29
  mutual. *See* enactments
  negative connotations, 29, 30
  one- *vs.* two-person models and,
    27–31, 55
  as resistance, 28–29
  role in psychoanalytic theorizing, 29
  self-expression through, 163, 166,
    169–171
    hugging a patient, 163–166
  as source of information, 28–29
  therapeutic role, 27
  as ubiquitous and unavoidable, 55
action language, 29, 45
action-oriented techniques, xii, 8,
    214, 218

vs. "active" techniques, 189n
  advantages, 200–202
  and analyst's stance, 223–225
  case material, 215–221, 261–262
  countertransferential meaning, 226
  defensive (counterresistant) use, 217
  in focused integrative psychotherapy,
    261–262
  "neutrally" introducing, 229–231
  as new relational experience,
    227–229
  problems and dangers, 226–229
  "seamless" integration of insight-
    oriented and, 240–242
  technical considerations, 221–223
  transferential meaning, 225–226,
    228, 236
  when to use, 217, 221–223
  working through and, 226
"active" techniques, 189n, 190–191
activity, analytic, 28, 189, 206, 207, 211
  defined, 27
  negative attitude toward, 190–191
  one- *vs.* two-person models and,
    213–214
actualization, 48
Adler, E., 207
Alexander, F., 68, 90, 132, 190, 191, 218
  on corrective emotional experience,
    72–79, 90